A MILLION REASONS

A MILLION REASONS

WHY I FOUGHT FOR THE RIGHTS OF THE DISABLED

to Father Bradley
with best personal
regards

ALAN LABONTE WITH BROCK BROWER

6.22.2010

HOTHOUSE PRESS

Permissions, Hot House Press
760 Cushing Highway
Cohasset, MA 02025

Library of Congress Cataloging-in-Publication Data

Labonte, Alan.
 A million reasons : why i fought for the rights of the disabled / by
Alan Labonte with Brock Brower.
    p. cm.
  ISBN 0-9700476-7-3
 1. Labonte, Alan–Trials, litigation, etc. 2. Hutchins and
Wheeler–Trials, litigation, etc. 3. Discrimination against people with
disabilities–Law and legislation–Massachusetts–Boston. 4. People
with disabilities–Employment–Law and legislation–Massachusetts–
Boston. 5. People with disabilities Legal status, laws, etc.–Massachu-
setts–Boston. I. Brower, Brock– II. Title.
  KF228.L23L23 2006
  346.744'61013–dc22

                    2006010221

Printed in the United States of America
Book design by Rebecca Krzyzaniak

Hot House Press
760 Cushing Highway
Cohasset, MA 02025
www.hothousepress.com

DEDICATION

This book is dedicated to my best friend, Lora, to my dear brother Bob, to my valued colleagues and mentors Michael Shwartz and Joseph Restuccia, to Drs. Edward Wolpow and Peter Gross and to all the family, friends and associates who encouraged me to write this book and provided moral support along the way.

In particular and for a million reasons, I offer this book and all the good that it will hopefully do on behalf of Maryann Antonia-Loy and William J. LaBelle for all those who suffer from chronic illness and disabilities.

Many thanks to my co-author, Brock Brower for his skillful construction and manipulation of the narrative story and to my publisher and friend, David Replogle for believing in me, for his tireless support and for his generosity in lending his considerable talent to the editing of this manuscript.

Finally, this book is dedicated, with heartfelt gratitude, to our friends and counselors, David and Diane Rapaport. Their adroit management of the legal transactions in my case allowed us to achieve a triumph for all disabled persons in spite of the incredible odds against it—without them, our story would be one of tragedy rather than inspiration.

Chapter One

I never wanted to sue. The most I wanted, ever really expected, was to settle the matter. Earlier on, after being summarily—and unjustly—fired, all I tried to negotiate was a decent severance. Enough money to cover my losses on our expensive move to the Boston area, keep my head above water while I struggled to reeducate myself, and learn how to deal with the sudden onset of multiple sclerosis.

They had treated me shabbily. In fact, they were breaking the law—even though they are a *law firm*, I had to keep reminding myself. "If Hutchins & Wheeler had ever behaved decently," my lawyer, David Rapaport, still remarks, with a marveling shrug, "I never would have met Alan Labonte." And that would have been a shame for both of us, but a greater loss to me—not in terms of my legal rights, but personally—because we have become such close friends.

As frequently happens, our wives were part of the team. "You can't leave the two wives out of this," insists my lawyer.

What David is talking about is what we all got ourselves into. It wasn't just me, but we became the Labonte Case. *Alan J. Labonte v. James G. Wheeler et. al.* All twenty-nine Hutchins & Wheeler partners were listed in the original action. But the actual starting numbers on the Labonte Case were just two couples, working together for some five years on what eventually turned into the last thing I would have thought I'd ever get involved with: a fight for civil rights as an American with disabilities.

After multiple sclerosis suddenly struck at my life in 1991, my wife Lora and I were in deep trouble. Trouble made far worse by my bosses turning my condition into an excuse to take away my very livelihood. David and his wife, Diane were two people who were going to do their best to get us out of trouble. They were partners in life as well as in their own law firm.

We tried to negotiate an amicable agreement with my employer, Hutchins & Wheeler (H & W), then one of the leading names in the Boston Bar. A *law* firm, always bear in mind—and a very prestigious one at that—the second oldest in Boston when I went to work there in 1990. Believe me, I kept my healthy respect for the legal prowess of H & W. That is why we tried to negotiate sensibly with them, at my insistence, thinking we might succeed through long patience, until the deadline loomed for entering suit under the Massachusetts handicap discrimination statute.

I still didn't want to go this litigating route. I have to admit to being a cockeyed optimist. "Alan always wants to believe the best about people," David will tell you.

I'd have to admit that David proved right. So, in the rigorous spirit of tough truth-telling, let me go to the night when the facts *did* sink in—when the Labonte Case, for me, began in deadly earnest. That would be the night of Wednesday, August 9, 1996. David had already called me the week before, to say we finally had a trial date—only a few weeks away—definitely time we got cracking. "I've been thinking," he said. "In order to better prepare us for trial, I'd like to set up a mock jury trial in my office. What do you think?"

"I think that's a great idea," I said, then added, a bit bubbly, "It will give me a chance to practice my courtroom etiquette."

Little did I know that a mock trial does so much more than that. It is a shrewd pre-trial strategy for spotting your courtroom strengths and weaknesses, and lots of money spent on testing how juries are going to react to plaintiffs, prosecutors, witnesses—the very gist of the case as conceived and presented.

We didn't have funds for a major event. The Labontes had our reduced-to-minimal family budget and some savings, and the Rapaports had their firm's limited credit, and at this late date, we were both nearly down to operating on fumes.

So, within severe economic parameters, David put together a mock trial with eight jurors—local friends, and friends of friends. They were hired for two hours on a Wednesday evening, at fifty dollars, plus a pizza dinner, to be delivered during jury deliberations.

But we sure paid them a lot of attention.

First off, David prepared a questionnaire that was sent to all eight mock-trial jurors beforehand. Five questions, the answers to which held some real surprises for us. But these responses helped guide our case.

1. How do you feel about the laws giving handicapped persons a right to "reasonable accommodation" in the workplace?

That was the crux of our case. After I told my superior that I had contracted MS and asked them to talk with my doctor, they failed to pay attention to the advice that they should make my working conditions accommodate my disabilities. All but one juror were solidly with us. "Long overdue," "They have a right to a decent job just as we all do," though "*reasonable* should be stressed," and "unless the company is so small that complying with 'reasonable accommodation' would present a burden." The one holdout was a research scientist, who wrote succinctly, "I don't like it."

2. Do you feel that an employer who believes an employee is doing a poor job should have to warn the employee before firing him? How strongly do you feel about this?

H & W's utter failure to do so was key to our argument that the firm had really fired me for my disability, and again these jurors were largely with us. "A difficult thing to do, but only fair—and humane." "Very important to give someone the opportunity to correct his errors." "It was at the least common courtesy." An employee should be warned "both in writing and in person" and "allowed reasonable time to improve performance." There was another "No" this time, besides the adamant research scientist's, but he qualified his negative answer: "I could be persuaded either way."

3. Would you hold an employer who is a large law firm to a higher standard in a handicap discrimination case than you would a large corporation such as Raytheon?

This was an exploratory probe after any likelihood that lawyers might be seen as especially culpable for not knowing and/or obeying the law. These culprits, again I say, were a *law firm*. But only one juror wrote, "Yes, since I feel they should be aware of the laws and handle each case according to the laws, not take advantage of their knowledge." All the rest were "No's," on the demanding basis—except for the scientist again—that we should "expect high standards from all companies large and small."

4. What are your feelings about lawyers who are partners in large law firms?

More exploratory probing that produced no ringing denunciation of lawyers. Nobody had "any particular feelings about lawyers." "My only contact is *L. A. Law!*"

5. Alan Labonte was earning $120,000/year at Hutchins & Wheeler. How do you feel about this, and how would it affect your consideration of his claim?

Alas, these brief riches were long gone, and hardly enjoyed, but David was concerned about any negative reaction to what might appear to be a high salary, far more than your average wage-earning juror might be making. Massachusetts juries are also notorious tightwads when it comes to awarding damages. But to our mutual surprise, they all answered that my salary was "irrelevant." One juror wrote, "If he earned the money, then it doesn't matter how much it was; as for it affecting my consideration of his case, he has just as much right to sue for discrimination as someone making half or twice as much money. The salary is not the issue." Another logged in, "It's a moral issue."

So we already had some profile of our mock jurors and their biases, though I confess I had not yet really looked to my own predilections as a witness.

I drove into Boston to meet this pre-assembled jury in David's shared conference room. I deliberately chose the seacoast route through Wollaston Beach, from our home in Cohasset. There is a mile or so that is open to the sparkling blue water, with a concrete walking area, and parking right along the beach. People like to congregate there, especially near the end of a long, hot summer's day. There were lots of different people, cooling down from a scorcher, walking, jogging, or just sitting and talking.

I had a fleeting thought I should pull over and park here, to get out myself and cool down. I was dressed pretty casually in an open-collared shirt, a pair of gray slacks, a beige sport coat, and brown shoes. But, I continued to drive.

Then I happened to look out to sea, across Massachusetts Bay with its circling islands, and caught sight of one of the commuter boats com-ing toward the shore from Downtown Boston. I started remembering the busy times, not just the late nights, but the early mornings when I used to ride that boat from Hingham around the dawn-struck Harbor Islands to Rowes Wharf. I'd get off the ferry and head straight for the big doors into the Boston Harbor Hotel.

But now it got painful to remember how I couldn't walk as fast as the others hurrying by me while I kept stumbling over those loose bricks in the sidewalks. The stumbles had to be, in retrospect, the first signs of MS, as I grimaced and pushed through the glass doors to take the elevator up to Hutchins & Wheeler's top four floors.

After work I'd just reverse it, grateful to be walking all downhill. I'd ferry across the black waves of Massachusetts Bay, late as the hour might be, pick up my lonely car from the parking lot in Hingham, and drive home in the coastal dark. But some nights my fatigue was so over-whelming that I barely made it to the car, collapsing into the driver's seat like a fold-up map.

Now I was suddenly seeing how different everything was. What a difference it made, seeing this unhurried stretch of beach road, so re-laxed, such a relief from what life had once been like for me.

So I was starting to feel pretty distant, and far away myself.

The next step, I arrived in the city to find the financial district deserted. I parked in the garage where I used to park when I was at H & W. One of the perks was a parking spot paid for by the firm, worth good money with downtown rates going at $20 per day. And from there, I headed around to One Boston Place to reach David's offices on the 33rd Floor.

It so happens I knew David's location only too well. Rapaport and Rapaport's cubicle was part of the *former* offices of H & W—which once covered four floors from thirty-two through thirty-five.

The door of the shared conference room, next to David's office, was slightly open giving off the only bright light on the entire floor. The mock jurors were sitting like a *tableau vivante*—so many living statues on the other side of this long table—all eight of them. I took my seat in a single chair, on the opposite side of the table.

This gave me a funny sense of feeling kind of *opposed* to the people who were the mock jurors. Even though they were mostly friends and col-leagues of David's, I found myself focusing on how I could remain even *more* distant from them. I was trying to stay aloof, thinking about how I was going to present myself. I felt sort of like somebody kneeling in the batter's circle, getting ready to step into the batter's box and hit away.

Then David started in, and he really loves this kind of lawyering. He thrives on the courtroom, where the action is. After graduating from Yale, he went to law school at the University of Pennsylvania, and soon joined Camden Regional Legal Services, a poverty law office in southern New Jersey. From what David tells me, Camden in the '70s really needed help.

In his hectic early career, David got himself involved with social activism, and later, criminal law. When he worked for district attorney Robert Morganthau in New York during the late 1970s, he found out that many of the other Assistant D.A.'s were happy to give him their homicide cases to try. He took as many as he could and achieved an impressive record of convictions. That led eventually to his heading up the litigation department for a small boutique international law firm in Boston, where he met another lawyer, Diane Neff. They soon decided to team up as Rapaport & Neff, and later married.

So you might expect something of a firebrand, at least the warm glow of banked embers, but that is not David's style. He is firm and incisive, always your dedicated advocate, but his manner is precise, carefully measured, if anything, understated, even mild. He will tell you that Diane has a better legal mind than he does, and how much he counts on her for "the overall scope, the feel, even the eventual disposition" of a case. But he is using his judicious manner, and his deportment, to disguise a sharp intelligence, and an adroit working of the courtroom.

And that's how he delivered his compact summary to the mock jurors. It was the two and a half years we'd been working together on this imbroglio, but instead of a book, it was an outline. Suddenly, the major issues were clear. Everything was succinct, rapid fire, done in five minutes, pure staccato. But given in his usual manner: carefully, thoroughly, and thoughtfully.

Then he questioned me on things I already absolutely knew.

Did H & W try to accommodate my MS? Did they offer to move me nearer the elevator?

I answered "No" to all queries. He wasn't directing me, but sort of guiding me through. What he was really doing was bringing my own case to courtroom life for me. He gave me the opportunity to be on trial without having to be in court. It was the dress rehearsal.

Except, as I was soon to learn, I wasn't dressed right.

Now up stepped a guy I'd never seen before, even though he turned out to be David's legal associate, Joe Limone, who also worked as an Assistant City Solilcitor. Since Diane had been raising their daughter Cary, she hadn't been able to concentrate on the details of every litigation. So David had been hiring part-time legal help to assist him. Before the mock jurors, David had directed Joe Limone to take every last shot that H & W were ever likely to fire at me.

Actually, this was the first time I'd heard *their* side of it, and Joe was very good. He had a whole script, well prepared, and made an impressive presentation. Up to then I had only heard all these flowery things from David, but now came the flip of the coin—heads, not tails—and I could feel my blood pressure rising.

Joe Limone stood very erect, but he didn't look at me. Or he sort of glanced at me over his shoulder, but really looked at the jurors. He did his presentation in maybe seven minutes, but a world of information came rolling out.

And he was downright disdainful, even rude. I took an instant dislike not only to what he was saying but the way he was saying it. His whole demeanor was kind of like, "You're not important, Mister, just answer my questions and don't give me any trouble."

I could see the awful—and distorted—picture he was painting, disputing all the points that David had made. For example, when David asked, "Did they ever make any accommodation to your illness after they found out about it?" And I had answered, "No, they didn't." This Limone guy would say something like, "Did you ever ask them to do anything for you?" So I was forced to say, "My doctors said I should have help." "That's not the question I asked you, Mr. Labonte, is it?" "No, it isn't." "You know the question I asked you was, 'Did you ever ask them to make any accommodations for your illness?'" And I was forced to grit my teeth and say, "No." And I started to get really angry.

Which, of course, was just what he wanted.

But I'd have to admit that while much of this anger was very real, some of it was acting. I'd gotten to thinking—part of that business of feeling so distant from those mock jurors—*I know this story, and nobody knows it better than me.* But in order to be convincing, I felt I needed to be this other person in front of these mock jurors. I told myself I needed to get angry.

That was a real mistake. After all those needling questions, I ended up looking like an antagonistic witness, my own worst enemy with a real head of steam. And how could that be in my own interest?

I don't remember how Joe Limone excused me, but I'm sure it was abruptly.

I didn't stay for the verdict. I was still confident that it was all going to be okay, especially after what started happening to me, driving home. I didn't go along the beach on the way back home. I was in a much different mood, still kind of steamed. I jumped right on the Southeast Expressway, to take the quicker, more direct route home. It would be about three-quarters of an hour, because there was still no traffic, and ample time to drive quietly and just reflect. I don't remember a lot about that trip home, but I do remember still being on the Expressway, when the revelation came.

For two and a half years we'd been pressing for a settlement with H & W, and I'd never really taken the charge of discrimination on account of my handicap seriously enough. I kept thinking of it as our negotiating ploy. But I had just tonight heard, sifted and considered all the evidence, and I saw the light. After all those months of second-guessing myself, questioning my own competence, going through all this soul-searching and seeking after some buried truth, it just hit me, right up front.

"You know what?" I said aloud, right there in the car. "Those sons-of-bitches really *did* fire me because I was handicapped."

And as for those mock jurors, or *any* other future jury of my peers, if I can see it—I harangued myself—they've got to see it.

Suddenly, everything changed. "Wait a minute," I told myself, "I've got to take this thing very seriously. I've got to steel myself for whatever it takes to beat these guys."

I didn't wake Lora when I got back to Cohasset. I went into my office to mull things over, then took a shower to calm down and got into bed. The next morning she had a lot of questions for me.

But I still wasn't worried, because for me, after I'd heard all the testimony—basically my own—the verdict had to be a foregone conclusion. We've got a real case, and they did me wrong, and we're going to have to fight them with everything we've got.

Then David called, sometime after nine o'clock. "The jury voted in our favor," he said immediately, "but the vote was five to three."

For a second, I took it favorably. Hey, we came out ahead. But then I realized that in an actual trial, we wouldn't have prevailed. It would be a hung jury as we had *three* against us.

"Wow," I said, in abrupt shock. "I didn't expect it to be that close." But what did I think I was saying? "Close" didn't even count.

And David came right back at me. "You can see it's not cut and dry, Alan. This is an indication. This indicates we can win this case, but we've got a lot of work to do."

He and Joe Limone had exited the "courtroom" at the same time I did. "We had the pizzas sent in," he later explained, "and left the jury to deliberate. Since we'd already used up close to an hour, and we only had these people for two hours, we asked them to stop after a half an hour and tell us their results." He repeated the bad news, trying to get me to see how we could turn it around into better news. "They were five to three for you."

But it didn't sound any better to me.

"Then we got to the most important part," David plunged ahead, "which was asking them *why* they decided the way they did. They gave us their thoughts and some advice. Then Joe and I followed up with more questions, and that was it. A wonderful way to get at least some reality check on what we've been doing."

He told me my two biggest mistakes, right over the telephone.

"You've got to act much more like the executive you once were."

They had suggestions to offer since they felt I had come on, way too casual. But the reason I had worn slacks and a sports coat was really my own mood. I was thinking, *That's the way I am now, and I should probably look like that.* The jury disagreed. When he goes to court, he should look like and act like the executive director he was hired to be by H & W. Otherwise he's not going to convince anybody he was ever really a competent professional.

So I made sure, when we went to trial three weeks later in the Suffolk County courthouse that I dressed just as I had at Hutchins & Wheeler. With the gold collar pin under my understated tie, the whole works.

"And don't be so angry!" David let me know, in no uncertain terms.

I ducked my head at that, and told him that I wasn't as angry as it might have appeared. "Some of it was feigned, you know," I confessed, to my own chagrin. And that was true enough—I've already admitted I was partially acting—because at the time I thought that's the way I *should* be in front of the jury. I shouldn't be just placid. Like, none of this is any big deal, I'm taking it all in stride. I needed to act like the angriest of the *Twelve Angry Men.*

But before long I discovered, under David's guidance, I just needed to be myself. I didn't need to make up a character for the trial.

"Just be yourself."

Even if it took many long hours with David to get to where I *could* just be myself. We spent a lot of time together, David and I, going over my upcoming testimony. "This is what I'm going to ask you, and how are you going to respond?" Then after I'd answered the best I knew how, he'd say, "Why don't you put more emphasis on this than on that? And don't say this, but do say more about that. Because that's very good, and this isn't too good. And don't even bring *that* up, it's off the subject."

The notes he had taken from the mock jurors' comments were perceptive, sometimes prescient, like buried clues to how to overcome our difficulties. *My* difficulties.

The three mock jurors who voted against me clearly had their reasons. The scientist remained adamant, "Alan didn't ask for accommodation, so the defendant has right to fire." Cheryl seemed to be saying I was in way over my head, "Job was very demanding, entirely different from his former field. A lot of people are terminated without warning." Lenny didn't see how H & W had done anything wrong, "All the facts don't show the defendant was happy or unhappy with him. No one said he was doing well. No one said, poorly." But Lenny did have some questions, "What does Alan's 4% raise mean? Was it automatic that everyone got it?" And David picked right up on that, adding his own note, "This is a key issue. Says it might have changed his vote. Show how Alan's raise compared to others."

But the other five mock jurors gave us solid support and promising leads. "If you do a good job, no one recognizes it," Valerie complained. "But the boss always tells you if you screw up." Jennifer charged, "They were trying to force him out by piling on the work." "Did Alan ask if he could get more people?" Audrey inquired, but Jennifer answered, "No one could help Alan with his job." I'd handled the challenge as well as anyone could. "Bring out that Alan is experienced, working with professionals," Jennifer added. "Bring out all *compliments* given to Alan."

David then noted "Fact that they are lawyers didn't affect most people." He wrote that another juror "says H & W should be more aware of the laws than others." But added caustically, "A law firm knows how to get around the law." Was that pretty clearly what H & W was trying to do?

Again, "Bring out that Alan got the highest raise," but "no one worried about Alan's energy level." "Alan didn't leave early," another said, "he had integrity." "Bring people in to say he didn't leave at 5:00," Jerry suggested. "Get the boat schedule," Audrey seconded.

David jotted down, "Jurors liked Alan personally." He quoted May: "Alan is a nice, ordinary guy." But he also noted Jerry's caveats: "Alan is a little smug on the yes/no questions. He should be as nice on cross as on direct. Don't be too defensive."

Overall, even the scientist had to admit that he "felt the law firm looked bad," and several had their own theories about what H & W was really up to. One said, "It was a put-up job from June on." "As soon as they found he had MS," another said, "they decided to get rid of him." "They didn't put him in another job," one reasoned, "therefore, wanted to get rid of him." "Make timing clear," insisted another. "One, got raise, two, next day MS, three, fired."

In contrast to all these shenanigans, one juror emphasized my "loyalty," adding he was "not concerned that Alan didn't keep asking for accommodations." "Alan wanted to fight MS," argued another sympathizer. "Go out and work all that much harder."

As for the other legal points of argument raised, such as breach of contract, David wrote, "People feel the discrimination [charge] is more powerful." Adding, "Jerry says to pick women jurors. They're more sympathetic."

All these helpful hints—after being "on trial," and finding so much support—that is what really galvanized me.

And David could see it happening. "You had more confidence," he later said to me. "I had that confidence before, so the mock trial was not nearly so significant for me as it was for you. It gave you a sort of lift, a real shot in the arm. We've got a case here! You could finally see that. There are people who believe in us. And they gave us good feedback, what the issues are, what to worry about, and what not to worry about."

What I worried about, immediately, was that five-to-three verdict. Clearly there were three people who didn't see it my way, and we had to have ten of twelve on the Suffolk County jury see it my way. This was reminiscent of when I was interviewed at H & W; when I had to convince several partners that I was the best person for the job. That gave me a mission, a real goal for the trial that was coming up.

And that was, frankly, to face up to accepting my own disability.

MS is really the invisible disease. People can in some sense see your fatigue, but it is much more brutally felt by the person with the actual disease. These days it's more obvious that I've got MS, since I now have to use forearm crutches to walk when I'm not on my electric scooter.

The irony is that the disease has to "progress" before most people can readily see the problem.

But I was still struggling *not* to show I was suffering from MS, and doing a pretty good job of it. David says when he first met me, I looked like any healthy, normal guy who walked with a limp. And that's how I was trying to present myself daily to the outside world. Lora and I had discussed the impact of my disability on our partnership. How she increasingly had to take on the responsibility for many of the physical chores that I had traditionally undertaken around the house. How difficult it was. But over time, I've come to know how much the lady I love still needs me just as she has always needed me. But she doesn't need me to clean the garage, mow the lawn, do this, do that, do all this stuff that we guys think that's what we're here for. What the woman I love needs me for, more than anything else, is to be her friend and confidant. That's how Lora could eventually come to accept my disability. And how I, in turn, came to understand and accept my new role in our relationship.

When I finally finished talking with David on the phone that morning, I went off on a very practical investigation, all on my own. In all that feedback from the mock trial, there was one clear directive: "Alan, wear your power suit." So I went around to our bedroom closet and started checking out my old wardrobe for Downtown Boston. Pretty soon I was yanking suits off hangers that needed to go to the cleaners. Then I was pulling my best pair of wingtips out of the dust puppies that were gathering on the closet floor.

I'm no clothes horse, but I like to be turned out as trim as the next gent, and I can tell you, shamelessly, where all this comes from. After I graduated from Worcester Junior College in 1961, I was surely headed for service to our country, and I decided to enlist in the Marines. Why? Maybe it was partially *semper fidelis*, but let's face it, it was really the uniform.

I loved those Marine Dress Blues.

The Marines also taught me how to spit-shine my boots, going over and over the toes with one finger wrapped in a wet rag. I used to do that with the shoes I wore to work at H & W.

And I guess that has never left me. Because what did I do that morning to begin getting ready to walk into Suffolk County Courthouse, to prepare for trial on the question of whether I could be summarily fired "for cause," when the only cause seemed to be multiple sclerosis, to defend my democratic rights as a citizen with a disability?

I started spit-polishing my wingtips.

Chapter Two

But believe me, I didn't slide into any high-polish life after I got out of the Marines. I returned to my blue-collar, Catholic roots in working class Worcester, where our Holy Name of Jesus parish was actually French-speaking. But at home we didn't speak French—even though my mother's family was French-Canadian.

When I got out of the Marine Corps, I got a job selling equipment for a company named Addressograph-Multigraph Corp. on commission, very low tech. I was pretty much jogging in place, exceeding my quota about half the time. But I did manage to meet Lora, who was working for a travel agency in Worcester, an agency where she would ultimately become the manager. Fate certainly smiled on me that day. I dropped by to arrange a family trip to Florida. She claims I asked her to rent me a Chevy Corvair at the Miami Airport, then I smiled and said, "Of course if I were taking you, it'd be a Corvette." I wouldn't deny that under oath, and she managed a wonderfully kittenish smile herself, one that has since gotten me through many a bad moment and tough times. We were married the next year.

Lora's parents were born and educated in Worcester. They moved from the city to a forty-acre farm in Leicester when Lora was just six years old. Petite and fair, Lora and her sister, Gail, could ride horses like the wind. They would rise at dawn on horse show days so they could ride to the appropriate town. After high school Lora had a brief career in New York City in the airline industry and then an even briefer marriage. Lora returned to Worcester and put her airline experience to work at the Worcester airport and then as a travel consultant in the city. We married within six months of our first meeting. In one day I became a husband, a stepfather to a three-year old and a technically excommunicated Catholic.

We petitioned the bishop in Worcester to recognize our vows, but nothing came of our plea. We never even got a response. Blessedly, I had Lora and her son, Jonathan, and my real concern was how to provide a better life for both of them. Selling for the Addressograph-Multigraph Corp. was strictly a Willie Loman job. But I was learning how to set up efficient office systems for my larger customers. In 1968, a close friend at Addressograph landed a job in the computer department at St. Vincent Hospital in Worcester; and he helped me get a job there.

It so happened that the Sisters of Providence sponsored St. Vincent. That put me back in touch with the Church, though I was still forbidden the sacraments. I did keep praying, but my sense of God was pretty remote. It came down to a vague worry about the legitimacy of my marriage, though Lora says nonsense, she *"always* felt married." My real problem was how to launch myself on a more fruitful career track—a couple, two, three steps nearer that well-beaten path to success.

Luckily I had the G.I. Bill, so I started going to Clark University, right in Worcester, at night. I worked a two-for-one combo, taking courses in information technology and other business related subjects. Between my night studies and my day job at St. Vincent. I'd wrap a lot of my hospital work into the project case studies I was assigned at Clark. It took me eight years, but I got an MBA in 1976.

I worked at night to obtain an MBA. That became a stepping stone. I was hired as an assistant administrator at Providence Hospital in Holyoke which—unlike St. Vincent—was owned by the Sisters of Providence. I must have made a good impression on the sisters who were board members at Providence. In 1979, they made me CEO of their most troubled healthcare center, Farren Memorial Hospital in Turners Falls. This time, I spotted a terrific opportunity.

To keep the place from going broke, we decided to rejuvenate its outpatient health care services. We put together a hospital-based group recruited from prestigious places like Albert Einstein in New York City and the Hersey Medical Center. I found a lot of young doctors, working in big city hospitals where they were unhappy with their lifestyles.

By coming into the area, they could have an exciting practice, but still raise their families in an idyllic setting, share coverage with each other, and have a life.

And I knew this would work because that's what Lora and I were already doing. Even developing our own fifteen acres of pasture and hillside, parcels of which we were eventually planning to develop as four housing lots. Lora was still commuting to her travel agency in Worcester, and the stress did bring on a medical emergency—a collapsed lung from an early form of emphysema. But the medical team I had helped put in place was superb throughout a long crisis. She had to have two operations, after her other lung collapsed, and spent weeks in the intensive care unit with several of her ribs surgically broken. But she toughed it out, made it through, thanks to our young doctors and a great local surgeon. Afterwards, she set up her own travel agency in Greenfield, named "Madelene Travel," after her mother.

So life, despite such setbacks, was good. As chief of a Catholic hospital, I was now attending Mass frequently. I loved being part of the healing mission of the Church, which only made me chafe more since I couldn't approach the altar to take communion.

But in any Eden, there is bound to be a snake coiling somewhere in the rustling leaves, and at Farren, it was beneath the hospital's financials.

We got caught in its strangle hold. I managed to make a profit one year, but the reimbursement system was so crazy that you never knew how much revenue was going to be taken away from you by Medicare or Medicaid. I had to tell the Trustees that I didn't see how we could make it through another year in light of the forthcoming, even more restrictive Federal reimbursement controls.

Sister Catherine, the president of the corporation that oversaw the operations of the Sisters of Providence facilities, came to see me one April night after a board meeting. Neither she nor I were able to concede that the small acute care hospital was being extinguished by the vagaries of the American health care system. As went the house calling physician, so was going the comfort of the small caring hospital. I was transferred to Sister Catherine's staff and a house cleaning CEO was hired for Farren. After much blood letting and a million dollar loss under his tenure, the sisters opted to seek its conversion to a chronic care hospital. Ironically, I helped get the legislation passed at the State House in Boston to allow them to convert Farren into just such a chronic care facility. Also, I ended up leading the statewide lobbying team that got an additional $95 million (annually) from the legislature for forty "low cost" hospitals in Massachusetts, several million going to those the sisters ran. I did well on these political visits to the Hub, working with my peers from the other hospitals.

In spite of my success at the parent corporation, I sorely missed the challenges of leadership. Just as the role of being a navigator couldn't replace the "esprit de corps" and excitement that went along with being a pilot, working in a staff position could never replace the "sense of self esteem" and excitement of being in a line position as a CEO or COO.

So I was ready for the call when it came from a Boston headhunter, saying a Downtown law firm was looking for an executive director. An out-of-the-blue opportunity to move back on to that path toward success, another shot at renewing my daily interaction with people in an operational setting. I've always loved the challenge of on-line problem-solving, creating more efficient systems and training superior managers to administer them. But then again, what did I know about running a multi-practice law firm?

"Stop thinking about it," Lora cut me off. "Just go for it."

At 8:30, on a March morning in 1990, I showed up for my interview with the management committee of Hutchins & Wheeler at 101 Federal Street. The firm resided in an impressive, newly girdered, Boston Harbor high-rise, dropped as if by hovering construction cranes right in the middle of the financial district. H & W had aggressively moved into its top four floors from their old quarters at One Boston Place. When I pushed through the swinging glass door at street level, I couldn't help wondering what it might feel like, walking through this high-glaze portal to rise upward, everyday.

I took the elevator to the 28th floor, walked through more thick glass, and was electronically released across yards of deep carpeting and polished stands of mahogany furniture. "Mr. Labonte is here," the receptionist intercommed, and I was ushered to a large conference room to meet among several others: Charles Robins, chair of the management committee, Jack Clymer, chair of the trusts and estates department, and Fred Grein, the firm's treasurer, who had both an MBA from Dartmouth's Tuck School as well as a law degree from Boston University.

They set about carefully sizing me up. The main player of this cautionary game was clearly Charles Robins, the partner whom I soon discovered brought in the most business, fully ten percent of H & W's billings. Someone, who in the jargon of law firms, is called a "rainmaker." He was scrupulously formal, conservative in both manner and dress, but smooth, even gentle in speech, though often, and pensively, silent. But then, so were they all, that day. The only thing Fred Grein ever said, after I sought to explain what my own financial experience was, "He's just saying he's not an accountant." I did well, much later, to remember that dismissive remark.

We plunged into a discussion of the difficulties caused by the dual relationship the firm had with its secretaries. Each secretary reported both to the chief administrator and to a particular attorney. That created problems whenever the administrator and the attorney disagreed on any secretary's performance evaluation. I said I'd gone through similar difficulties in evaluating members of my own staff, who also worked individually for a hospital-based physician. I was beginning to find and strike analogies between my labors in the healthcare system and professional relationships within H & W.

I said I always sought compromise and fairness, but emphasized that I was averse to any prima donna who fouled the links in the chain of command, that I did not work well with people with "big egos." "If you want somebody who will cater to someone's ego," I told them, "hire somebody else. I'm not good at it."

Did they hear me that first day, loud and clear? Too early in the deal to tell, since they were looking at four or five other candidates over the next few weeks. Two would be selected as finalists, then one offered the job. Meanwhile, the interviewers were waiting on another member of the management committee, Anthony Medaglia, off in Florida. I also had to wait for Tony Medaglia, who would meet with every likely candidate upon his return.

This turned out to be, as I would learn over time at H & W typical of Tony. He and Robins had the two corner offices on the 29th floor, overlooking the Boston skyline in equal splendor, located where they could most conveniently get together. Tony Medaglia was also a rainmaker, bringing in eight percent of the firm's income, and he always managed to meet with everybody, including Robins, one on one. What the rest of the firm did by committee, he handled strictly *mano a mano*.

Within a week, on a very windy, rainy, spring morning in Boston, I found myself running down the flooding State House steps—after doing more of the Sisters' business—trying to wave down a taxi for my appointment with Tony. By the time I got into a cab, I was soaked. I had studied my notes carefully, preparing for the interview, but I looked like a wreck. My hair and coat were drenched, my pants had lost their crease, and the shine had run off my shoes.

Tony, as usual, was impeccably dressed. A nicely starched shirt, suspenders and hand-tied bow tie, with his manicured nails buffed to a gleam. He had a very polished manner of speech, but a brusque, standoffish, rude if need be, style. He was Harvard Law School, and it was patently clear that he'd gone there to become some firm's dominating partner.

I took my seat in the handsome leather chair he offered, and tried to apologize for my bedraggled appearance.

"We're not hiring you for your sartorial splendor," he allowed.

Then he went through much the same questions I'd been asked by the management committee, glancing at a document on a small table beside him. Since the script was familiar, and I'd reflected carefully on my previous answers, I improved on my performance over the next half an hour, I felt I was giving an impressive interview. Only once did Tony come down hard. "Do you think you're tough enough to do this job?" I had an instant impression he was looking to hire an enforcer. I nodded, almost by reflex. Then we went on to something else, until I got my edge back. "You asked me if I thought I was tough enough," I backed up. "I think I'm smart enough to do this job."

He made a note, the only one I saw him take.

So I remained in the running, despite my soggy display, and returned for follow-up interviews. Robins explained they were creating a new position of Executive Director, a member of the management committee, with full powers of Chief Operating Officer. Thus, I would have to be approved by all department heads.

At this point, I was one of two finalists. The other candidate came from a law firm, so it was up to me to argue the value of my own past expertise. I kept drawing job-related parallels. For example, I had overseen a hospital's medical library, online with the automated Index Medicus, so I could take charge of their 28th-floor law library, online with Lexis.

Again Tony took me quietly aside and alone into his office, confided that I'd done a great job interviewing, and assured me I would probably get the job. "So long," he added, "as you don't act like a pig."

That was Tony's zinging contribution to the salary negotiations. I was asking for $120,000 with a company car, while the firm was offering $115,000 and no car. If I would take their salary without a car, they would agree to a signing bonus of $20,000. Their benefits package included a month's vacation, fully paid Blue Cross Blue Shield medical insurance, life insurance, and long-term disability coverage. My head was spinning at my suddenly improving prospects, but I hung onto a last few cautions.

I needed to see H & W's own financials, if I was going to be handling them, so I had a final meeting with Robins to go over the books.

I saw the firm was owed many millions in accounts receivable and income from work-in-process, those yet unbilled hours on cases open and pending. A sizeable cache, but the true value of these tenuous assets was questionable.

A downturn in business everywhere around Boston reflected in slower payments to the firm. In the affluent 80s, lawyering had kept pace with the booming economy, the high tech growth and all the new ventures involving complex corporate restructuring that went into what Governor Michael Dukakis called "The Massachusetts Miracle." But the Miracle was over.

Collections on H & W bills were running so far behind expenditures that at least $4 million was long past due. When suddenly aware of this yawning short fall, I almost didn't take the job. But Robins assured me that all the senior partners would be my stalwart allies against the financial threats the partnership faced.

On April 27, 1990, Robins faxed me an employment contract, with a severance clause providing for six months continuing salary if I left the firm. I immediately signed, and faxed it back. I hadn't felt such relief since my discharge from the Marine Corps during the Vietnam War.

I was due on the job in June, but met everybody from the firm during a Cape Cod outing in May. So I left the Sisters after 22 years for the topmost 31st floor at 101 Federal, where I too was given an office with a sliver of a view of Boston Harbor.

There was one other large perk on the 31st floor—an in-house, gourmet restaurant, the 101 Grille, with a chef and two assistants, operated solely for and by H & W. Once a month, a terrific dinner was prepared for the partners, after which the business of the partnership was conducted. That July, I was asked, as a command performance, to report on their fiscal future. I handed around packaged reports that highlighted what I now calculated to be $5.5 million in accounts receivable plus another $7.5 million in unbilled work-in-process. I reminded them that their own consultants had warned this was twice the amount of un-billed work and receivables normally carried by other law firms.

I'd already decided to write off $500,000 in bad debts and engage Dun and Bradstreet to go after other defaulting clients, in order to stimulate collections. With my staff of eight administrative managers, I had also begun spotting small savings that could turn into large gains. Just as a symbolic gesture, we'd already turned back two unused parking spaces in the garage by One Boston Place. Peanuts, barely $1000 a year, but even small savings had a way of adding up over time.

Ultimately, I said, they would have to apply the "golden rule" to their own situation. That is, "He who has the gold, rules!" That got a laugh, and I then urged a concerted campaign to collect a much needed $4 million from their delinquent clients. I'd already talked to each of the partners about whom they needed to approach about timely payment. That potential cash flow would pay off the worst of their own debts and allow for a substantial cash distribution to the partners. I got a nice hand for that hopeful prospect, and several compliments afterwards for the quality of my comments.

During the summer, H & W had its annual outing for the partners and their spouses at the Ipswich Country Club. This was the first time they had an opportunity to meet my wife, Lora, and she could not have been more warmly received. Early in August, I contacted the State Street Bank to start the renewal process for H & W's line of credit, which provided $2 million in annual working capital. It was paid off at least once annually, usually at chaotic year's end, but H & W was becoming dependent upon these millions for continuing operations. The partners also had another $2.7 million loan with State Street for furniture, office equipment, and other furnishings to their plush new offices. So that by the end of June 1990, H & W was into their chief banker for almost $3 million, with another $2.6 owed to other lenders, including the Bank of New England, also a client.

The State Street Bank officer was friendly and receptive, but wary. She didn't like the level of accounts receivable any more than I did, nor the cash drain from one vacant floor out of the four we still leased at One Boston Place. I told her we were working hard on collections, and might even sue one past due client. What I *didn't* tell her was that in addition to the $50,000 per month H & W was losing on its old leased quarters, we were also coming to the end of our honeymoon with the landlord at 101 Federal. After September we were obligated to pay $38 per foot, and that times 73,000 square feet, plus operating expenses came to over $300,000 rent every month. I figured the bank officer was already looking dubious enough. But I had to warn the management committee that State Street, as a condition of extending the line of credit, was considering imposing conditions on how we made distributions to partners in the future.

They said State Street was always acting too "white shoe," so I recommended that we start looking elsewhere for a line of credit.

John Thomson and I did manage to negotiate a quick lease for that empty 33rd floor at One Boston Place. We checked the tenant's bank references, had the principals sign personal guarantees, got $20,000 up front for the first month. But that's all we ever received. A couple of months later, we realized we'd been stiffed. They were only buying time until their next dark-of-night jump, wherever they were taking their scam, and we soon had the empty floor back on our hands.

To keep on top of this big, new, but frustrating job, I decided to take a temporary apartment in Boston. Lora and I figured we'd delay any move from Greenfield until we were sure the job was working out. She came into town one weekend to help me find a rental—at the Devonshire, only three blocks away from 101 Federal—and then we went sightseeing around Downtown Boston. I enjoyed myself, but found I couldn't walk too far without getting fatigued.

Lora noticed, and worried why my endurance was so low.

"I guess I'm just feeling a little tired today," I tried to brush aside her worry.

But I was already beginning to feel those first tinges from MS that I naturally took to be the rising stress and strain at the office. I was faced with recurring crises, large and small, that led straight into the pitfalls of office politics at H & W.

These blips could be touched off by the least unguarded remark. Initially Robins—and I presume Tony—had decided to drop Fred Grein from those weekly management committee meetings, since I was now on board. But Robins planned to tell Grein privately, in his own good time. Inadvertently I let slip this news, which got back to Grein, who was incensed. Robins called me into his office, livid himself, and warned me to keep strict confidentiality about what was said at management meetings.

It was my own fault, but the incident marked a small break in the smoothness of my relationship with Robins. He had been stopping by my office every morning at eight A.M. to pick up a one-page summary of the previous day's cash position. We'd talk over the next collections, in easy and pleasant sync. But now I saw he could be cutting, even demeaning, and I vowed to watch my step.

This daily cash summary had fallen to me because the head bookkeeper, Eleanor Lanes, was out on extended medical leave, convalescing at home after an operation on her leg. I called her early to offer my sympathy. She was grateful and offered to do some work at home and have the accounting department prepare a one-page cash position summary for me, so I could have it to discuss with Robins.

I thanked her for that significant help, only to discover that there was a move afoot to fire her, since she had been absent for so long from the firm. H & W was continuing to pay her salary and benefits, which came to $6000 per month. I was being asked about her recovery, and for several weeks I hedged. "She's making progress and doing work from home. I'm certain she'll be back very soon."

Her name came up again at the next week's management committee meeting. Charles Robins looked grim and defaulted to me. I took the plunge. "Eleanor is a long-term employee. In her illness, she has continued to demonstrate loyalty and dedication. Her counsel is of great value to the firm—and to me. I want to see her through this crisis, if possible." I called her that day and said I needed to know, *now*, when she would return to work. She promised to talk to her doctor and get right back to me. A week later, I was able to report she was planning to be back at work on October 22nd.

Everybody looked very surprised, while Robins looked very relieved and very pleased.

Eleanor returned to become, to all appearances, my close co-worker and immediate friend. She would even bring me little pastry treats. With her help, I pulled together a highly detailed expense budget and cash flow analysis for the coming year, 1991. We also did a detailed forecast of expenses for the rest of 1990. It was the first operating budget the firm had ever had, and I invited Eleanor into the management meeting to defend our rationale, and respond to questions. Not only did management sit still for it, they agreed to our guidelines.

Though I did notice a sudden, early hole in my day. Robins no longer dropped by to see me for the summary and chat about our cash position. He and Eleanor had resumed their prior morning meetings.

Margaret Hadley—like Eleanor, another longtime employee, both around fifteen years with H & W—was director of human resources. She came on warm and friendly, offering me much advice. But despite her grace and diplomacy, she remained oddly reticent. Behind her introspective mien, I could never be sure what she was really thinking.

One morning I came into work, and Margaret informed me that our in-house telephone system was "down." The phone system was her responsibility. She reported that no one in the firm could place or receive a phone call. Charles Robins came by, extremely upset, protesting the enormous cost in lost client time and billing. By his estimate, $17,500 per hour. I got hold of the service people, who had the system up and running within several hours, but a few days later, it happened again. I called, then wrote the president of Northern Telecom, the company that had installed the whole mess. I detailed the impact of the breakdowns, and demanded a more reliable system. All the partners' names ran in phalanx off the letterhead, warning that it might not be too wise to get into a dispute with this bunch of disgruntled Boston attorneys. The phone system was quickly upgraded, and began functioning smoothly. The upgrade cost $25,000, but the free service provided by the embarrassed company offset the expense. Another small saving toward an eventually large gain.

I soon discovered that the firm's entire computerized billing system required an upgrade in order to speed things up, improve operating efficiency and reduce cost. And that brought me into uncomfortably close contact with Charlie Gaziano.

Charlie Gaziano had previously been performing many of my functions as the interim firm administrator but chose to turn down the job of executive director. Boston law firms, he forewarned me, don't let top administrators enjoy a lengthy tenure. He preferred to stay administrative head of both the trust and tax departments. When I came aboard, he did offer to help me make the transition, and at first I confided in him. But soon enough, I found him trying to manipulate me, along the lines of his own agenda of how he had done the job and how I should do the job. He tried to use me rather than really help me.

Charlie had developed his own hybrid computerized system for the trust department, which he jealously guarded internally, and designed systems and offered his services as a consultant to outside law firms. Charlie even used H & W personnel to convert and automate other law firms' trust accounting systems. He did compensate the firm with a share of the profits, from his lucrative consulting practice.

What disturbed me was the partnership allowing Charlie to report to another member of the management committee on a "sweetheart" deal, over which I had no control. Here I had been put in charge of all four of these employees: Eleanor Lanes, Margaret Hadley, Charles Gaziano, and Ruth Clarke. They were half my administrative staff of eight departmental directors, including the excellent Mike Dunham as mail room manager. I had to build my working relationship with them from a flat start, for instance, by moving Eleanor nearer my own office on her return. But Charlie always took his own lead, often blatantly, as when he came to ask me to raise a member of his staff's salary. The increase was outside the limits that had been set, at my urging, by the management committee. I was attempting to bring equity into the firm's employee compensation program, as I had suggested should be done with the secretaries during my first job interview. I wanted more structured performance evaluations that treated everybody the same, under a uniform set of standards.

"Look, Alan, this isn't anyone asking you for this," he whined. "*I'm* asking you, and if I were still sitting in your chair, I would do this."

"I'm sorry Charlie," I insisted. "I can't help you."

And he was gone from my office with an abrupt goodbye and menacing body language.

I realize these machinations sound petty compared to the firm's grander actions in court, under the blind majesty of Justice—all the deft arguments and high pleadings, and many billable hours, that went into the daily practice of the law by twenty-nine partners and their associates. But from my own daily observations, I could see how critically near to shipwreck, through imminent financial foundering, the firm itself was sailing. And if I couldn't get things righted below decks—if only operating as the ship's purser—how long would we remain afloat and shipshape?

Early one morning in October, Tony and Robins called me into a meeting of just themselves. They were acutely aware—from our financial projections—that H & W couldn't cover operating expenses and meet the desired compensation levels for the partners. Desired, though not necessarily deserved. As one economy, could I reduce the number of non-legal staff? I said we could since the level of services we now provided to clients had plateaued after the firm's rapid growth in the 80s.

I brought Margaret Hadley in on the secret, and she came up, none too happily, with recommended cuts in staff. Then together we went to the management committee with our proposal to eliminate nine positions. After Margaret left the room, Tony complained that these reductions were coming more from Margaret than from me!

Of course they were, I responded. I'd been with the firm only five months, and Margaret had recruited the staff we were cutting. She knew better than I where, and how best, we could eliminate people without adversely affecting the services we offered. After some discussion, with Tony still unmollified, the committee approved reducing the staff by nine.

Margaret took charge of the lay-offs. Her office was next to mine, and I soon gathered, from her distressed demeanor, how very difficult all this was for her. Again I tried to help her through the ordeal. We provided letters of reference and one week's pay for each year served.

But no lawyers were laid off. In fact, at the very next management committee meeting, Tony immediately announced, "It's time to feed the donkey."

What on earth did that mean? I was momentarily puzzled, but not for long. I could almost hear the braying inside the 29th Floor conference room. They were going to award the partners their bonus compensation, even though insufficient funds had been collected from billings. The funds would have to come out of their State Street line of credit. And I was enraged.

"Look, we can't keep doing this," I burst out. "It's up to the partners to bring in the cash when we need it. I've got to send State Street our quarterly report in the next few days, and they are going to go wild when they see this in our financials." I even added, not like me: "We are going to look like a bunch of assholes."

Tony looked straight at me. "I don't care."

He then called for a vote, and the committee affirmed his decision to make the distribution.

I was shocked, but all I could do was hope and pray that the cash would be forthcoming from the firm's frantic year-end closing process. I'd been slyly warned by Charlie Gaziano that the period from December through the holidays into January was a hard-driving and stressful one of playing catch-up. We were clearly dealing with an under performing computer system, but we also had a lot of procrastinating, even dilatory lawyers. The workweek was soon extended to "billing Saturdays" when all the attorneys were supposed to come into the office to prepare their long-overdue client bills.

Again I was thankful that Eleanor was back at work, doing the books. I showed up for every "billing Saturday" myself, but my role was more symbolic than practical. I made the rounds of their offices, to follow up on every outstanding account. Within the circle of Boston's law firm administrators, this is called "beating them up." If you bugged them enough, they'd do the work just to get rid of you. Also, this gave them a chance to complain about any administrative problem—straight to my face, standing right there in their doorway. "Look, I can't fix it," I was fond of saying, "if I don't know it's broken."

During these hectic months, I reported directly (and only) to Charles Robins as chairman of the management committee. Robins saw to it that the committee stayed focused on the firm's financial problems and encouraged open discussion to face what I foresaw as looming disasters. But it soon became apparent how much Tony Medaglia disapproved of "all this self-flagellation." Sometimes he would huff and puff himself up out of his chair, right in the middle of a heated exchange, and announce he was "going for a walk." He had a short fuse, really didn't like being cooped up in meetings, especially with people over whom he couldn't exercise an iron-fisted control. Tony would occasionally move that the meeting go into "executive session." A polite way of asking me to leave the room, but Robins would have none of it. With his busy practice, Robins had to schedule himself very carefully, but he made time to see that he and I reached consensus before any disputed matter got to the committee.

Because the firm was going through tough times, I tried to keep well in the background, when time came to share in the benefits. H & W had always given Christmas bonuses, and I told the committee it was important to do the same this year, in light of the recent lay-offs, to keep up staff morale. I submitted a list of eligible employees, who had all made significant contributions. Jack Clymer looked over the list, and asked why my name wasn't on it. I said I was new with the firm, already well compensated, and I didn't feel justified in asking for the traditional bonus. The committee voted to approve the Christmas bonuses, and instructed me to add my name to the list. I ended up receiving $4400.

I took this as definite approval of my own performance midst the rising seasonal chaos. We were soon into that short "stub period" of two-to-three weeks in January when the books are kept open—after December 31st—so that lawyers can still collect from their clients. Such additional cash would be credited toward their yearly compensation on one set of books, and calculated in their share of profits from 1990.

This created piles of work for Eleanor's accounting department, who had three closings, two year end and one monthly, within a one-month period. The bind came when we closed the stub period on January 25th and tried to catch up on the hourly billing of clients for January. Eleanor's staff had only a short time to process the lawyers' diary entries (those hours worked by attorneys for specific clients) that had accumulated during the stub period. These entries were electronically stored in that Wang computer cave, using software designed long before my arrival at H & W.

Yes, it was accessible, but slowly, cumbersomely, taking three days to gestate, grind out, and grudgingly disclose those billable hours. And at that, those hours were still not billed because Ruth's system couldn't process the diary entries and compute the bills simultaneously.

So we billed very few clients in January.

Robins was upset and angry since we were now off by almost a month on budgeted cash flow. I should have anticipated the problem, he argued, but all I had to go on was Ruth's predictions of a smooth and timely transition. We recovered by February through Herculean efforts, but I could no longer put my trust in Ruth's predictions.

When we closed the stub period on January 25th, the 1990 profits were not nearly as large as everybody had hoped. That pointed to an even harder year ahead. I continued to hunt down small savings, including one that was especially gratifying—a credit of $42,000 for misallocation of operating expenses to H & W by the landlord at One Boston Place. John Thomson and I had uncovered this discrepancy, which pleased the management committee and relieved some of the tension over our failed rental of that 33rd Floor. Altogether, after Eleanor and I prepared the final summary of the 1990 operating statement, I was able to show that expenses were $300,000 below what we had estimated three months earlier. But looking ahead, I saw the firm still had to come up with additional cuts of $500,000 in projected 1991 expenditures.

That, I knew, was going to be tough sledding because we couldn't get there by my planned changes in the firm's benefit plans and further cuts in non-legal staff. The attorneys had to cut their own legal support staff. I proposed that we eliminate another six non-legal positions, and awaited their proposal to cut many associate attorneys from the firm's roster of lawyers.

This tight situation was brought home to the management committee by State Street Bank's stringent limitations on any future credit. State Street would renew the $2 million line of credit, but only if H & W agreed to have partners pay greater attention to past due receivables before any further distributions were made to the partners. Exactly as I had warned them. I used my financial cash flow model, feeding in recent historical data from the firm, to demonstrate the impact of these stipulations, i.e. how they might curtail the management committee's control over its own decisions. The committee was sobered by my analysis—as the State Street bankers had been—and voted to accept my recommendation to seek a new line of credit elsewhere.

To whom did management turn, at Tony's urging? To one of their own clients, the Olympic Bank, which has since disappeared, shut down by the FDIC in June of 1992. Olympic set up a $2 million line of credit in February, without a murmur of stipulation.

In more and more cases, Tony seemed to be affecting outcomes. Margaret Hadley and I put together a program to give merit increases to non-legal staff. It provided moderately larger increases for the firm's administrative managers because they were expected to be far more committed to the firm—through longer, harder work schedules—compared to other administrative personnel. But Tony would have none of this, demanding that everybody should be evaluated on the same scale. We went back to the committee three times, in an effort to compromise with the Medaglia position. As usual, I felt that I had consensus with Robins. But Tony was adamant. And while Robins was still powerful, when Tony stamped his foot often enough and hard enough, Robins deferred to him. We had to concede.

That April, I decided to face up to the dysfunctions of the H & W computerized billing system. It was already a hot potato since a prior committee of attorneys had paid a hefty sum for an improved software package. Only, they hadn't involved Eleanor Lanes, who found the software couldn't perform the functions required to keep the two sets of books needed to integrate the firm's tax liability with its profit distributions. An impasse, which I was assigned to break, since I had experience in computer systems analysis. I approached the assignment warily, preferring to find an outside consultant, one that was an expert in both Wang and Digital computer systems.

I got one name from Margaret Hadley—someone in private practice who had the credentials we asked; who knew the wobbly nature of our

Wang equipment, the ins and outs of the software package; and who had long experience doing exactly this kind of evaluation for other law firms.

Another name came from Tony—that of Chris Medaglia, his son. Chris worked at Hale & Dorr, another prestigious Boston law firm, which had an in-house system group that did outside consulting. Tony urged me to call Chris, inquire about a consulting arrangement.

In the end, I did what I always hoped I would do. Looked to the merits, and decided, as I explained to Tony privately in his office, I had to do "what was best for the firm." The individual consultant appeared to be more qualified to do the detailed analysis, and the cost was far less. Tony listened intently, but gave no hint of how he felt. He was totally non-committal, and left me wondering—as I left his office—where I really stood.

Heartily sick of city living on top of all the daily pressure, I decided to move out to the more beautiful South Shore of Massachusetts. I'd been confined to quarters at the Devonshire for almost a year, with newly acquired twinges of bodily fatigue that were hints of MS. So I took off, on a Saturday morning in late April for Cohasset, and found a seaside apartment, in a white colonial complex, overlooking Black Rock Beach. I stood with the landlord in front of the large picture window, and just let its full stretch of shimmering glass reveal the beautiful spring day out there over the blue roil of Massachusetts Bay. I rented the place on the spot—for a couple hundred dollars less than the Devonshire—set to move in on May 15th.

This would also be Lora's pied-a-terre, away from Greenfield, where she could come and start looking for a more permanent residence in Cohasset. I felt confident that I was in good standing at H & W and this was confirmed for me by the evaluation I received at the end of my first year as executive director. I believed I had made my mark by my all-out effort to impose fiscal discipline, and Charles Robins said as much in my annual review in June.

He had been my mentor, and the firm's leader, providing the political underpinnings that buttressed my day-to-day operational reforms at the firm. Robins offered some constructive criticism of my performance—minor in nature—and gave me a raise of $4,600—greater than that which any other administrative person received. Charlie Gaziano was next at $3000. I was grateful to Robins for having included me in all aspects of the firm's business, regardless of the sensitivity of matters under discussion. And I thanked him, then and there, for his openness, help and support.

Each month now, I carefully compared actual financials with the budget forecast we'd prepared for 1991. The forecast was surprisingly accurate on sales, i.e. billable hours, receipts from fiduciary work on trusts, and expenditures. Everything was in balance, except cash flow, which depended, as always, on the lawyers bothering to collect their hourly fees and disbursements. I talked myself "blue in the face" at every monthly dinner meeting in the large conference room with dinner provided by Grille 101. The partners wiped their sleek chins and nodded agreement and went on avoiding the embarrassment of bluntly asking to be paid for their services, even though several of the partners were not helpful in collecting overdue fees from there clients.,

In May, I gave Margaret Hadley her annual appraisal. I told her she had done a great job, shown poise and grit in stressful times. I gave her the maximum allowable raise of $3000, and said I thought she had real executive potential. I went so far as to promise to train her to be my successor if she was interested. She took what I had to say with her usual reserve, maintaining her habitual reticence. "I'll think about it."

Undaunted by all this well-mannered recalcitrance, I plunged ahead with my major effort to restructure the firm's healthcare program. This is where I felt I could rightly call upon my own expertise, and Margaret's assistance was invaluable in gathering first-hand information about employee needs and desires. We had further help in evaluating our healthcare coverage from a large insurance agency that happened to be Jack Clymer's client.

The firm presently offered two choices: an indemnity plan from Blue Cross with full coverage of all medical expenses, or an HMO under the Harvard Community Health Plan. The indemnity plan was very expensive since it included the right to choose any physician or hospital in Massachusetts. The HMO was less expensive but limited selection to a dedicated panel of physicians and hospitals. Premiums were paid by the firm with a certain proportion charged back to participating employees through payroll deductions. But partners ended up paying the full cost of premiums, so that many of them had actually chosen the HMO option, and, as we found to our surprise, they were satisfied with the services they received.

On this knowledge base about outcomes, I recommended the adoption of a single managed-care plan, financed through self-funding from the patient pool within the firm, rather than have medical expenses paid by a third party. I proposed to act as the plan's administrator, as I had previously done for 4500 employees, also self-insured, within Providence Systems. Access to all claims data would allow me to craft and manage a benefits package that would meet both employee and partner needs while minimizing costs. I wasn't trying to pinch pennies. I wanted our people to have high quality care through access to outstanding physicians and the best hospitals. But I knew from long experience in healthcare management that you could fund a high quality benefit plan and still save a lot of money.

On May 8th, I presented this self-funded, managed-care plan to the management committee, estimating that first-year savings would come to $150,000. Robins and others were keenly interested, and the committee endorsed my proposal. I was told to meet with Michael Gengler, a healthcare attorney who had recently joined H & W, so he could advise on any potential legal complications, particularly for the partners.

Around this same time, I also recommended changes in the firm's life insurance benefit plan. We had been able to negotiate with the insurance carriers, and I could offer a $500,000 policy for each partner at a weighted cost of only $90 a month. A dramatic improvement over their existing plan, and since this was a group plan, any member of the group would be insured regardless of health status. Again, the committee was enthusiastic and approved the changes. Only, how much should each partner then be charged? I proposed the weighted average of $90, because one of the reasons behind insurance was an equal sharing of risks among the group. They turned and looked at me like I was demented. Finally somebody moved that each partner pay his own premium based on his age. If these people are really a partnership, I remember reflecting, they sure don't act like they share much of a common bond.

I began to worry more and more about stumbling on my way to work, after deboarding the Hingham ferry. It's only stress from the job, I kept telling myself. But in the midst of revamping the firm's healthcare coverage, I got to wonder about my own health. Was I really taking proper care of myself? I'd gone to see one neurologist, then talked to my primary care physician in Boston. He had sent me along to an orthopedic surgeon, who couldn't find anything wrong with me either. Maybe I was not accessing the right doctors, among all the medical talent for which Boston has long been famous.

One morning I went down to Tony Medaglia's office to ask him—very privately—if he could recommend a good physician in the Boston area to evaluate my problem. Tony was actually empathetic—a rare moment in our relationship—and gave me the name of Dr. James Wepsic at New England Baptist Hospital. I didn't know it at the time, but *wouldn't* you know it? Dr. Wepsic was one of Tony's clients, too. He also had all the right stuff. Examining me routinely, he found I had an "upgoing toe" on my right foot. The "Babinski Reflex," which he triggered by scratching the inside arch of my foot, a stimulus that normally causes the toes to clench *downward*. He also detected a slight distortion in my speech. Which symptoms required that I immediately travel to Cambridge for a Magnetic Resonance Imaging scan of my cranium.

I have to admit the MRI was a frightening experience. I've got claustrophobia that goes back to a childhood sledding accident, which caused a terrible concussion. But it had greatly increased after my crash-landing water training in flight school. They strapped you into this cage we called the Dempsey Dumpster, and you went down a long chute into a swimming pool. The cage hit like a downed airplane, tipped over, sank to the deep bottom. You had to wait, sit there, upside down, in your full flight gear and helmet, until the cage settled. Then you were supposed to unbuckle your seatbelt, pull yourself out, and head up to the surface.

I've always felt claustrophobic any time I get held down and I can't get away. So I didn't wait long enough, and struggling to get out of the cage, my parachute harness got caught. The divers had to come down and release me, push me sputtering to the surface. Then I was sent back up the ladder, right to the top of the chute again, and I made my decision right then and there. I don't care, if I'm out of the program, I'm not going to drown for these people. And I glared at this corpsman who was strapping me in, and I said, "Look, I don't want to do this." And he said, "Sorry, sir, we're too busy." Wham, he hit this big red button, and down the chute again. This is it, they're going to kill me. To hell with it. I just gave up. I'm dead, so what? I'll just drown, and that will be the end of it.

And the cage rammed down into the pool, flipped upside down again, and I just sat there, totally complacent. Very soon, it settled. All the bubbles stopped. I decided that I must have drowned. So I reached down, unstrapped my harness and kicked myself out. The divers gave me a "thumbs up" and that was the end of it.

The MRI was twice as scary as that Dempsey Dumpster. What should have taken maybe forty minutes lasted an hour and a half. The technician, a woman who was a lot more sympathetic than that tough corpsman, kept fanning me between trips down into that narrow, dark, deep-end tube.

When Dr. Wepsic read the radiologist's interpretation from my MRI, there was a potential problem. A flag—a white spot on the computerized image—had shown up. I needed to see a neurologist, and he referred me to Dr. Edward R. Wolpow, at Mount Auburn Hospital in Cambridge. Dr. Wepsic's secretary warned that Dr. Wolpow wasn't accepting any new patients, and Dr. Wepsic immediately said, "I'll call Ed Wolpow and ask him to see you." Then he cautioned, "Be careful going down the hill to your car."

It was a God-send that he sent me to Dr. Wolpow. I felt an immediate confidence in the man. He was tall, with a compelling gaze, but what really spoke to me were all the photographs he had hung on his office wall—portraits of doctors who had been his teachers at Harvard Medical School.

"A lot more appropriate to show *them*," he told me, "than some piece of paper with my name on it."

That's the moment that kindled our friendship. I'd known too many doctors who never could get their egos and priorities straight. Dr. Wolpow went right to the heart of my case, agreeing with Dr. Wepsic's preliminary findings and setting up a schedule of further tests. An Evoked Potentials Study, an EMG, another MRI and other lab work. I hastily pointed out I'd already had an MRI.

"Not here," Dr. Wolpow insisted.

"Oh boy," I thought.

When I showed up for this second MRI, I tried to explain how panicky I'd been during my last trip down the tube, and what precautions had been taken to help me. But I was up against another corpsman. "We can't do that here," he said. "You'll have to lie still for the entire exam." If I couldn't manage it, they'd have to cancel. So what I did was will myself back into flight training. If they were going to strap me in, I would just go ahead and drown, and that'll be the end of it. "Okay," I said, "I'll do the best I can." And everything happened the same way it did during that water-crash test. I became totally complacent, said a few prayers and it all worked out fine.

The other tests mystified me. The Evoked Potentials Study took several hours with a very gentle, considerate technician, who kept zapping small jolts of electricity through pathways of my central nervous system. They tingled gingerly and ominously. He tested my visual responses to a flashing pattern that left my right eye badly fatigued, unable to focus. Dr. Wolpow himself administered the EMG by zinging higher whacks of electrical stimuli down various nerve paths. He spent a lot of time checking out the median nerve in my right hand. "It's weak," he told me, "but it's there." I had no idea what he was talking about, even less where any of these galvanic whiplashes were leading.

On Friday afternoon, June 28th, I went to see Dr. Wolpow to discuss these test results. I had already figured out what he was going to tell me, that I would have to have major surgery on a cervical disc, to repair damage from that sledding accident back when I was only five.

Dr. Wolpow came right to the point.

Though it was a different point altogether, and an abrupt shock, followed by deep confusion.

My test results were consistent, he told me, with a diagnosis of multiple sclerosis.

Out of the fog of this shock, I began to perceive the reality of the things Dr. Wolpow was telling me. The MRI scan had revealed multiple lesions in my brain, areas of damage where the MS virus tricks the immune system so that it generates cells that attack the myelin that provides a protective sheath around the nerves in the central nervous system. Once the myelin sheathing is damaged, short circuits can occur—same way they occur if the insulation wears away from household wiring. These "shorts" can interfere with walking, writing, vision, etc., depending on which nerve is affected.

Epidemiologically, the disease could have come from many risk factors, among them those to people who live in the northern most latitudes, like Worcester, Massachusetts, including some who have been exposed to sick animals during their childhood. I told Dr. Wolpow I could never have a pet because of my father's allergies and asthma, but I did love animals, and spent a lot of time as a kid at a neighbor's house, where the family ran an animal hospital out of their home.

Dr. Wolpow explained that any such virus encountered during childhood could lie dormant until triggered by some later physical or emotional event. That brought a flood of speculative memories that rose like the sudden ghosts of life's mischances.

Of course I didn't *know* that they may have been early symptoms of MS back then. How could I? But as I sat there, stunned by his diagnosis, trying to think back farther, I began to recall other warning signs. And dear God, my chronic inability to manage well in situations of extreme stress! Such as high school football or when I overshot the first third of the air strip during flight training, or nowadays whenever I stubbed my polished toe along the uneven Boston streets or fumbled to get my right leg's lag to catch up with my left leg's strut.

And in all of these stressful times, I knew how my mind could shut down into a swirling mental fog. That very same fog I was now fighting off, under the menace of Dr. Wolpow's prognosis, that seemed to settle in, like desperation made visible.

Before I left, Dr. Wolpow advised me to obtain a book—*Multiple Sclerosis: A Guide for Patients and Their Families* by Labey Scheinberg— and said a final word about the total unpredictable nature of MS.

"You mean," I tried to hold on to some vague hope, "I could wake up tomorrow and be walking perfectly?"

What else could he professionally reply but "yes"? Though I was too well aware of my own whistling in the dark.

That Friday evening after work, I met Lora at the Hingham Pier where the ferry comes in. Her sister was coming for the weekend, and Lora was anxious to meet her at our apartment. But driving back toward Cohasset, I couldn't restrain my own larger anxiety. I told her I had something really important to discuss, and on an impulse, I turned off and stopped at a parking area.

Lora looked at me, a little quizzically, and I came right out with it. I'd been to see the doctor, and he says I have multiple sclerosis.

Count on Lora for calm. She immediately wanted to know how this would ultimately affect my health, but who knew? All right then, how is it going to affect *us*? Should we maybe put everything on hold? Was it still prudent to sell our house in Greenfield? Shouldn't we just stay put and see how things worked out? She tried to reassure me that we could both keep steady in all these uncertain currents, if we stuck to our own straight-forward but cautious course.

I said I just didn't know what to say right then, I had to think about all that had happened, we'd have to keep talking. I knew that didn't come near being an adequate response, but she gave me a warm hug, like a great big wish for happiness. She told me she loved me, that she knew everything would be okay, that we would work it out together.

That got me through the weekend, and back into the office on Monday, and through a week-long wait to be sure that Dr. Wolpow's diagnosis was confirmed. Lyme's Disease had to be eliminated. Nothing developed to contradict Dr. Wolpow's findings, and I got only one surprising piece of news.

Tony Medaglia had been elected chairman of the management committee.

Apparently the committee had gone into executive session. Robins had stepped down, and from now on, I reported to Tony.

Chapter Three

I knew I had to tell somebody at H & W, and soon. Once I had Dr. Wolpow's agreement to talk candidly about my condition, I took the short walk down the hall to Charles Robins' office.

I knocked, and he motioned me in. I closed the door tightly behind me, and sat down, and took a deep breath.

"I know I don't report to you anymore," I started in, "but I've got something I need to share, and I'm more comfortable sharing it with you first." He nodded in that silent way of his. "I've got MS, Charles."

He nodded again. Same silence, but looking very grave.

"I'm not going to kid you, Charles," I said, determined not to kid myself, either. "This is a major-league illness, and you need to think about its full impact, very carefully." I moved nearer to the nub of the matter. "And how it might affect my health in the future." And my work, I might have added, but retreated into the formalities. "I've authorized my physician to speak with you about my medical condition, so that you can be fully advised." I gave him Dr. Wolpow's name and number, and sank into silence myself.

"I'm sorry, Alan," he finally said. Out of that gravity that can sometimes stand in for kindness. "I'll communicate this to the management committee, and we'll be in touch."

Then I went back to my own office, set right to work, and waited upon my fate.

One by one, over the next week, each member of the management committee dropped by to see me. Mary Ellen O'Mara, with her no-nonsense but very womanly sympathy, James Westra, a new member who had a relative with MS and recognized what a sudden blow this had to be to me, and Jack Clymer, who kept up his always friendly solicitations after my well being. All of them listened to my explanations quietly, pledged their support, and said how much they "wanted to help." Then, after this warm display of management concern, Tony himself came by my office one morning, and surprised me even more.

He and Robins had paid a visit to his friend and client Dr. Wepsic. Tony said he wanted me to work a less strenuous schedule. Some of my work would be shifted to Fred Grein. I should put in fewer hours, try to conserve my strength. And he promised to be helpful whenever he could. "I'm speaking for the firm. Let's just see how it goes," he announced, then offered me this solid reassurance. "We have a good long-term disability program. You really don't have anything to worry about."

I was totally taken aback, almost numbed, I'd have to admit, by Tony's hail and hearty sympathy. If only what he said during that drop-by had ever turned out to be true.

But I wasn't thinking warily, or even straight, at that moment. I was in a naked panic over whether I could still do my job. That is a typical reaction among abruptly surprised MS sufferers. I asked Tony and the other committee members to keep my medical problems confidential, not to make my illness known to the office generally, and they readily agreed. That gave me a veil of official silence for self-protection, and deluded me into a curious and unfounded sense of fresh opportunities opening up for me. I plunged back into my dutiful work schedule—the same, and sometimes more, hours, long past five P.M.—with warm feelings of both camaraderie and closure, from the moral support offered me by the committee. I knew I loved this job, every aspect of its high-level Downtown Boston buzz, right down to the gold collar pin in my crisp shirt that went along with it.

"These are great people," I actually told myself. "I'm going to do the best for them I possibly can."

I immediately embarked on another cost-saving campaign, this time to stop the firm from paying clients' costs, those legal expenses, clerical charges, filing fees, often due on a judicial deadline, other out-of-pocket disbursements, that were all immediately payable.

I'd been monitoring the amount of money that H & W was liberally investing in these upfront outlays for clients. Attorneys at H & W had always sent along these bills to our accounts payable department, to be covered as a courtesy to their clients. Later these paid charges would be added to client billings at the close of an action. Or, more likely, in the chaos and confusion of the end-of-year "billing Saturdays" and the "stub period." I found over a million dollars sitting in accounts receivable for these firm-paid disbursements.

This black hole was helping to sink us further since we were always running short on cash nowadays and borrowing from the firm's new line of credit with Olympic. But I could actually do something to stop this hemorrhage. Since I signed all checks under $5000, I adopted a new policy: I would not approve payment for any such disbursement unless it was approved by a partner. Usually I wrote a note on the bill, "Please send to client for payment." And rerouted it to the originating attorney. There was a lot of grumbling at first, but within a very short billing time, the amount owed to the firm for these disbursements dropped by $200,000.

It helped that we had finally, per our consultant's advice, brought the firm's billing system entirely in house. We purchased new Digital hardware, including a high speed printer, with a license to use integrated software for timekeeping, billing, and accounts receivable. We ran the old system and the new one together for a short test period, and everything balanced to the penny. The conversion cost $40,000, but it brought down monthly expenses by $13,000, so we had a payback within three months.

Then I hit a snag, surprisingly on my own healthcare proposal. The new self-funded insurance plan was scheduled to go into effect on August 15th with cards already available from the Tufts Total Health Plan. At the last minute, one of the younger attorneys, Carol Brown, spotted a potential tax problem for the partners. How, I still don't understand, but this last-minute glitch meant the new plan had to be delayed. The legal nuances were beyond my ken, but that didn't stop my embarrassment when Tony had to apologize to the partners at the next monthly dinner.

At that same dinner, I had to get up, yet again, to badger the partners about collecting monies variously due from their dilatory clients. On the financials, I could report new savings from controls I'd instituted to curtail overtime expenses for non-legal staff. Another $36,000, but that wasn't going to pull us out of the red. I warned they were looking at immediate problems of paying their quarterly taxes to the IRS and the Commonwealth of Massachusetts. After that dinner, I went around to each partner—with detailed lists of how much each of their clients still owed, how long they'd owed it—and urged them to call personally and ask for prompt payment.

Once more, collections fell woefully short.

What could I do but keep trying? Keep bird-dogging our expenses to conserve what little ready cash I could. From the landlord at One Boston Place, I got agreement to our reserving another $30,000 pending correction of their allocation of electrical charges. Finally I took a more active role in going after delinquent clients myself, scraping together another $20,000 by dunning several deadbeats. But it was all peanuts, nothing like the cuts I knew I could accomplish through establishing our own self-funded health plan.

I had quickly developed an alternative approach to address the tax problem raised by Carol Brown, and kept bringing up this new plan at the weekly meeting. Jim Westra was conferring with me regularly to work through any further difficulties, but it soon became clear that the real stumbling block was Tony.

He hadn't liked the idea from the very first since it would require his family to change doctors. He wanted to keep his freedom of choice under the Blue Cross indemnity plan. I tried to argue how much money his freedom of choice was costing the firm, that a self-funded plan, using the physicians under the Tufts arrangement, would still provide us top-quality healthcare at very considerable savings.

But Tony turned a deaf ear. "Hey, I don't want to keep talking about this every week." He wanted whatever was best for him. And others were grumbling about leaving their doctors under the Harvard Plan, chiefly, I'm convinced, because they were more comfortable with an HMO entitled "Harvard" than one less elegantly labeled "Tufts."

"We've got to resolve this matter," I kept plugging. "A lot of money is at stake, and I'm having a hard time getting extensions of coverage from our existing carriers."

I was following up with Dr. Wolpow these days, since my symptoms were more evident. My walk was unsteady, and the discomfort in my right hand so pronounced that I had to wear a hand brace at night. I might require surgery for carpal tunnel syndrome. He sent me to an internist at Massachusetts General Hospital and set up an appointment with a surgeon to operate on my hand.

But other impasses, besides my uncertain health, were beginning to affect the pace and morale within the office. To my amazement, I was finding doors often closed when I went to call on my managers. Sometimes I would have to wait an hour before one or the other of them would emerge from whichever office they'd chosen for their tete-a-tetes. To my chagrin and disgust, I was watching an office cabal form right under my nose, and had little doubt that Charlie Gaziano had to be chiefly responsible.

Then, at the end of September, Margaret Hadley abruptly resigned.

She came by to explain, with her usual grace, that she felt she had been in one place too long. She needed a change, an opportunity to work for a smaller firm in Boston that was in a growth mode. By implication, instead of one which kept contracting by firing people. She reminisced about her early days at H & W during its rapid, late-blooming rise in the 80s, how exciting it had been to work in that growth environment. And she left as much of a mystery to me as ever.

But stubbornly, I refused to believe I wasn't up to the challenges I was setting for myself, so Lora and I had finally decided to move permanently to Cohasset. With the help of another H & W partner, Kenneth May, also in the real estate department, we'd sold our home in Greenfield, and purchased an atypical colonial—a salt box with a sizeable extension added—on Forest Avenue, very near the shore. Ken May had the office next to me, and oversaw the negotiations. I'd been on the phone for hours every evening with the Greenfield buyers over the complexities of the protective covenants.

On October 10th, Lora closed on the sale of our house in Greenfield, and she and her brothers loaded all our belongings, along with our golden retriever Strider (named after the lad in *The Lord of the Rings*), into two large rental trucks, while I closed on the Cohasset house. They were the extended family Lora had brought into my life, and we all met the next night at my apartment on Black Rock Beach. After dinner, the boys curled up in front of the TV with Strider, and Lora and I settled in the bedroom. I knew this was an emotional crunch for her. She was leaving behind a very peaceful stretch of our lives together, and the small travel business she'd managed to build up again, after our departing Worcester.

Lora got up during the night, went out to where the boys were asleep, and found that Strider had suddenly died. He was an old dog, suffering from cancer, and the move had just been too much for him. She cleaned up after his death throes, and I woke to find his body lying on the kitchen floor. I leaned down and patted him with my troubled right hand. The first duty we saw to when we went over to the new house was to bury Strider in the backyard.

I settled back into the ferry commute to Boston, but at the end of October, I got sudden word that my father, now retired down in Clearwater Beach, Florida, had to be operated on, for complications from his colon cancer. I flew down for a post-operative visit, along with my older brother Bob, and my blue-collar father joked about my new career in Downtown Boston.

"If you want to know how to make money," he ribbed Bob, "talk to your brother. He'll show you how to do it." Then he lifted his eyebrows at me. "He'll show you how to spend it too." I could sense he was thinking about that costly move we'd just made to the South Shore. I did my best to reassure him, with a tricky hug and kiss among all the wires and tubes that entrapped him. But his difficulties, brave as he was about facing them, seemed to pile on top of my own burdens from the insidious progress of MS and the hectic conditions at the firm.

I flew back to Boston, right into the midst of our negotiating arrangements with the four attorneys that were joining us from the bankrupt Gaston & Snow. It was reported that bankruptcy occurred because several partners were paid exorbitant compensation, far more than the income of the firm ever justified, or could possibly cover. Gaston & Snow partners had been subsidizing these over-the-top distributions by using the firm's line of credit with Shawmut Bank.

I wondered if our guys might be getting the point, but I was both too busy and too cautiously circumspect to raise it. I was sorely missing Margaret Hadley, since I had to do a lot of her work as well as my own, while I was still finding some office doors shut tight against any intrusion.

Then, on November 1st, everything stopped for me when my mother called from Florida, choking back tears. "Your father's very bad, you better come down here." I had those four Gaston & Snow attorneys right there on the 28th Floor, literally moving into our trust and estates department at that very moment—eleven A.M.—along with their four staffers the entire party very apprehensive. I could not just up and abandon them, or the pile of work on my desk. I called my brother Bob, told him I'd get down to Florida as soon as I could, and would keep him posted. Then I opted for a flight out of nearby Logan Airport to Tampa at three P.M.

Luckily it was a Friday, so that everybody soon settled into making the new people welcome, then turned to the last of their week's work. I could clear my own desk, leave a voice mail for Tony so he'd know what was happening, call Lora to tell her I was out the door, grab my coat, and catch a quick cab to Logan.

But before I left, I called Charlie Gaziano in trusts and estates and asked him to look after the new attorneys in my absence. I went over the detailed arrangements Mike Dunham and I had already made, so things would go smoothly. "Don't worry," Charlie said, "I'll take care of everything."

Three-and-a-half hours' airtime to Tampa provided some opportunity to reflect on how much life had changed for me in the last four months. I saw myself still at a peak of activity if I could only keep up my strength against MS. But here was my father, surely near the end of his own life span, struggling with the complications of his recent illness. I went straight to the hospital from the airport and asked for my father's room number. The volunteer-receptionist in the front lobby said that she couldn't find it in the computer.

But I knew too much about hospitals, not to sense immediately and acutely what had already occurred. "I'll call the nursing supervisor," the volunteer lady said, "and see if she can help you." Soon enough, I was sitting with a nervous nurse supervisor staring hard at her computer screen.

"Have you checked on his discharge status?" I asked professionally. She looked again, without comment.

"He's expired?" I asked, without quite really raising any question.

"Yes, I'm sorry."

So I knew, and after I drove out to my mother's place along Clearwater Beach, I went straight in, to find her sitting sad and somber in her easy chair. "I've just come from the hospital," I said.

I knelt right down to hold her, and she cradled my head in her hands. "Don't cry, Alan," she tried to soothe me. The phone rang, and she got up to answer, and it was my brother Bob. I got up hastily and went into the bathroom to wash my hands and face, feeling mightily embarrassed. I could hear her saying, "He cried like a baby."

Dad had always insisted, "The only way you're going to get me back to New England is in a box!" He made my mother promise not to spend a lot of money. "A crying shame to bury a beautiful piece of wood in the ground!" So we flew back, with Dad resting in his coffin in the cargo section. Two days later, the mass was said for him at Holy Name of Jesus Church in Worcester.

All this amounted to a very long weekend, with a couple of precious days missed from work. Several people kindly came by to offer their condolences, but my desk was already piled high. I decided it would be a good idea to come in Saturdays, no longer crediting Tony's earlier words urging me to take time off. I intended to put in those extra hours, whatever it took to get the job done.

Financially, there was no leeway. H & W's unrelenting liquidity crisis had now come down to the age-old question, "Who'll pay the rent?" Not only did we still have that vacant top floor at One Boston Place on our hands, but were paying more dearly for our top four floors of 101 Federal Street. That got the management committee to initiate pleas to their Federal Street landlord for concessions, and Tony was to head up the negotiating team.

It was the first time I found myself excluded from a top-level meeting. Instead, Tony took along Fred Grein, as the partnership's treasurer. Maybe that was Grein helping ease my workload, but Tony still came by my office, demanding certain computer-generated financial reports that he had to have immediately for these confrontations with the landlord. They were detailed and extensive, basically the careful summaries we produced each month when we closed the books. Our computer system was at last in fully accountable trim, but it still took most of an evening to generate all the data Tony requested.

But when I gave him the reports, Tony grew irate.

"These make us look too good," he snarled.

"What can I say?" I gestured at the reports. "These are the numbers you asked for. They represent our financial position, as of today. What do you want me to do?"

"I don't want *you* to do anything," he fired at me. Then he walked away, leaving me standing there in the corridor where we'd met. "Never mind," he shot back over his shoulder. "I'll get my own numbers."

Before Margaret left, Tony had come by my office to ask that his secretary be given an additional pay hike. He claimed Margaret Hadley didn't like his secretary, hadn't given her an appropriate increase at the time of her merit review. I got in touch with Margaret, and she stood by her decision and furnished me a complete list of all the other partners' secretaries, their salaries and number of years with the firm.

From this list, it was obvious that undiluted favoritism had ruled in the past. Secretaries who worked for the more influential partners got higher wages than others with comparable years of service and capabilities. One of the glaring inequities I was trying to weed out.

I explained to Tony that he and I should *want* to use the same wage scale and criteria when evaluating employees with similar job descriptions. But he wanted what he wanted, and that was that. I urged him to try to work with me, said I was sure we could arrive at some arrangement that was acceptable. He said he was going to the management committee with his request, which he subsequently did, and immediately got their approval to raise his secretary's salary.

His total control did far worse damage when the management committee finally got around to a decision on the firm's healthcare plan. Over my strong but futile objection, they voted in favor of Tony's recommendation to abandon any idea of a self-insured health plan and instead, offer two options to employees, either an HMO under the Harvard Community Health Plan, or indemnifying medical insurance through Bay State Health Care, which was adamantly Tony's own choice.

I was in agreement, though reluctantly, that the Harvard Plan would be offered, but I was deeply concerned over the financial stability of Bay State. *The Boston Globe* had reported a negative net worth of Bay State at $24 million from the insurer's own financials. As a healthcare professional, I could see that Bay State's premiums were too low to cover actual medical costs incurred by its members. The plan was going broke, and I didn't want to see H & W employees suddenly left without coverage.

But I swallowed my disappointment and prepared very positive letters announcing the changes. I'd negotiated new contractual agreements with the carriers, so I could take some pride in the knowledge that, because I'd pushed the management committee so hard, steps had been taken to reduce health care expenses by a projected $130,000. When I introduced this new coverage, I raised the amount paid by employees toward the cost of care, saving the firm another $50,000.

Still, it was a high-risk solution, best regarded as short-term, like so many other fixes around H & W in these perilous days. I had already set out to find a replacement for Margaret Hadley. She had given me some names herself from other Boston law firms, and I checked around, until I had resumes from some twenty candidates. After reference checks, I selected three possible candidates, then brought those down to two finalists, who interviewed with the management committee. I also asked Charlie Gaziano and Eleanor Lanes to see these two candidates. After hearing everybody's comments, I made a few discreet inquiries among individuals I knew who had knowledge of their work experience, style, and accomplishments. Only then did I select the person whom I wanted to hire.

But, of course, Tony had not been at the management committee meeting when this candidate had been seen. Inevitably, I had to ask him to interview her before making the offer. He did so, *mano a mano*, and came back with word that he'd also called someone at the firm where she worked, and gotten a poor reference. Tony then told me not to make the offer.

Abruptly, flatly, no further explanation, which was vintage Tony. I informed the management committee that I was going to place an ad in *The Boston Globe* and engage the services of a personnel agency since I was far too busy with other matters, including doing most of Margaret Hadley's work myself. On the plus side, I informed the management committee we were currently saving over $5000 a month on Margaret's salary and benefits.

But of all the missteps I had with Tony, the worst, or certainly the most aggravating, was over the firm's annual Christmas party. I started out with my usual good intentions, suggesting we best not blow a lot of money playing Good Saint Nick this season. In the recent past, the Yuletide affair had been catered, at large expense, by the staff at the Meridien, a posh French hotel near our offices. Since we were laying off people, cutting corners everywhere, wouldn't that send the wrong message to our employees?

"Just because we're in trouble," Tony bridled, "doesn't mean we can't have Christmas."

Granted, but we could have Christmas in a less expensive venue with equal wassail. Lora had arranged many such events as a meeting planner for large corporations, and she could put together a gala event at the Boston Park Plaza Hotel, not that far away, at what I projected would be half the cost.

So Lora plunged ahead with the arrangements, starting just prior to Thanksgiving. My widowed mother, who'd been staying in Worcester, came down to Cohasset to spend Thanksgiving with us, then decided it was time she got back to her home in warmer Florida. I went to Tony and asked for a week off to take her back myself, and he frowned. Busy year-end period, not the time for anyone to be taking time off. "You're needed here," he insisted, "but I'll leave it to you to do what you think is best."

I cut back on the trip, missing only three days of work. Because, yes, we were into that December crunch again, when a quarter of H & W's annual collections occurred. But that didn't stop both Tony and Charles Robins from taking their regular winter vacations in Key Largo and Boca Raton, lasting ten days to two weeks, right in the middle of this crunch.

But they were both there for the Christmas party, on December 12th. I was tired from a full day's work, since the disease was beginning to inflict its own fatigue, but I still decided to walk over to the Boston Park Plaza Hotel, stopping along the way to buy two expensive cigars. I popped into the main ballroom, where the party was already booming, and saw immediately what a grand job Lora had done with the festivities. Instead of everybody being crowded into two or three small rooms at the Meridien, thoroughly subdued as they had been last year, they were happy with room enough for everybody to "kick back" and enjoy themselves.

Except Charles Robins and Tony, who were standing together, out on the edge of the ballroom.

I went up to them, and presented each with a cigar.

They were cordial but distant, and I'd have to say, cold. They stayed right where they were, the entire evening, quietly talking together.

But the rest of the crowd—nearly 150 people—had a wonderful time. And told us so. At the end of the evening, they came up to Lora and me, said what a great party it was, how much fun they'd had, and how much better it was than previous galas.

I was delighted, but pretty much done in, so when Lora and I got back home to Cohasset, I didn't quite get what she was telling me.

"Alan, something's wrong."

How could that be, didn't everybody have a ball?

"I didn't get the big warm reception from the partners. Not like in the past. And once, I caught Jack Clymer's eye, unexpectedly. He was looking at me, *very* sympathetically. It really made me feel uneasy. And when I tried to catch Tony Medaglia to ask him a question about the open bar, he turned his back on me at least three times. Are you sure that everything's okay?"

"Far as I know, everything's fine." I shrugged. "The partners are under a lot of pressure. I guess it's beginning to show."

The next day, I handed out the Christmas bonus checks, took compliments on Lora's Christmas party, and felt a genuine boost in morale from these two seasonal lifts.

But not from Charlie Gaziano nor Eleanor Lanes when I stopped by with their checks.

Their bonuses had been my latest set-back before the management committee. I'd been determined that we take care of the people with the greatest burden of responsibility for keeping the firm together. I had emphasized that Charlie and Eleanor should be well compensated for their hard work and enormous dedication in these difficult times. Again I asked *not* to be given a bonus, that any moneys intended for me should be divided equally between Charlie and Eleanor. I made it clear how strongly I felt about splitting my share between them.

The committee then voted that all non-legal staff be given the equivalent of one week's salary, including me.

That meant that I had to hand Charlie and Eleanor about half of what I had wanted them each to receive. They were both disappointed, but Charlie was extremely bitter. Though I tried to explain, with some chagrin, how I had been overruled, I doubt he believed me.

Still and all, I was rightly confident that we were making some headway against the firm's debt load. I'd finally found a likely tenant for that empty floor at One Boston Place, a minority law firm that specialized in discrimination cases under civil rights law. When I took a look at their financials, I had to tell myself I only wish ours looked as good. That lease was in negotiation, and later in December, the management committee announced a move with which I thoroughly agreed, that in January Fred Grein would take a newly created position as managing partner of the firm.

Both Fred and I had our offices on the 31st floor, and we'd steadily developed a good, sensible working relationship, so that I saw his appointment as an answer to unspoken prayers. "At last I'm going to get some help," I recall thinking. "Someone who has the political clout to get things done. Someone accessible to me, who I can work with, who can help get the changes in client billings and collections that have just *got* to happen."

Fred even dropped by, in friendly fashion, and said he wanted to start signing the checks as a way of getting up to speed on where all the expenses were actually occurring.

I thought this a bit odd, but was happy enough to get rid of a one time-consuming task among many.

Then Fred asked me to attend a special Saturday meeting of the management committee to review my 1992 financial projections. This was shortly after the Christmas party, so I had a chance to ask around the table how they all thought it had turned out.

"I thought the desserts were great," Jack Clymer replied. With what seemed a certain hesitancy in his voice. Or was I just picking that up from Lora?

Should I reserve the Boston Park Plaza for next year?

"No," someone popped off. "It's in the wrong part of town."

The committee then agreed on a return to what they obviously considered a more proper Boston location, declaring that next year's party should be held at the Marriott Long Wharf or the Boston Harbor Hotel or, better yet, just down the street at the Meridien Hotel.

Passing hastily on to more immediate matters—after my venture into this holiday social gaffe—the committee then asked for my financial projections for 1992. I'd prepared carefully, since I knew how daunting a short fall we faced on next year's operating budget. We were projected to face another tough year due to continuing high rent and flat sales volume. With receivables of questionable quality, as it was already December and collections were lagging, Tony presented a stark view of our situation. No question, we had to cut back somehow if we were going to survive. I pointed out that I'd already reduced non-legal staff down from 141 to 118 positions, a cutback of seventeen percent, but that the legal staff had not been cut anywhere near that deeply. I had a sense that all those in the room were finally ready to reduce the number of legal staff personnel in order to save their own necks.

I was then asked where additional reductions could be made in non-legal staff. I offered some few suggestions, but warned against a proposed further ten percent cut across all departments. I knew from experience, I told them, such arbitrary cuts, at this crisis point, would threaten the operational well-being of the firm. All this potential mayhem, mind you, was being discussed in civil tones. Tony, for once, the most cordial of them all.

The committee complimented me on the quality of my presentation, and Tony thanked me for coming in on a Saturday—and moved that the committee go into executive session.

It was the first time I'd actually been asked, no, *told* to leave the room—ever—let alone in the midst of deliberations critical to my own endeavors.

But I held on to my stubborn belief in my own ability to contribute, until another Saturday morning in Fred Grein's office—one of my working Saturdays—when I happened to say I hoped we might eliminate the "stub period" in the future.

Fred squinted hard, and said, "We're going to eliminate the stub period right away."

I was elated. I counted it as one of Fred's effective moves. I knew that the management committee had been weighing that choice. I blurted out, "I'll tell Eleanor right away, so that she can stop the work she and her people in accounting are doing."

"No," Fred reacted, very firmly, "I don't want you to do that."

I was flabbergasted. If Fred Grein didn't want Eleanor informed, it was not my prerogative to impart this vital intelligence to the accounting department.

With the result that, a week later, Eleanor marched into my office, very angry, to ask why I hadn't told her the stub period had been eliminated. She and her people had been working day and night, on what had all turned out now to be wasted effort. I had to explain that Fred had instructed me not to tell her. She listened quietly, then walked out of my office, clearly very upset. And once again, I found my staff behind closed doors with Charlie Gaziano.

A few days later, Charles Robins called me down to his office. He had received a complaint. He was concerned—*aghast*—that I had not informed Eleanor the stub period had been eliminated. Eleanor had been working very hard during the year-end closing process, he lectured me, then added that Eleanor had been forced to assume additional work on payroll since the departure of Margaret Hadley.

She felt, Robins declared icily, I had been very inconsiderate.

I could see my relationship with Robins slowly dissolving, with the comfortable, old alliance between Robins and Eleanor shaping up into an attack on me. I told Robins flatly that Fred Grein had specifically told me *not* to tell Eleanor Lanes, but it was clear he didn't believe me and chose to believe his partner.

What was happening to me here? I was right back where I started, defending my trustworthiness to Robins, only arguing that this time I'd exercised discretion over candor. And it was deeply humiliating not to be believed. This whole dispute was causing me to lose my credibility with both Robins and Eleanor, on whom I had long counted to support me in my work.

So I did what I too often do, I over-compensated. The next day, I went to Eleanor and told her how terrible I felt that she hadn't been informed earlier about the stub change. I asked her to teach me how to do the firm's payroll, so I could provide her assistance in these tough times, even take over for her when she went on vacation. It so happened Eleanor was a big Boston baseball fan, loved to go down to Florida with her sister to watch the Red Sox during spring training. I fantasized any way to be helpful, and over the next two weeks, spent eight to ten hours with Eleanor going over the ins-and-outs to learn her payroll system.

I was doing the same thing with H & W's threatened budget. I found a more economical way to handle the large cost of our malpractice insurance. Why get hit with the entire lump sum of $400,000 for the whole year's coverage? TransAmerica Insurance Company would let us stretch out the payments over monthly installments, at an interest charge slightly below prime lending rates. Even this little relief at these trying cash junctures might help us hold together over the long haul. The management committee approved, and I went giddily forward with the conviction that I was still helping us all to stay afloat.

Until Monday morning, January 27th, at around ten A.M. I'd just finished interviewing a candidate for Margaret Hadley's position, when I got a phone call from Robins' office to get down there ASAP.

I hurried down to the 29th floor. Robins invited me to sit down with Tony Medaglia and Fred Grein, then closed the door. The three of them, lined up primly, pretending to See No Evil, Hear No Evil, Speak No Evil.

Naturally it was Tony who finally looked at me, and spoke for them all.

"Alan, it's not working." The first outright word I'd ever heard of any dissatisfaction with my work. "Your decision-making is not as crisp as it needs to be. You're going to be terminated."

And "for cause," yet.

Tony pushed two legal documents at me that outlined a severance agreement, along with various covenants I was to abide by. He then advised me to seek legal counsel and consider filing a claim with the Union Mutual Insurance of America, known as UNUM, the firm's long-term disability carrier.

I was in shock, but lucid enough to notice this was the first time any of these sleek gentlemen had made any outright reference of my "disability" since my one talk with Tony.

I couldn't believe this was happening. *No way.* Yes, there had been arguments, disagreements, but I'd had absolutely no warning that anybody thought I wasn't doing my job. I hadn't had a performance appraisal since receiving high praise from Robins that previous summer. Yet they sat there in their grim reserve, full of austerity and well-groomed hauteur, somehow convinced they were going to make me out to be the problem.

I started talking—the first fiery words of a blazing blue streak. "Ever since Charles Robins stepped down as chairman, there's been no clear leadership. Especially for me."

I fixed my eyes on Tony. And my anger. Wasn't he supposed to be the guy in charge?

"And it's not just loss of leadership." I drew a long breath. "In that same time, I've been diagnosed with MS, as well as lost my own father. You want to know what that does?" I couldn't stop my pent-up feelings, had to be heard for a change. "It brings on real emotional devastation."

They just sat there listening, like so many plaster Brahmins, and I got more animated. *You may have called this meeting*, I told myself, *but I am taking charge.* "Ever since I joined this firm, I've had to face one crisis after another." I ran through them all, naming names. "I haven't had a quiet moment since I got here."

But it was getting real quiet now.

I fixed on Tony again, trying to shift into some equanimity. "Look, after my father died, I felt very angry and bitter inside. And I might have misdirected some of that at you. If I did, I apologize."

He shook his head. "That has nothing to do with this."

Okay then, what *did?* "A couple of years ago, you fired your administrator, right? Then you offered the position to Charlie Gaziano, and after he sort of temporarily filled in, did the job for a year, *he* refused to take it! And now you're getting rid of *me.*" I drilled it right at them. "If you want to know what's wrong, don't keep blaming your administrator. Just look in the mirror."

What would they see? A triumvirate sitting aloof, together in their grey suits, all the civilities in place, backed by the Ivy League, and the Downtown Boston Bar, like the busts of so many Roman nobles. But they were really nothing but a three-man junta, being led by the nose by their strong man, Tony Medaglia.

Charles Robins blurted something like "That's enough." But I had hit full stride, and was not to be stopped.

"This firm has a very serious liquidity problem." I kept looking straight at Tony. "And *you*—as chairman of the management committee, with full knowledge of this crisis—you have over $400,000 in client accounts that have been due for over four months."

Tony actually ducked his head down and for once muttered, "You're right."

"There's a total lack of a common vision in this partnership. In spite of all these financial crises you're facing, the partners are unable to focus on the need for timely billing, let alone ever bothering about collections!"

Then I turned on Robins. "How the hell am I supposed to maintain any standing as executive director when Eleanor Lanes reports to me but keeps your personal finances plus checking account and discusses the firm's balance sheet privately with you every morning?" He didn't move. "Then she gets shafted on the stub period by Fred here, and somebody complains to you about me! And you call me down to chew *me* out instead of even giving me the least benefit of the doubt!"

"I had a complaint," Robins tried weakly, "and I wanted you to know about it."

"Okay, here's *my* complaint." I kept going. "None of you even had the courtesy to thank my wife Lora for the effort she made in arranging the firm's Christmas party. At which, despite your killjoy presence, a lot of people had a lot of fun. I guess they just didn't know they weren't in the right surroundings for proper Christmas cheer.

"And may I remind you, Lora and I took a big hit of $100,000 when we moved to Cohasset only three months ago." I let loose. "We'd never have taken such a major step if we had any inkling you were dissatisfied with my performance."

Then I leveled off. "In spite of everything I've said . . . " Why do I say these things? "I will leave peacefully and work out a smooth transition with whomever is going to take over."

Somebody then said, "Charlie Gaziano has agreed to serve as interim administrator."

Incredible, but absolutely true to form.

I then excused myself from this meeting.

"I have done everything you asked me to."

With that clipped but useless truth, I got up and headed back to my office. I was shaken by the enormity of their betrayal, but already thinking what this blow would do to my future and my family. I went into a minor panic—my right leg began acting up on me, as I walked back into my office—but after sitting a few minutes, I saw partially through the fog. "God, I need time to work this out. What can I do to get more time before these guys toss me out in the street?" I quickly devised an alternate plan that would be good for the firm, good for me, and hurried back down to the 29th floor.

When I knocked on the door, Robins said hesitantly, "Come in," and I walked right in to find him and Fred Grein huddled over the table with Charlie Gaziano. They all looked surprised to see me, especially Charlie.

"I want to let you know I'm willing to stay on a while for a short transition period." That got their attention. "I can make all the staff adjustments . . . " In other words, announce more layoffs. "And do any of the other unpleasant tasks before I leave. That way, the staff will be angry at me." I smiled right into their own tangled double-dealing. "Not Charlie."

Nobody said anything, until Robins managed to utter, "Thank you."

I went back to my office, and continued to ponder my future. Until along came Charlie Graziano.

I tried to pick up from where I'd left off earlier that morning.

"I need at least two weeks to get through this," I told him.

"I don't think you have that long."

"How long do I have?"

"The rest of this week."

All along he had sneered that I had a sucker job, it was a thankless dead-end. That was why he hadn't accepted the position at H & W when it was offered to him. And never would. And all along, when I'd been interviewing for the job, he had recommended the other candidate over me.

He tried to lean on me. "I think you should sign the severance agreement."

I ignored that.

"You know, I could have handled this job if my health weren't impaired."

He looked back at me and said, "Yeah, you probably could have."

He showed me the memo to be circulated throughout the firm, announcing my resignation for reasons of health. I read it very carefully and signed it.

Then Charlie hustled off, to be told his next bidding. I soon learned there was a special meeting of the partners at 5:30.

Jim Westra came by that afternoon to offer his sympathy. He seemed to be truly sorry that I was leaving the firm, and talked again about his relative who had MS. I told him how bitterly I had "lashed out" at Tony, Charles, and Fred, but I wanted him to know that generally I had to respect everybody's judgment. "It's made me realize I have to accept the limitations this disease is placing on me," I half-confessed.

My emotional state was wobbly, but then I began to build back my courage out of a slowly dawning surprise: the sudden show of sympathy I was getting from all sides. Several other partners stopped by my office, and many of my own staff, throughout the rest of that long and agonizing day. They were sorry, they would miss me, they truly wished me well.

People kept dropping by, many in sorrow and puzzlement. I felt free to tell them I had MS, that the disease was affecting my work, let alone my life, that I'd been instructed to step down, that yes, I was unsure of my future. And they said how clear it was to one and all that I'd done my best.

Just before the partners' meeting, Charlie was back. Then, once again, tried to lean on me.

"I really think you should sign the severance agreement."

I'd already read the agreement and its accompanying libels several times over. The language was direct, even brutal. I was being terminated for "willful misconduct." Therefore, the documents further stated that "even though the firm had the right to dismiss me without compensation," they would pay me $60,000, the severance that was due me under my employment contract, provided that I agreed (1) not to bring legal action against them in the future and (2) to maintain strict confidentially in all that I knew about the firm.

"Charlie," I answered him, fully and finally, "if I were on my death bed, I wouldn't sign that agreement! Okay?"

Chapter Four

When you are suffering the hidden ravages of MS, you are really caught in a triple bind. The disease itself is insidious, secretly undermining your health, but its course is exacerbated by any stress. And that stress comes as a double whammy, sometimes physical, sometimes psychological, often both. I've already said how vulnerable I am psychologically, so that last week at H & W and the next several months brought a maximum rush of mental hell.

Before I left on February 4th, I did manage to slip away long enough for that first visit to David Rapaport. His name happened to be on the top of a list of three lawyers I'd gotten from a health care attorney I knew who said David Rapaport had an outstanding reputation in matters of employment law. I told H & W that I was going to check out that vacant 33rd floor at One Boston Place, which we were at last about to rent for a hefty $300,000 annually, a deal that John Thomson and I had brokered. The office manager introduced me as "the guy who calls about the rent," and I immediately explained why I wouldn't be doing that anymore, and handed David Rapaport my severance agreement and employment contract.

"My employer has asked me to sign this agreement," I said. "I need your advice before I do."

I spent twenty minutes on the iniquities of H & W. David was congenial, but had a lot of paper stacked around his small office, obviously a busy man, and proved very efficient at skimming my documents.

"At a quick glance, this seems like an equitable agreement," he concluded. "They're offering you six months salary and benefits, which is consistent with the stipulation in your employment contract, and a pretty good deal as these contracts go."

Then I mentioned I'd been diagnosed with MS, only a few months ago.

That raised an eyebrow. "Did Hutchins & Wheeler make any accommodation for your illness?"

"What does that mean?" I asked, in my then large ignorance.

"If you are a handicapped person, by law your employer has to make a reasonable effort to make things easier for you. For example, since you have difficulty in walking, did they make any attempt to move you closer to an elevator?"

Was he kidding?

"No, they didn't."

David leaned back in his chair, looked directly at me and said, "Then you may have cause to bring a claim for handicapped discrimination."

That was the only hint of the future I took away from our first meeting.

Lora was shaken but not surprised by my sudden forced resignation, and we had decided to make the best of it, stay put in our new home for the moment. Your first impulse in a crisis like this is to sell the house, get rid of the costly mortgage, rent something less expensive, but I did some quick calculations at home. What with any realtor's commission, sudden capital gains taxes from the sale of our home, other sales expenses, we'd be taking a big hit if we sold at that moment—actually, a sizeable loss. Lora was proud of me for helping us keep our heads on straight in that initial rush of panic.

I woke up February 5, 1992 to the delayed shock of having been brutally fired. It only hit me then, and hard, because I didn't *have* to get up and go into work. There had been an abrupt change in my daily reality. What I had to do was go into Boston and file a claim for unemployment from the Commonwealth of Massachusetts.

But not today. I needed a little time off to think and rest my weary bones. I slowly got up, and went into the small office near our bedroom. Downstairs, I could hear Lora sharing coffee and morning TV and early buzz with her brother Fred. Fred was a young man at loose ends, who had asked to come live with us—in that ever extending family we seem to gather—because he said he wanted a more stable environment.

I shook my head ruefully at our situation which surely needed immediate reassessment. Everybody in this supposedly stable household was now unemployed. Jonathan was down in Florida. Fred had just left his girl friend, the community college he was attending, and a part-time job in an auto parts store. Lora had already moved six times since our marriage. How was she going to start up her travel business, yet again, out of our home? And I was at the lowest emotional point of my life, with a progressively debilitating disease and rapidly diminishing self-esteem.

I slowly realized I had to accept the fact that I was no longer the quick-witted manager, the can-do executive, the rock, or the bridge—the one who was always there for everybody else. I had to learn my limits, probably lower my expectations, even consider the chances I might become an invalid—God forbid—unable to care for myself.

And as far as the household finances went, nobody knew better than I how rocky they were. I'd left H & W with a last paycheck for $15,000, two weeks' salary plus four weeks of unused vacation. I hadn't had time to take a vacation. The only vacation days I'd used were to visit my dying father and help return my mother to Florida. We had some equity in her small house in Clearwater, Florida, but we weren't going to put my mother out in the street. We also still owned land in Greenfield—two building lots remained—but new construction was abysmally depressed. Our house in Cohasset we'd bought with $60,000 down from the sale of our Greenfield home, but we were carrying two mortgages for $180,000 long-term and $100,000 short-term. And I'd already decided it would be too big a loss to sell. We had savings of $130,000 that I had diligently set aside from my various paychecks, first with the Sisters—a tax-sheltered retirement of $115,000—then a 401K with H & W for $15,000.

So, with $280,000 in mortgages, and $30,000 in a bank loan against $130,000 in savings, it was a bleak financial scene. I might be able to collect partial disability from UNUM—which would be 60% of my final salary—but what future employment would fill in the gap? All my professional training and experience had gone into a career of high-stress managerial leadership, which my doctors said I could no longer handle. And Charlie Gaziano had almost gleefully warned me against seeking a job at any other law firm. "Boston's a small town. Word gets around real fast. No other law firm will hire you."

At this agonizing moment, I didn't feel I really had the strength to go job hunting. I didn't believe in myself anymore, after the maiming I'd been through at H & W, where what I'd believed I was accomplishing turned out to be grounds for firing me "for cause."

I knew what I was feeling.

Disgraced and totally depressed.

Mental confusion from MS was causing me to think I was maybe losing my mind. "It's the only explanation," I said out loud. And I had a bleak vision from the TV games that every little kid was playing back then, absurd as it seems . . . that this ravaging army of circle-faced, jaw-snapping "Pac-men" were chomping around inside my head, gobbling up the myelin, eating my brain tissue, and gulping down my intellect.

And as I sat there, shaking, I had my blackest thought. There was still a way I could take care of my family financially, relieve them of the burden and expense of caring for me in the threatening future. I reached into my desk and pulled out the insurance policy I had bought, just prior to joining H & W. It paid a death benefit of $250,000, with double indemnity—$500,000—if my death was caused by an accident.

How could it best be done? A car accident? I'd have to plan it carefully at a spot where no one else would be injured, in a way that no one would suspect my subterfuge. The car would go off the road, careen down an embankment. But what if, by some awful miracle, I *wasn't* killed? What if I survived in even worse physical shape than I was now?

Then again, what if I was *successful?* And that got me to thinking along those lines of *Hamlet* that I knew so well from high school English. "Ah, there's the rub, for in that sleep of death, what dreams may come when we have shuffled off this mortal coil?"

That foreboding got me in even deeper. I hadn't been much of a Catholic, as I've admitted, but I'd been raised by God-fearing parents and knew my catechism and the Church's teaching on suicide. There could be no worse sin. It would cut me off totally from the love of God, who was already keeping His distance. Did I want to push Him even further away? Psychologists describe suicide as the act of someone who has a greater fear of living than of dying. Had I gotten to be that afraid of life? Once the armor of self has been stripped away so brutally, was death all that was left for me to contemplate? And I grasped, then and there, the terrible reality of a life cast off, what enduring pain that abandonment can cause in the hearts of those left behind, like my mother and Lora.

I came out of my stupor with a heady rush.

"What am I thinking of?" The fog scattered. "No matter how bad it gets, this isn't the answer." I shivered, and stuffed the policy back in the desk drawer, and that morning called up my new Boston internist, Dr. Peter Gross, to schedule a complete physical.

Dr. Gross saw me immediately, and concluded that while I was in pretty good shape, I was suffering from obvious anxiety and depression. He was also concerned about the growing physical weakness in my right hand and right leg from MS. He ended up referring me to John Purcell, the psychiatrist I soon began seeing at Mass General.

"You may not need his help," he speculated. "But if you don't, considering what you're going through, you'll be the exception."

I stopped at Dr. Purcell's very small office in the middle of February, and from then on, showed up every two weeks at an appointed time. I never saw a receptionist or a secretary or even another patient. I just arrived, sat down, and waited to be called. It was an eerie vigil. But strangely welcoming.

John Purcell is a tall, quiet, and empathetic young man, who turned out to be a huge basketball fan. He'd fly off anywhere, for an exciting night hoop-side. And that's all I got to know about him because our sessions were very much about me. Inside his small inner sanctum, we would talk. But it wasn't really a conversation, just an opportunity for me to vent. And vent I did. I was spilling my guts about everything and everyone I loved passionately, about all my fears and regrets.

I spoke about my father, who seemed so long gone, how much I had cared for him, but how difficult it had been for either of us to say, "I love you." How we had never really connected emotionally, because we were both too private, incapable of adequately expressing love for one another, either in an embrace or in simple words.

I spoke about my mother, the bonds we shared. Her unbounded forgiveness, her courage and wisdom, her gentle touch. And I spoke about Lora and the difficulty that my illness had initially created in our relationship.

I finally ventured back into Boston, to face the music, which was going to be a lot of sour notes. My first trip was up the escalator at the Shawmut Bank to visit Todd Baker, a loan officer, about my $30,000 personal line of credit. I explained to Todd that MS had forced me to resign my job, but didn't go into any further details. Not to worry, Todd said, if worst came to worst, the bank would set up a term loan, with an extended period of time to pay off the balance. Until I got back on my feet, I could pay the interest only every month. I was grateful for such sympathetic treatment.

Heading back down the escalator, I stopped at the ATM machine in the bank lobby, to make a deposit and withdraw some cash.

It took me half an hour to complete these two straight-foward transactions.

I was that distracted, feeling so unsure of myself, so low in self-confidence that I could not handle that simple sequence of punched-in entries, on which the machine did all the required calculations.

I walked out of the bank, feeling rejected by an ATM, on my way to another worrisome destination: the Boston unemployment office. It was just down a few blocks. All this was too familiar territory, since a glance across the street—yes, Federal Street—went directly into the glass doors of what I was already beginning to think of as "my old office building." Shawmut Bank stood just opposite 101 Federal, and I could hardly bear to walk past those spotlessly shining portals, ducking my head and hoping nobody who worked at H & W would see me.

I scurried into the mawkish, melancholic crowd at the State Division of Employment and Training and joined a line to fill out an initial application for benefits. The woman who helped me was polite, but overwhelmed by the number of applicants who needed her assistance. Everywhere, distraught people were standing in queues, sharing sad stories, waiting resignedly for their names to be called.

What a relief when you were called, but that was only the prelude to a more desperate quest. Still more forms had to be filled out that would bring at most a benefit of $200 per week for thirty weeks. Hardly a replacement for the salary I had been making, but like every distressed soul gathered there, I knew it would bring at least some income home.

I went back several more days to wait in line, fill out further forms, attend a briefing on how the system worked. This brought on growing physical stress, since the diminished strength in my right leg made it hard to stand for long periods, hoping to be called. The indignities of the dole made all of us brief comrades, and out of boredom and despair, people plunged into their wrenching personal narratives of the injustice in finding themselves suddenly jobless.

I found it hard to bear their stories, and my heart went out to these people beaten down by the system, who, for one reason or another, didn't fit in, were simply discarded by their employers. On average, they weren't that attractive or articulate, but their plight surely mattered. They left me feeling even more depressed but at least grateful that my own situation, at its very worse, even with the problems from MS, was far better. I was advised I would receive my first check, that next week.

When I returned to sign in, I was actually feeling pretty positive for the first time in days, at the prospect of having managed one step forward. But when I got up to the counter, I was told I couldn't be paid. Talk to one of the hearing officers, if I wanted to know why. Another lengthy wait, on trembling legs, until I was ushered into the office of a middle-aged man, who pulled my file out of a nearly tottering pile.

"Your former employer states you were fired for cause," he snorted. "So you are ineligible to receive unemployment compensation."

"My former employer might be saying that," I hissed back, "but it's not true." I could feel my gorge rising, hot with a bitter grudge. "They fired me without any warning, claiming my performance was unsatisfactory."

The hearing officer's eyebrows went up slightly, and he reached for his telephone. He called H & W, and to my utter amazement, asked for Margaret Hadley.

She wasn't available.

Margaret Hadley?

How could she even be available . . . *at all?* But her name was on the reply form that H & W had filled out after I filed for unemployment. I started feeling sick to my stomach.

"If you want to ask for a hearing on this matter," the man explained, "I'll set one up for next week. Meanwhile, I'll keep trying to reach Ms. Hadley for an explanation."

I quickly requested the hearing, and thanked him for his time, after he slipped me a paper with the date and time, next week.

How could Margaret Hadley be back at H & W? Had Charlie Gaziano called her the day I left? Was it all some devious plot?

"These people are unbelievable!" I kept muttering, all the way home to Cohasset. Their insensitivity, sitting up there in their little glass kingdom, in their plush offices and fancy clothes, totally oblivious of what I was going through, and not giving a damn. "We'll see what they have to say next week." How could they justify what they were claiming? By just jotting down some pat phrase like "for cause" on a piece of paper. "I'm not going to let them get away with this," I swore bitterly. "Not without a fight."

But when I showed up at the hearing room, loaded for bear, nobody else was there. I was sent to see the same hearing officer, who greeted me pleasantly, and immediately signed a sheet of paper. "There won't be any hearing," he managed to smile. "We've cleared up the situation with your employer. Take this over to the payment window and collect your check."

I was ridiculously elated. Once more I thanked the man, and he gave me a good, firm handshake. I could tell he was pleased for me.

"Guess I still have some fighting spirit left in me," I let both of us know.

I walked over to the pay-out window, got a check for two weeks compensation, and you'd have thought it was for $10,000 instead of only $400, I was so happy to head home and brag to Lora and Fred. I strolled out of there, without allowing myself the least hint of a limp.

The following week, I went back into Boston again, this time to the UNUM office to file my disability claim. The irony was not lost on me that here I was at rock bottom, one of the little guys seeking help through the endless warrens of a benefit plan for people with health problems. A disability plan I had overseen for two employers. If I looked closely at my topsy-turvy life to date, I could see how I had started out as one of the little guys, strove to become one of the big guys, made it, or almost, only to fall precipitously back into the precarious stature of an even littler guy.

I'd have to say I was humbled, but rapidly gaining in street smarts from these daily experiences that proved the bureaucracy, for all its faults, could be made to work.

At UNUM, I found myself asking for help from the very woman who had been my contact when I was a big guy at H & W. She was young and extremely pleasant, enormously helpful, but she threw me into a panic when she told me she would soon be leaving UNUM and handed me off to another woman in the office. As a suddenly belittled guy, I desperately wanted to stay with somebody I knew when I was a big guy.

In these panicky circumstances, I kept turning to David Rapaport. When I got home from my visit to UNUM, I called him immediately to go over the application forms. David advised me not to state anything on the UNUM forms that might jeopardize my legal right to file a claim for handicapped discrimination against H & W in the future. I didn't want to sue, but since learning that Margaret Hadley was back at work again, I was growing increasingly suspicious as to what had really precipitated my dismissal.

"They know that they owe me the $60,000," I complained. "They just want to see me grovel and give them a blank check release, to let them off the hook." David always listened sympathetically. "They never should have let us move down here. Lora left her business behind. We had a wonderful, affordable home in Greenfield. Now we're hanging in the breeze, in a new house with a big mortgage that is filled with boxes we haven't even unpacked yet, and I'm out of work."

David had put all these losses together in a letter that had gone out to H & W on February 14th. In addition to asking that the firm pay for professional outplacement service and provide me a neutral reference, he listed:

Loss on sale of home in Greenfield, below market value	$18,000
Anticipated loss from forced sale of home in Cohasset	$28,000
Loss to the value of Madelene Travel	$50,000
Six months severance pay, original contract	$60,000
Miscellaneous legal, other expenses	$12,000
TOTAL	$168,000

Since H & W had imposed a deadline of February 7th on their "for cause" ultimatum, we requested a one-month extension to March 6th. When that day came, without any response from H & W—and even though we had not yet heard if I would be granted partial disability by UNUM—David wrote H & W to decline their $60,000 offer. That really was the day the dispute began—March 6, 1992—with only the faintest hope of our ever turning back. But I was still fearful of going forward with legal expenses that I couldn't afford against H & W, a large, well-established, high-powered law firm.

And here we were, already worrying about balancing my claim for partial disability against any right I might have to sue for handicapped discrimination. David, very wisely, sought out expert legal advice on the subject of disability insurance, which tended to support our cause.

Luckily, as I now further found, I was included in the insured group comprised of all H & W attorneys, with far superior coverage to that provided to the firm's other employees. UNUM would compensate anyone who could not perform their usual duties because of a disability, but who could do another, less taxing, but still challenging job. This *partial* disability would cover sixty percent of any beneficiary's prior salary until age sixty-five. Since I was then fifty-two, that held great attraction for me, far more than full disability that would limit my future work to some mindless occupation at best, or menial endeavors at worst. In fact, in order to receive these partial disability payments under the policy, the recipient had to be gainfully employed, which stimulated me to get moving on establishing a consulting practice.

We carefully drafted my UNUM claim according to my physicians' evaluations of my MS. We argued, per Drs. Gross and Wolpow, that I could no longer perform the stressful and demanding work required of the executive director of Hutchins & Wheeler "as the job was structured at the time of onset of my disability." But that did not preclude me from claiming, in a later lawsuit, "that I could have done the job," had H & W restructured the position, i.e. made an accommodation for my disability, and revamped the duties of the executive director. That might be a bear to prove, but such proof lay far in the future, on that still distant battleground we had yet to reach. For now, we all agreed that securing approval of my disability insurance claim took precedence.

"But if we're going to sue for handicapped discrimination," David explained, "we will need to file with the Massachusetts Commission Against Discrimination within six months of your dismissal."

Everything seemed to be within this six month window, so this would be our strategy. We would seek to negotiate an out-of-court settlement with H & W—upwards of $200,000—during the six months it would take to gain a positive response from UNUM. I needed that guarantee of financial support from UNUM before we could ever enter upon any litigation that might well last for years, with great uncertainty about its eventual outcome or even likely reward.

I took a deep breath and said, "David, we'll just have to see how things work out. Thanks for all your help."

David answered, "You're welcome," as he presented me with a $10,000 legal bill.

That indicated graphically how soon I had better find work. I already had to report periodically to the unemployment office, in writing, how I was seeking gainful employment. Also, as noted, to receive any partial disability payment from UNUM, I would first have to show employment. I decided to form my own consulting business—AJL Associates—and revive the many dormant contacts in healthcare I still had around Massachusetts. I was fairly well known for the role I had played in gaining passage of that almost $100 million in funding for

Massachusetts hospitals, so I picked up from there, networking with old friends and colleagues.

Within a few weeks, I popped into the office of David Hannan, the CEO of South Shore Hospital, located in Weymouth a few towns from Cohasset. Dave and I had worked together at St. Vincent back in Worcester during the 70s, when he was an administrative director, and I was working in their information systems group. Now he was building a solid reputation for South Shore Hospital, one of the few hospitals in Massachusetts that was actually growing, and only twenty minutes from my front door.

Talking to Dave was a test of my nerves. He was balder, my curly hair was whiter, and we laughed about "the good old days at Saint V's." But once I got started on my story, the tone changed abruptly. Dave's demeanor turned deadly serious as I told him about my MS and being fired by H & W.

That worried me until his secretary came in to hospitably offer coffee and pastry. I settled for an orange juice. Dave creaked back in his chair, and began brooding on the problem at hand, as I'd seen him do so often at Saint V's.

It seemed that his executive VP was out on short medical leave—elective surgery, available at their own clinics these days—but Dave felt safe in saying, on a preliminary basis, there were two or three key projects they were conducting—which could certainly use my help.

Within a week, I was back there under a year-long consulting engagement. Dave wanted me to select a computerized decision support system for the hospital, as well as to conduct a competitor analysis. I would be paid $40,000 for two to three days per week, and South Shore Hospital would provide me an office in the executive suite with access to a secretary. "By God," I congratulated myself, "I'm back in the saddle." I was soon donning executive attire again, at least for part of every week, and familiar tasks were helping salve my damaged ego, raising my sense of self-worth.

And I was delighted to pay my last visit down to the unemployment office to tell the State Division of Employment and Training I would no longer be needing their services.

Of course, $40,000 was only a third of what I had been earning at H & W, but in my newfound exhilaration, I was already launching out on another brave venture: To earn my doctorate in business administration.

I can't exactly explain how I grew this suddenly bold attitude, coming straight off the unemployment lines. But the idea had long been lurking in the back of my mind, ever since my days as CEO at Farren Hospital, when I'd taken two graduate-level courses at the University of Massachusetts School of Public Health in Amherst. I had loved the unstructured learning environment, and felt this spate of advanced education had increased my intellectual grasp, and had made me a more informed and better manager.

Now I took it a step further. It might someday make me into a useful teacher.

So I sat myself down with a reference guide to all the programs in advanced education in the USA.

The closest was Boston University, so I arranged a meeting with Joe Restuccia and Mike Schwartz, two professors in the Operations Management Department at the BU School of Management. Over lunch, we discussed my background and aspirations. I said I'd always wanted to pursue a doctorate, but earning a living—which meant holding down a full time job—had taken precedence. Now that I had gone into my own consulting business things were different. I kept the matter of my health under wraps; didn't feel that it was necessary to disclose anything at this juncture.

Joe and Mike were friendly enough, but hesitated to encourage a man of my age to become a full-fledged doctoral student. The course of study I was proposing would be long and difficult. If I only wanted to teach, why sweat the ordeal of a doctorate degree?

But I was adamant, explaining why I was after more than a teaching post. I wanted to advance my knowledge in order to discover solutions to problems that contemporary managers daily and desperately confronted, especially in health services. I'd faced so many of these quandaries myself. I was intrigued that they might be solved more readily and fully, by using a more scientific method based on sound theories instead of the constant trial-and-error approach that was all too common in managerial practice.

They shrugged politely and introduced me to Janelle Heineke, a former health care manager, who had nearly completed her doctoral work. She was cordial, and listened patiently as I ran through my aspirations and goals again.

"Your goals seem very broad in scope," she diagnosed my case. "You're going to have to focus your interests and energies much more within a specific area of study. And be prepared to work hard. It's taken me nearly five years to get to a point where I am ready to defend my dissertation."

And that was considered to be record time in a setting where homework was measured in pounds of paper, not inches.

I took these broodings back home, where I caught a glimpse of flurrying fur, gone flashing down the hallway, and heard the scuffle of claws, and the rush of little, fumbling feet.

Better check this out, I figured, and stepped into the corridor to find Lora and Fred standing at the top of the stairs, laughing at a small, very blond, golden retriever puppy scurrying away from me. The pup saw me, turned around in a swirl, and sprang back toward me on four short, fat legs. I slid down the wall, and caught his long red tongue, panting and wet, full in the face.

"His name is Mr. August Baggins," Lora smiled.

Another visitant from Middle Earth. It had been a long time since we lost Strider. All three of us fussed over Baggins, romping and cuddling and playing with him in turns. After he jumped into Lora's waiting hands and thoroughly washed her face too, I grabbed him and hugged him and felt how easy and good it was to be laughing again.

I went to bed that night, still smiling over my better feelings. I was grateful to everybody who was trying to help me, for just giving me the fun of having a dog back in the house.

I was coming out of a long, lonely, cold winter, frozen at times by my own depression, but spring was breaking up the harsh, binding clime that had emotionally gripped me. I went around to see Dr. Wolpow again, and got an encouraging report. The one-day surgery I'd undergone for carpal tunnel repair had decreased the numbness in my fingers, improving the dexterity in my right hand. And Dr. Wolpow wrote that my plan to do a moderate amount of consulting while working toward my doctorate showed that this patient was "setting out to do a very reasonable series of activities in his life."

But despite this upbeat note, my walking was getting worse. On leaving a visit with John Purcell at MGH, I had to stop two or three times to rest. The muscles in my right leg felt tired and weak. I couldn't arch my right foot, and kept struggling just to raise my toes. I started to stumble, more than I ever had coming off that Hingham ferry, and had to plop down on the curb that wraps around the lawn edge of MGH.

I waited for my ebbing strength to return. Then stopping and starting like a broken pull toy, I managed to haul myself out to Cambridge

Street and careen into a nearby pharmacy. It was medically well-supplied, so I immediately purchased a cane. I picked one made of sturdy aluminum but fashioned so that it easily broke down into a three-piece package that could be stuffed into a large briefcase or travel bag.

You only have to use it when you need it, I told myself, but it sure made walking those next several steps a lot easier. When I got to the doorway of the pharmacy, the guy in front of me stopped to hold the door for me. "Thanks." Hey, I decided, this isn't going to be so bad after all.

It is the end game from the Sphinx's riddle to Oedipus. What creature goes on four legs at dawn, two legs at midday, and three at sundown? A man, of course. And a cane is that third leg, so just be glad you have one by your side when you need it. I began using mine to take the pressure off my right leg, so that I could keep a better and safer balance on three points instead of only two.

Since I'd gone so far as to buy a cane, I got to considering other easements. A few days later, I called the MS Society in Waltham and asked to speak to someone about getting a handicapped placard for my car. "The hell with my pride," I decided. "If I'm going to do all this other stuff, I've got to do whatever it takes to conserve my physical strength, so I can preserve my energy and quality of life."

The operator switched me over to a Ms. Purcell, who helpfully told me what I needed to do to obtain a handicapped permit from the Massachusetts Registry of Motor Vehicles. At the end of our conversation, of course I had to ask if she was related to Dr. John Purcell at MGH.

"Yes," she laughed, "he's my husband."

This brought to mind Mark Twain's comment, "Coincidence is God's way of remaining anonymous."

I filled out the application the RMV mailed to me, got Dr. Peter Gross to complete his portion on my handicapped status, then went around to the registry office in Quincy. I walked in there with my cane, but not really "in there," since the long line of people waiting for service already extended outside the entrance doors onto the sidewalk, and on around the block.

De ja vu, the unemployment lines all over again. "Is this the way all the Commonwealth runs," I pondered, "or is this just my own personal misfortune?"

Impulsively, I decided to take operations management into my own hands. I refused to endure one more moment of hardship, standing there in line on shaking legs. I excused myself to everybody who gave me a questioning look, and walked straight through the crowded doors, all the way to the head of the line, and behind the service counter. I sat down in the first available office chair.

Some minutes passed before a woman came over to me, out of whatever back room offices the RMV had. She looked slightly shocked, but asked, "May I help you?"

"Yes, please," I said, and handed her my completed application.

A startled look came over her face—a mix of immediate recognition of duty and embarrassed chagrin at my difficulties.

My application was processed on the spot, while I got up to have my picture taken. Then, making full, perhaps intrusive use of my cane again, I walked back out to my car—a rented Volvo that Lora had insisted on—and slipped the handicapped placard around behind the tinted glass and looked hard at my latest picture through the slightly dirty windshield. Now I was the one who was shocked, registering what had just happened to me inside the RMV.

I had been officially recognized as a handicapped person. Yet I hardly recognized myself—didn't know this far older, more vulnerable, tight-lipped face, which had somehow replaced the youthful, confident visage of all my past official photos.

I caught sight of something I had seen many times in other faces, all my life as a bureaucrat: pathos.

I called Joe Restuccia at BU, to ask how my application for doctoral studies was coming along. Joe was chair of the Operations Management (OM) Department, so he had been able to convene a full departmental discussion of my case. The faculty was convinced of my sincerity, but noted that it had been sixteen years since I'd gotten my MBA. A lot had changed in management studies, and some questioned whether I was up to the rigors of what would essentially be academic rehab.

Joe had a proposition to put to me. Would I be willing to take four doctoral-level courses over the next academic year, beginning in the fall of 1992, with the proviso that if I did well, I would be formally accepted into the Ph.D. program in 1993?

Yes, I said, so long as those four courses would count toward my doctorate. "They would," Joe assured me, and a few days later, I got a letter of acceptance as a "guest student" at BU. Joe ended the letter: "I am sure I can speak for Mike, Janelle and the rest of the OM Department, as well as myself, in conveying our excitement in working with you in the doctoral progam." I was delighted but reflected soberly that no one in the OM Department knew that I had MS.

My disease came more sharply into focus in July when David Rapaport forwarded the draft of another letter he was ready to send to H & W, this time putting the firm on notice of my legal claim. It was powerful. David outlined the legal justification for our charge of handicapped discrimination under Massachusetts Statute, Chapter 151b, as well as a common law claim that H & W had improperly failed to forewarn me that my job was in jeopardy. He wrote that the potential award from a court judgment against them could reach $1,000,000 for back pay, front pay, legal fees, emotional distress, and punitive damages. Finally, he gave notice that, if we did not reach a settlement before the end of the month, we would be compelled to file a claim with the Massachusetts Commission Against Discrimination (MCAD)—within the legal limit of six months after my firing, which would be July 27th—and proceed to civil suit.

Off the letter went, with my and Lora's firm approval. But for all this bravado, I was still hoping, realistically, for the $200,000 settlement we'd proposed earlier.

But the stark truth is, both the Labontes *and* the Rapaports were facing challenging financials, though David never quite let me know his problems in the way I had to share mine with him. We'd only just met David's wife and partner Diane. All I knew then was that Rapaport & Rapaport had been doing increasing business over eight years, but the fact was that Mr. and Mrs. Rapaport were carrying a large financial burden.

I decided that if matters moved beyond the incentives I had offered David for settlement, and we actually had to sue, I hoped he would agree to a contingency agreement. One third of any judgment would go to Rapaport & Rapaport since that was the only way that Lora and I could take on the financial rigors of a protracted lawsuit.

But it's one thing to work through these thoughtful conclusions in the comfort of home, quite another to take the actual, physical steps, especially with MS.

So up the cobbles of Beacon Hill I climbed to One Ashburton Place, just across from the gold-domed State House, on July 20th. David had received no reply from H & W, and he had made the appointment for me with the Massachusetts Commission Against Discrimination. He also accompanied me. With cane in hand, I hobbled along the narrow, twisted sidewalks. As I struggled to pitch my right leg forward, I suggested that we might bring a class action against Boston for the outright failure of its streets to provide access to people with disabilities. But David said it wasn't worth it, since the city had capped its own liability. Boston couldn't be sued for more than $5000.

David left me alone in a small room at the MCAD, and a dark-haired woman came in shortly to talk with me. She was one of those patient troopers in the stalwart but resigned cadre of the Boston bureaucracy. The Minutemen have long since been replaced by the Many-Houred Women, and she asked politely why I thought I had been discriminated against. Good question, I had a sudden impulse to say. It was high time I pulled together a succinct and effective answer. I had my facts down pat, told her all about the positive job appraisal, the salary increase and bonuses I'd received. "I thought I was doing a good job," I said to her. Then came the disclosure in July of 1991 that I had MS, the relocation of my family to Cohasset in October, and my sudden firing in January. But I just didn't feel "pat" about any of this, any longer. I felt used and a little pathetic and, far worse, violated.

She took some notes on a lined pad, then looked a little sadly but directly into my eyes, and asked, "Were you ever given any warning that your job performance was not satisfactory?"

"No," I replied.

She made another note, stared straight at me again, and asked, "You did not have any warning, either written or verbal?"

"No, I didn't."

With that, she raised her eyebrows—certainly had to be a key point in mooting these cases—and got up. "I'll be back in a minute."

She came back with David, and had me sign the State form that officially entered my charge of handicapped discrimination. "Your case will be assigned," she almost sighed with official patience, "to an attorney on our staff for follow-up."

"Mr. Labonte will, most likely, be filing a civil suit in this matter," David quickly informed her.

She turned to him, quizzically. "Who will be representing him?" she asked.

"I will be," David replied.

A hint of bureaucratic relief, no more than a blink, came into her patient but stolid gaze. "And you are?"

"David Rapaport."

That caused her to take one more note, which was the last of her involvement, or that of the MCAD, in the subsequent years of litigation.

It was the warmest moment in the entire interview. She understood—with a gratitude she could barely disguise—she was off the hook.

"Good luck, Mr. Labonte," she said and shook my hand.

David walked me down Beacon Hill more easily than up. "You did a good job," he assured me.

"I'm glad it's over," I admitted. "I feel like I just climbed a mountain." Or was that altogether the best metaphor for a potential litigant with MS? "I'm ravenous. Let's get something to eat."

That tough climb up Beacon Hill was enough to send me across the Charles River to Somerville Hospital, four days later, to see Dr. Andrea Wagner. I'd seen her a year ago, at Dr. Wolpow's insistence, so that she could evaluate my walking. Back then, she'd cleared me for sidewalk traffic, but this time, she decided I definitely needed a brace on my right leg. She sent me off with a prescription to a Boston brace-maker.

So now I knew why.

The brace, lightweight and comfortable, made a tremendous difference in my stability. It cuffed the back of my leg, just below the knee, extended down around my heel and under my arch to the ball of my foot. It fitted inside my shoe, like a stiff, transparent sock that was held up by a Velcro strap. When I stood up, my pant leg all but covered the brace, so you'd hardly even notice it. And I didn't need my cane anymore, since I found I could walk just as confidently without it.

"You're standing nice and straight now," Lora smiled broadly, "and your walking has *so* much improved."

And lately I was learning how to take a compliment whenever one was really meant.

In fact, the only place where I seemed to be falling behind—seriously losing ground—was on our monthly payments in support of the Labonte household. Despite the added income from my consulting for SSH, we were going in the hole every month. I regretfully had to turn to our tax-deferred savings accumulated over twenty-two years working for the Sisters of Providence. I took out $37,000, paid the taxes and penalties for early withdrawal, and ended up with $30,000. That was enough to bring our payments up to date, satisfy what was owed to Rapaport & Rapaport, and still put a little aside for future expenses.

But it was depressing to withdraw that money. I'd worked hard to build up this retirement fund, and here thousands of dollars were being rapidly siphoned off by the societal vacuum we were caught in. I'd always been a planner, my eye to the future, hedging against the uncertainties of life. Suddenly those uncertainties had arrived on our doorstep, stripping away all the security I so cherished. But we had to do what had to be done, and trust that everything would come right in the end.

Then, on August 12th, I received a letter from UNUM stating that my claim for partial disability had been approved.

Lora and I were ecstatic. So was David. This new income, equal to sixty percent of my former salary at H & W, combined with my consulting fees, would put the Labonte budget back on an even keel. Everybody at UNUM had been great. They were respectful in all their dealings and sensitive to my situation and needs, while doing their job for the insured H & W. My account had been assigned to one Sharon Labonte, a benefit specialist, who would keep track of my status through physician reports, earnings statement, etc. from here on out. She was as struck as I was by the coincidence of our names.

But what my newly won financial security really meant was that we could confidently move forward with a legal action against H & W. Not that problems didn't still loom. My disability income, for instance, now raised the legal question of my very right to sue. It had not yet been decided by the Massachusetts courts whether a person with a disability had the legal right to sue for handicapped discrimination if he or she was already receiving compensatory income through disability coverage. Could such parties be estopped—that was the legal term, which came down to meaning "prohibited"—from seeking damages for prior acts of discrimination, thus trumping the remedies provided under Massachusetts Statue, Chapter 151b?

But now, I could at least tell David to proceed forward with raising such issues, without any fear of our landing in the poor house. We filed suit against H & W in the Suffolk Superior Court on September 11th, 1992. September 11th has since taken on far larger connotations, but it remains for me the date when the malaise of my MS-induced foggymindedness lifted, and I began to take charge of my own life again. We named every partner individually as a defendant, by running down the whole letterhead, but the top line officially read: *Alan J. Labonte versus James G. Wheeler et al.* And since Boston is still a small town, bad news travels fast when a big firm gets into a legal tangle.

David had a copy of our claim hand-delivered to attorney Mary Marshall at Stoneham, Chandler & Miller, the firm that had been chosen to represent H & W.

But I was much more fascinated with how our suit would be greeted in the lofty offices at 101 Federal.

I could imagine a brief furor at our audacity, but that would quickly subside into a general disdain for our vain and feckless pleading. By and large, it would be sloughed off as a nuisance and a joke. But Charles Robins would be more serious-minded about the matter, as would Jack Clymer, whom I knew to be a good friend of attorney Alan Miller at Stoneham, Chandler & Miller. I could even imagine Miller advising Clymer that they were going to be juggling a hot potato in the days ahead, best be on their guard.

But, I decided Tony would undoubtedly prevail over any and all doubts before the management committee. I realized in retrospect how much he must have come to hate my guts, how much he must have had to do with my termination. He was not going to hand me any $250,000 without a fight. I gritted my teeth and swore under my breath, "And it's a fight you're going to get, Tony, my boy!"

Chapter Five

Once our suit was officially docketed, the uncertain, hesitant course of my life abruptly changed. Almost as if what lawyers call the "cause of action" had actually set in motion a new and demanding but exhilarating course of events, which caught me completely by surprise. Among the first was my unexpected exit from the welcome comfort of therapy.

I'd gone into MGH to see John Purcell for another of our bi-weekly sessions. As usual, I did 99.5% of the talking, this time at a highly emotional pitch. I described my mother's holding my head in her lap after my father's death, how I had broken down and cried. I knew she needed me to be strong, but I couldn't be strong. I was feeling so vulnerable and frightened. Right there in front of Dr. Purcell I broke down and started crying all over again. In desperation, I surrendered myself totally to him, unveiling my deepest fear. "Does everyone have so many troubles, or is it just me?"

That's when he gave me his one great piece of advice, that we all have to abide such pain. "Alan, If you want to live in a cave like a hermit, essentially sealed away from the world, then you can avoid these problems. But if you want to live in the mainstream of life, then they're really unavoidable. This is part of it."

I immediately felt better, wiped my eyes, managed a smile, and murmured "Thank you" from the bottom of my shaking heart.

And the very next session, during which I kept better control, he stood up at the end and said, "I don't think we need to see each other anymore."

Instead of feeling let down, I experienced a deep sense of relief. "Good luck, Alan," he wished me.

And I thought to myself, "He trusts me. I'm going to be okay. I'm not crazy after all. Just going through a tough time. Just struggling like anybody would be in my situation. Thank God!"

I was so exhilarated when I arrived outside at the top of the hospital steps that I had an urge to take them all in one leap, despite my MS. "Easy, Alan," I warned myself. "One step at a time."

Dr. Purcell's quiet, patient, and wisely one-sided consultations had opened me up, psychologically. How wide open I didn't yet know, but when I look at the past, I can see how he brought me back into self-balance, so that I could navigate, on my own, to the verge of what turned out to be my true spiritual life. The real leap I was preparing to take was one of faith.

At that moment, however, I was still too involved in facing tough life choices to notice where I was headed. I'd register for two classes at BU under Joe Restuccia's guidance: a doctoral seminar in operations strategy and a statistics course in Multivariate Data Analysis. My classmates were often fellow New Englanders who had also worked in business and industry, and they too were furthering their education to take up academic careers. But they were easily twenty years younger than me, and in far better health.

I found the classes daunting with material that was hard to grasp. I was definitely an old dog learning new tricks—from a master who gave commands in a new jargon, that of "academic-eze."

The grind made life extra stressful. I was learning this new language on the constant run, back and forth, to my "day job" two or three days a week at South Shore Hospital. I was also refurbishing my computer skills. Luckily I already knew that jargon, and the concepts, and soon enough, got into my newly purchased PC and had it performing like a new wind-up toy that did smarter and smarter tricks.

The income from SSH helped, but it wasn't nearly enough, since we'd run up a lot of credit card debt over the first six months after my departure from H & W. And now I had to face rising legal costs like court reporters fees from David Rapaport's pursuit of H & W by deposing the key members of the firm.

So I took out a five-year loan of $50,000 on my retirement plan with the Sisters—our nest egg—and called in what I had in my 401K at H & W. I wrote the woman attorney in charge, asking her to send me a check for $16,000. I deliberately noted to her that I understood I could roll the $16,000 into an IRA to avoid any tax consequences, but had no intention of doing so. I cashed the check immediately and paid the tax. I just didn't want anyone at H & W to know how desperately I needed the money. It was already becoming that kind of cat-and-mouse game. Two poor church mice up against a very fat, well-clawed cat.

Then we got an early and important call from one of the older H & W partners, Tom Paxton, disclosing that he and three other partners had been forced out of the firm, barely days after my departure. Could they possibly be dropped from our complaint?

I was shocked, but not really surprised. I'd heard enough at management committee meetings from Tony about some partners not "pulling their weight."

"David," I said, "they're in the same boat that I'm in. Sure, they were around when I was canned, but my leaving was probably presented to them as a medical necessity, something that I had to do for my health. Look, these people aren't to blame," I said. "I'd just as soon let them off the hook."

David, as usual, struck a wise compromise. "I agree with you, Alan, but we have to consider liability here. If we excuse them, and then ultimately win a large judgment, it may be difficult to collect what's rightfully due to you from the remaining partners." He was already envisaging legal consequences, far ahead. "Why don't we omit them now, but tell them we reserve our right to name them in the future if need be?"

I went for that. "Sounds great. Let's do it." And because we did, out of my growing suspicion that the management committee had set in motion a far broader plan than my small destruction, we gained friends. One in particular, Ken May, ended up testifying on my behalf at trial, out of H & W's real estate department.

We were planning courtroom strategy, though I still trusted that we would never have to go that far. I hadn't really gathered the inner strength for such a brutalizing struggle, and the way in which such strength finally came to me was—the only word I can find for what occurred—providential. I'd never been much of a believer in divine providence. On the contrary, I claimed to be a realist and planner, a futurist of sorts, a make-it-happen kind of guy. But I have to confess, flat-out, that what happened to me was a religious conversion—if not exactly overnight, right out of the dark night of my own soul.

It's a long story, better told elsewhere, so I will only give the highlights as they affected my outlook, and our mutual conduct, regarding the Labonte Case. My excuse is, that's how I treated the entire religious experience I underwent throughout my legal ordeal. I never even told David. During all those lunches we shared together, I didn't mention a word about the mission I'd undertaken, nor the travels I'd gone on, deep into war torn Bosnia.

All of this started out as a kind of busman's holiday to Washington, D.C. A friend invited me to join him on a lobbying trip in support of Hillary Clinton's healthcare program to see how much support her program had. I ended up with a few hours to spare before my return flight to Boston.

Since I'd already seen all of the monuments on the Mall, I decided to visit, my first time ever, the Basilica of the National Shrine of the Immaculate Conception, that great Catholic treasure out on Michigan Avenue. I was really just gothic-hopping, wandering around the crypt through the shops, under all that magnificence, when a paperback in the window rack caught my eye. It wasn't the cover, only the picture—a softly focused, slightly dimmed photo of a young girl's face. But with bright red lips, glowing skin, and dark, sloe eyes in a valentined oval.

I felt an instant sense of recognition, though I couldn't possibly have told you from where, or why. Nor did I have a clue who she was.

A block of cover copy ran next to this pleasant face. I picked the paperback off the rack and read down the side of the picture. "On June 24, 1981, six children in the mountain village of Medjugorje in central Yugoslavia reported that the Virgin Mary had appeared to them on a hillside. Allegedly she has been returning everyday since."

The book is called *MEDJUGORJE The Message* by Wayne Weible—a devout Lutheran—who describes the sighting on that memorable June day, from many testimonials, in these words:

Ivanka Ivankovic, 15, and her friend, Mirjana Dragicevic, 16, having finished their field chores had gone for a walk on the dirt road that wound from their hamlet of Bijakovici, along the base of the hill known as Podbrdo. On their way home, Ivanka happened to glance up and was startled to see the shimmering figure of a woman up on the hill, bathed in a brilliant light.

"Mirjana, look: it's Gospa!" (Our Lady) she exclaimed without really thinking what she was saying.

So it was *Gospa*—the Croatian name for Our Blessed Mother—who appeared on the cover. From a photograph taken by a Catholic nun during an apparition inside the St. James Church at Medjugorje, where a group of Franciscan monks—very much at odds, at first, with the Communist regime and, later, with the presiding bishop and the Holy See itself—took charge of the six children who variously shared in the vision of Mary on that June day.

Yes, Medjugorje and the Message—its almost daily messages—are very much the modern mediated miracle. Both passionately believed, and equally doubted. Over the past two decades, thousands of pilgrims have flocked to Medjugorje to witness the visitations that *Gospa* supposedly still makes to some of these now very grown children. The nun took her photo, in a small sacristry to the side of the altar at St. James's Church, focusing on the crucifix on the wall above the visionaries kneeling in their revery. When the film was developed, the image of *Gospa* amazingly appeared. Modern candor has to admit some likelihood of a double exposure, even the possibility of a hoax. At the same time, I myself share Weible's sentiment that among all the pictures of the Holy Mother, "this one would always be my image of Mary."

A worldwide organization has grown up around Medjugorje, especially in this country, but you can also read widely in the Catholic press how unsubstantiated by any credible evidence this continuous Message from Medjugorje is regarded by the official Church.

When I returned from D.C., I settled back into the BU day job routine. To my surprise, I did well in my courses at BU and was admitted to the doctoral program. We also managed to relocate my ailing mother from Florida, back to a Worcester senior care center, with her only surviving sister. And I had the preliminaries of our lawsuit to focus on.

But I couldn't stop reading, and re-reading Wayne Weible's book.

A terrible longing arose in my heart to travel to Medjugorje. And I didn't even know where it was! Somewhere near Italy? I got hold of a world map and found it way over on the other side of the Adriatic. "Get a grip on yourself, Alan," I brooded. "You need to go to a place and you don't even know where it is?"

But June 24th happens to be celebrated in the Catholic Church as the birthday of John the Baptist. And my middle name happens to be Jean, after my father whose middle name was Jean de Baptiste. And one day, sitting in my office at home, I took down the calendar and highlighted the week of June 19th to June 27th. And then, on the inspiration of the moment, I decided to take that leap of faith, though it was much more like a hop, skip, and a jump.

I called Lufthansa and booked a round trip ticket to Zagreb for that highlighted June week.

"If I can get that close, I can do the rest of the trip by land," I half-kidded myself. "And if the Blessed Mother really wants me to come, she'll send me the money before this reservation expires."

The next week got very busy, and I pretty much forgot about the deadline. That Friday, I met with Joe Restuccia at BU to discuss a consulting project he wanted me to do for $2000. "And Alan," Joe smiled, "I've been able to come up with another thousand dollars for you."

When I got home that afternoon, Lora said I'd had a phone call from somebody in Chicago about my paying off a government education loan. Actually I'd already sent in the pay-off check to a Boston agency, but I called the guy in Chicago anyway, and he said he could save me $1500 if I could pay the loan off through him. I made a quick call to Boston. My check hadn't been processed, and they could see their way clear to sending it back to me.

I rushed to tell Lora that we were $1500 ahead on our tight household finances, and she was delighted. Then I remembered the deadline—this very Friday at midnight—and realized I actually had $2500 in newly found money, which was enough to pay for my trip!

"What trip?" Lora frowned.

Sheepishly, I told her about the reservation I'd secretly booked to Zagreb, and she was aghast.

"Honey," she sighed, "don't you know there's a war going on there?"

I did, kind of, but I really hadn't connected Medjugorje with the hostilities in Bosnia. Of course, Medjugorje was very close to Croatia. But if I'd looked more closely at the world map, I would've seen Mostar, that was only seventeen kilometers away from Medjugorje, already in flames with the Croats now fighting against the Muslims, who had originally been their allies. Horrendous and bloody confusion, as Lora was telling me in no uncertain terms.

"How will you get there? You don't speak the language. Who's going to take you there? You certainly can't go alone."

"I'll just let the deadline lapse," I angled. "But I've got to tell you, this is getting scary. I really think I'm supposed to go there."

I let the ticket go, but then got hold of a pamphlet on Croatian Relief, known as CR. I phoned CR to ask how to find somebody, anybody to take me to Medjugorje. Contact a woman in Wichita, Kansas, named Nives Jelich, I was told. She had emigrated from Yugoslavia with her family, but she escorts groups of pilgrims back to her homeland. Right after dinner, I went upstairs to call Wichita, and Nives Jelich answered.

She responded warmly, as if we'd known each other for years.

"Oh yes, Alan. We have a group going in June, but I can't talk to you now. Ivan is visiting us."

"Ivan?"

"Yes, all the way from Medjugorje."

"Ivan Dragicevic?"

"Please call me at the office in the morning," she said politely, but clearly under unusual pressure. "It's almost time for the apparition."

In Wichita? I silently gawked.

I hung up the phone, hurried to the stairs, and in my careless haste to descend, almost collapsed at the bottom.

"I'm going," I cried out.

"You all right?" asked Lora.

"It's all set." Both tears and laughter. "I'm really going."

But I decided I had to make some contribution, and the CR bulletin said medical supplies were especially needed. Well, wasn't I a health-care professional? I called Catholic Relief Services in Washington and was told they had an office in Mostar, where "penicillin, amoxicillin, and ampercillin are at the top of our list."

"How would I get them there?"

"The surest way is to bring them in a suitcase."

I got a list of major drug companies and started calling several who manufactured the products I needed. Did they have a program that would donate drugs in a crisis situation? Yes, but they customarily routed shipments through charitable organizations like the American Red Cross, not through individuals. When I called Wyeth-Ayerst, my plea finally got a more sympathetic hearing. Wyeth was willing to sell me the drugs at a wholesale price, but they still needed to see some official authorization. So I started in on another spate of phone calls, and soon found out what I was up against. At least three government agencies, not at all ready to do business. And I didn't have that much time, with our departure date only sixty days away.

But what good is living your life as a healthcare bureaucrat, if you don't have some life still left in you? On our next lobbying trip to Washington, I made other negotiating rounds. I spoke to my congressman, Gerry Studds, with officials at two of those three federal agencies, representatives of two humanitarian organizations, and several stone faces at the Croatian Embassy. That night I again dropped exhausted into my hotel bed. I realized I would have to stop pushing. If God wanted me to take medical supplies to Bosnia, He would work out the details. All I had to do was my best to cooperate.

I began to feel, just generally, more at ease. While still troubled by the many uncertainties we were facing, I kept myself more open to new experiences like the fresh faith I could put into this pilgrimage. I stopped thinking about all those -cillins, until five days before my departure, when I got a personal phone call from an official at one of the federal agencies. He sympathized with my plight but insisted, "Mr. Labonte, we can't allow you to receive the drugs directly." Instead he asked indirectly if I might happen to know any physician who could order them from the manufacturer . . . for some future purpose?

"I know a *lot* of physicians," I couldn't help replying. "Are you saying that if a doctor could get the supplies to me, I could just put them into my suitcase and *go?*"

"Basically," he answered, "yes."

I called a physician friend who immediately agreed to act as the go-between, and then phoned Nevis Jelich to let her in on this capricious caper.

She sounded very excited. "Alan, how much will this cost?"

"For $2500," I replied, "I can obtain $20,000 worth of antibiotics."

She took me totally by surprise. "Alan, we have some money in the relief fund. I can send you a check."

I was flabbergasted, as much as anything by her complete and immediate trust.

I called Wyeth-Ayerst and arranged for the shipment to my physician friend. Then I went out and bought the biggest suitcase I could find, even got a fifty percent discount. Three days later, I had my brand new suitcase packed with seventy pounds of medical supplies for the hospital in Mostar, along with two other bags and a knapsack, plus a gigantic bottle of spring water—a staple for MS sufferers. And that's how I made the journey with sixty other pilgrims via airplane and busload into the mountain vastness of Bosnia-Hercegovinia, using my folding cane—one minute to save my balance, the next as a makeshift grappling hook.

That very first morning, I set out early up the road to the top of Podbrdo, the hill on which the six children had first seen their fateful vision, back in 1981. I dug my cane out of my knapsack and hurried off before the sun got too high.

Somehow it pleased me to recall that, in less fraught times, the girls had gone sneaking off here, after their chores, to smoke cigarettes and listen to a portable radio. The boys who were later called to witness the girls' sudden apparition were already busy up a tree, stealing apples.

The steep road soon crumpled into an uneven, rocky path that yawed up the hill. I pushed myself along with my cane, grateful I was one of only a few out on the hill at that hour.

But each time I rounded a bend, I came upon another bronze plaque, all fourteen Stations of the Cross, signifying Christ's passion at Calvary. I could empathize, wondering if I would make it to the top myself. Nearly there, I stopped to rest and pray at the ninth station where Christ falls for the second time, and heard a tinkling sound coming eerily from above.

"Oh God," I caught myself half in a trance, "am I about to have some kind of religious reverie?"

The tinkling came closer and closer. Exactly like the communion bell used to sound at Mass. I could feel my heart pounding, arythmically, when a head suddenly peeped over the grassy rise behind the station.

Then a small beard.

With horns.

A little goat, as surprised as I was, pranced around me, and hoofed on down the hill, tinkling its bell all the more frantically.

It took me two hours of hesitant climbing, but I made it. I kneeled down among many wooden crosses, reciting the rosary with other pilgrims who began arriving around me. I felt the relief of the cool, balmy breezes above Medjugorje, its white houses and red roofs clustered below.

I realized, despite myself, I had been half expecting a miracle, and had just been given the goat instead.

I was also facing a crisis of faith, in the midst of two days of rising celebration in thanks for the visionaries' messages of love and hope. Despite the war, only as far away as seventeen kilometers in embattled Mostar, pilgrims were streaming into Medjugorje, many families walking six to eight hours to reach the overnight campgrounds around St. James Church. Dozens of priests sat out in the courtyards, hearing confessions in the open air.

After some agonized soul-searching, I found a priest beside a sign that said "English" and went over to him and sat down.

"Father, it has been thirty years since my last confession," I began. "I was married outside the Church. I love my wife, and we have a good marriage. I want to go to confession. Is this possible?"

That was a hard mouthful to pull out of myself. The priest looked back at me and sighed. "Why weren't you married in the Church?"

"You see, Father, my wife was married previously for a short time."

His expression became more gentle, even slightly sad, but he had to say, "I can't hear your confession in light of the current situation. When you get home, go and speak with a priest in your local parish and discuss your problem with him. I'm certain that something can be done." He shook my hand and gave me his card. "My name is Father Kevin." An American. "If I can ever be of help, this is where you can reach me. God bless you."

But I needed his help, right then and there. I managed a smile and walked away, sunk in the despair that overcame me whenever I faced this inner conflict. It had haunted me for so many years, yet even this renewed urgency couldn't help me resolve it. My love for Lora was strong and sure. Nothing could change that. But my love of God—this longing to share in His sacraments—burned within me. I loved them both, but couldn't have them both. How could I choose between them? The answer was simple and devastating. I couldn't.

I was also frustrated to see the suitcase full of medical supplies still sitting in the hallway of our guest house. Finally, I confronted one of the Franciscan priests after his saying Mass. "Father, I've brought medical supplies for the hospital in Mostar. Can you help me get them there?"

"You can't go to Mostar," he warned, in alarm. "The fighting is terrible there. If you go, you will be killed. You must leave this in the hands of local people. They will get these drugs to where they are needed."

He flung his arms around me in a bountiful blessing. I vowed to leave the suitcase in the hallway—and its eventual disposal in *Gospa's* hands. I feel sure—though, to this day, I don't know how—it got to Mostar.

Then I remember wandering the next day into my first evening Mass. Originally, I had thought I'd be one of very few people crazy enough to travel to this war torn region, but there were so many thousands of pilgrims waiting on wooden benches that had been extended into the field behind St. James, in front of an elevated, circular platform that bore the altar. I was lucky to find an empty seat. Most of the crowd were standing, or sitting on the ground, and when the tinkling bells rang for communion, almost like that goat, the priests left the altar, moving down among the people, like overseas missionaries.

I thought of the embrace of the Church, reaching out to everyone to share in the body of Christ, and I yearned to receive Him. But I just sat there, stuck in my seat, as always, unwilling to break the rules, feeling unworthy, over so many years, to partake in the Eucharist.

But no, I decided, not tonight.

I rose and faced the aisle that opened in the parting crowd, making way for the band of priests, come down into the multitude, each one bearing a golden cup filled with the sacred bread. It was near dusk, and I faced a setting sun, lowering among clouds, behind the giant concrete cross atop Mount Krizevac. At this hour, a green-yellow luminescence seized the sky, the way sailors sometimes see the bolting sun strike a green flash from the ocean's sunset edge.

I prayed for some sign to guide me. My eyes were drawn back toward the sun, still behind that veil of mountain clouds. I let go of all my anxiety, and surrendered to the mysterious, dancing light from that fiery halo.

As I stared into it, I felt the emotional clutch of an embrace. A hug.

When I looked away again, I saw Father Kevin approaching, giving communion nearby. But he soon turned off, moving away from me.

My resolve all but vanished, but a young priest abruptly broke into the aisle and began walking directly toward me. Our eyes met, and he seemed to look into my very soul and see my confusion.

In that split second, the world stopped. Then the young priest chose to reach out to me. He strode down the lines of people waiting for communion, and stopped right in front of me. Then he placed the Eucharist in my mouth, and moved on, having lent mercy to my conflicted soul.

I sat down and cried, sobbing for a long time. *Gospa* had guided me to this place, this moment in time, then provoked me, and stepped aside. Nobody could keep me sitting out God's love any longer.

After that epiphany, I plunged passionately into the village life around me. The war still raged, and refugees were pouring in, out of the north in Bosnia. I met as many as I could, and their rescuers.

After losing so much—my job, my father, my prospects, my health— I had found true happiness in a faraway land, in a country agonizingly at war, among crowds of strangers.

Had I expected something more holy? Had I come in vain hopes of what is too easily, often selfishly called a miracle? Did I perhaps believe Medjugorje might heal my illness in the fashion of Lourdes or Fatima?

I feel certain in saying no, I never realistically had any such hopes, or even such predilections. But I will admit to believing that marvelous events *do* occur around Medjugorje, midst the rich human surroundings of a religious life. And if anything "miraculous" did happen to me, it would be this very slight glitch in the universe, on my return to our guest house that evening.

Dinner time at Marinko Ivankovic's home was always a feast, when the pilgrims gathered to drink the tart, homemade wine and enjoy the Balkan dishes so lovingly prepared, along with the wonderful melons. We filled our stomachs with this tasty fare, and our souls with tales of the daily mysteries.

This night, our table was blessed with a pitcher of fresh and mountain pure water. I took up the pitcher and poured, filling a large glass to the brim. But something held me back from drinking it. I kept reflecting on how hot the day had been, how much I yearned for this sweet water to quench my thirst by its cooling cascade.

Then something slight but wondrous happened. One of the kitchen women brought out a bowl of ice and set it on our table. Others took up the metal tongs and helped themselves. I knew how much the cold ice would ease me. The sharp cold diminishes both the mental exhaustion and physical fatigue brought on by MS. But I still held back. Long enough to close my eyes in a brief silent prayer of thanks, offering up my suffering.

And when I opened them, my glass was brimming with ice.

I asked those around me if anyone had put ice in my glass. They scoffed, said no to a man, and went right back to their spirited gabble.

I drank. I luxuriated. I crunched the ice in my teeth, tasted the coolness, and wondered, "Is this going to be my Medjugorje miracle? Some trick with a glass of water?"

I went off to my room, to get packed for our departure the next morning.

It was then it came to me. The miracle at Cana when Christ changes water into wine for the wedding feast. Only here, instead of the sweetness of *grappa*, there was the coolness of the ice. And what does *Gospa* say after that miracle? *Gospa* says to the servants, "Do whatever He tells you." (John. II. 5.)

I flew back to the daily troubles and legal throes of our suit in Suffolk County Superior Court. From Split via Vienna to Boston, and home. But I could not escape the mystical hold that *Gospa* keeps on those who have come to Medjugorje to hear the children deliver her messages.

"Do whatever He tells you."

Over the course of the trial through the verdict to the final ruling, I managed to return to Medjugorje as often as I could.

* * *

I arrived back in Boston, my faith deepened, and my soul at last my own, but still unsettled. I knew I was breaking the rules by taking communion, and that troubled me as a Catholic, but so, I realized, were a lot of other people breaking the rules. Constantly, collusively. It was high time I took a hard look at what had really been going on—and gone so much against me—during those traumatic days at H & W.

I phoned David Rapaport for an update—though I didn't tell him where I'd been—and got an earful. He was deep into the discovery process, which was turning nasty. He was also greatly frustrated by the deliberate delays in H & W's delivering information to which we were legally entitled.

"These people are dragging their feet at every opportunity," he groused impatiently. "It's taking forever to get the stuff we need to prepare for trial."

"Typical Tony tactics," I told him. "He will absolutely not give us anything we ask for—until he's forced into it."

After I hung up, I thought back to the day of my own deposition, back on June 11th, ten days before I'd flown to Medjugorje. It had been conducted by Mary Marshall in the conference room of Stone-ham, Chandler & Miller in a tall, modern, ugly-looking building with an all white façade and funereal black windows. "Entering enemy terri-tory," I remembered brooding. I'd had trouble sleeping the night before, struggled hours through the tedious Boston traffic to get there, then couldn't find a parking spot.

At the time, I remember Mary Marshall being a small, attractive woman who was very stern and definitely all business. I learned later that she had been in the midst of a divorce. She definitely kept taut control over her demeanor. Her trim stockings had a kind of steely glaze to them, and even sometimes when she strode forth, I could hear an audible hiss.

"Mr. Labonte, if at anytime during the course of this deposition you feel tired, or you would like to take a break, simply say so," she started off. "Okay?"

"Thank you." We'd agreed, early on, that my interrogation would not last longer than three hours on any given day. So her solicitousness was a nice gesture. But it sounded more like setting up a record than like any sincere expression of concern.

Over the next three hours as David and I sat there, I took a couple of breaks to go to the bathroom, but really to clear my head. She tried hard to catch me at some mentally weak moment, to pick up lapses that could be used to embarrass me during the trial. But David had pre-pared me well on how to act my best. Among his tips: "Concentrate on the question being asked and make certain you understand it. Answer only the question being asked, and *don't* volunteer information. Never guess or speculate, and don't be afraid to say 'I don't know' if you don't. Listen carefully when I object to her questions. And above all, tell the truth and stick to it!"

She asked me questions to test my memory—where I went to school, my job history, dates, and responsibilities. I got through her quiz with all correct answers.

Then she asked me about the interview process at H & W, the job description, the work outlined, the duties demanded, and the high ex-pectations held by the firm's partners for their new executive direc-tor. Clearly she was attempting to lay down a record that would show I hadn't accomplished what the job description specified, that I was unable to perform the "essential functions" as detailed in that job de-scription, due to MS. But through my honest answers and forthright defense, and David's alert objections, I met her blunt challenge to my capacities and competence.

At one P.M., she allowed, "I think this is a good place to stop," and I left enemy territory unscathed. As we walked out together, David pulled me aside to tell me I'd done a wonderful job.

"If she's a good attorney, she will advise H &W that you are a very good witness, one who will be skillful and believable in the courtroom." He smiled. "And this may help us get an offer to settle."

But there was no movement from H & W. I was summoned for further depositions on August 13th, 19th, and 27th. Mary Marshall kept digging into all my numbers from the financial plans and projections I had drawn up for the firm, steadily tapping into my head to find some flaw in my reasoning, some error that would ring out the false notes of my supposed incompetence. But I kept alert and cool, always dead certain of my facts. She was next planning to depose my physicians—Doctors Gross, Wolpow, and Purcell—and had already subpoenaed their office records.

Meanwhile, David had deposed the members of the management committee, a few other H & W partners, and the three key administrative staff who had reported to me. I gasped when I saw the bill from the court reporters for their transcripts, running $372.50 for Robins and $424.75 for Tony. Worse somehow was having to pay for the transcripts of my own depositions ($1,177.88), for the session in June and those three in August, and yet another day of sparring with Mary Marshall still to come.

David had been holding his depositions at One Boston Place, in his 32nd floor offices, which were of course H & W's former offices, now subletted per the leases I had overseen for the firm. This irony was not lost on David, who found the partners much discomfited when called upon to defend their conduct on their own previous premises.

"You can't believe the stuff these guys said," he marveled. "I'm not certain Mary Marshall prepared them." He was most rankled by Tony Medaglia. "Pretty nasty and evasive, and very uncooperative. But wait till I get this guy in court."

"David, they are not taking us seriously," I said, yet again. "I doubt they invested much time in preparing for their depositions."

He grinned at me. "They will taste my steel."

* * *

Lora had taken a job as a real estate broker, but she hadn't sold any houses yet. We decided to put the house in Florida on the market, now that my mother was resettled in Worcester. I felt guilty, knowing how important it was to my father that we hold on to the house for our own retirement after he and my mother passed on.

The slow market eased my conscience. Sales were just as bad down in Florida as they were up in New England for Lora's prospects. The only deal we ended up doing immediately was to refinance our own house in Cohasset.

Then Joe Restuccia invited me to another of those fortuitous meetings in his office. While I was working hard in the doctoral program, the woman who had been administrating his Agency for Health Care Policy and Research Grant had suddenly left for the Harvard Community Health Plan. To my utter surprise, he offered me her job.

"I don't know what to say, Joe," I agonized. "I'm very complimented, but there is something you need to know before we go any further with this conversation. I have MS."

Joe looked surprised, and I quickly tried to back and fill over my own chagrin. "I haven't mentioned it before now," I confessed weakly, "because there didn't seem to be any reason to." But there always turns out to be some reason to.

Joe leaned forward in his chair and looked me up and down, earnestly.

"I'm sorry to hear that," he said. "How do you think your illness might affect your performance?"

And this time, I bit the bullet. "The main problem is fatigue. I cannot work more than six hours at a time. But most of all, I need to have a flexible work schedule."

Joe sat right back again, and immediately relaxed. "That will not pose a problem. We can give you all the flexibility you need. Your salary will be $2750 per month plus fringe benefits. Will you accept the job?"

By God, I realized, Joe or BU or somebody is at last willing to accommodate my disability.

I leaned across his desk, put out my hand, and croaked, "Let's go for it."

I went home to Lora with a new job, and we danced—with certain accommodations—for joy. I felt I could now face up to a task David had assigned me, over which I'd been procrastinating. He wanted me to read over all those transcripts from his depositions, so I could help him better understand the position H & W was taking on my dismissal, what possibly valid or patently false rationale they had to offer. I was reluctant to do so, since I knew this sworn testimony would contain a lot of criticism of my performance. I didn't want to re-experience all the emotional pain that sank me into the doldrums that blue Monday morning in January of 1992. But I had a lot more inner strength now, from my spiritual revival out in those mountains around Medjugorje. And I knew David needed my insights, so I pulled the first transcript off the large pile, now stacked in my home office.

John C. Thomson, senior partner in the real estate department, had been a good friend, helping me enormously with the management of those leases at One Boston Place. Hadn't we gone through that boondoggle the scam artists pulled, faced the embarrassment together? Hadn't we worked in tandem to get that 35th floor finally rented to the minority firm Fitzhugh & Associates? But from the transcript, you'd have thought we barely knew each other. Without emotion, he stated that I had, in his opinion, done an "adequate" job. He did not remember any criticism of my performance by anyone in the firm prior to my discharge. But when David pressed him, he simply replied, "I don't recall" or "I don't remember."

I closed the document and muttered, "So much for friendship."

Next, my mentor, and source of support, Charles W. Robins. If Thomson's deposition had lasted a scant forty-five minutes, Robins took over three hours to do nothing but criticize me in the extreme. He could not recall anything I had actually accomplished as the firm's executive director. He not only distorted the facts to make me look bad, but blatantly manipulated situations where I'd made real contributions.

Somehow bringing the firm's record-keeping and billing in-house ended up being all Eleanor Lanes' and Charlie Gaziano's doing.

He had to admit the management committee did substantially increase my salary after my first year, on the heels of a generous Christmas bonus. But he refused to say I'd been given a raise. He characterized this wage hike as "an increase in my base compensation."

When he finally got around to my last seven months with the firm, Robins began withholding information by selectively playing dumb. On any reasons for the long hours I worked, or the heavy responsibilities I bore, his memory was weak. "I wasn't on the management committee and, therefore, I don't know." But his memory revived conveniently whenever he wished to knock my performance, even if it turned out to be—at a generous estimate—faulty.

He had the nerve to state that no operating budget had been prepared during my tenure. A total falsification, since he knew that I'd prepared—with Eleanor Lanes leading the accounting staff—highly detailed revenue, expense, and cash-flow projections over two fiscal years, for which he had specifically offered me praise at the time. On one occasion, I remembered him telling me, "We've never had anything like this."

Most riveting were the words of a memo Robins had written on January 9th of 1992: "C. S. Gaziano came to see me regarding a major personnel problem in accounting. Apparently Alan failed to inform Eleanor Lanes about the fact that there would be no 1991 stub [period]. Eleanor had spent considerable time and effort. . . ." Gritting my teeth, I muttered under my breath, "Judas." I had always found it difficult to believe that Eleanor had been the sole objector to complain to Charles Robins.

Here it was in writing that the movement to get rid of me clearly involved Gaziano and surely Medaglia and probably Margaret Hadley but not necessarily Eleanor. A tidbit of relief, even though I was so emotionally upset that I felt, frankly, nauseated.

"Look, Alan, I know this is painful," David soothed me, "but I need your feedback on all the depositions. You've got to keep giving your side of the story, so I can prepare our case. If you think they're distorting the truth or covering up, tell me why. That way, I can put them on the spot during the trial."

With that promise in mind, I picked up the transcript of Tony Medaglia's deposition. Four and a half hours, 151 pages long.

After reading a few pages, my spirits perversely lifted. Following Tony's testimony was like trying to keep on course in a stormy sea, with Medaglia deliberately, like Neptune, raising every wave higher. In some ways, it was downright exhilarating. He was doing what he did best, the master of obfuscation. He kept asking David for clarification, forcing him to rephrase his questions. Tony even left the room to consult privately with Mary Marshall as well as requested reference material to refresh his memory, asked for coffee, and to go to the men's room.

Initially his shenanigans thoroughly disrupted the interrogation. You could tell from the transcript how frustrated David was getting. But gradually he took hold, knowing how to handle a difficult witness. He got sharper, and Tony had to ease off and settle down. While he was baldly critical of my performance, his comments were far too general for their vicious nature. He wasn't putting any substance behind his denunciations and kept referring to notes he said he had prepared.

Two thirds through his testimony, Tony started talking at length about "a continuum of dissatisfaction" with me that had begun in the spring of 1991. Not realizing what he was admitting. It was important for us to establish that Tony and others had their doubts about my long-term future with the firm all along. And here he was, saying so, under oath, that he was dubious almost a year before I was fired, yet never communicated those doubts directly to me. Would I have moved my family to the Boston area if I'd ever understood the depth of his supposedly "duly noted" dissatisfaction?

That was a bombshell, and it repeated itself explosively throughout other transcripts. Grein, O'Mara, and Clymer all stuck to a common theme. They all suffered from amnesia. Nobody remembered anything I had ever done right. They were, to a man or woman, dissatisfied with me, but couldn't recall ever speaking to me about their dissatisfaction. And no one thought that I'd pursued a demanding work schedule. I never worked very hard, came in late, left early and generally malingered.

Thoroughly disgusted, I took a two-day respite before reading the depositions of the key employees who supposedly reported to me.

What struck me dumb about Charlie Gaziano was the extent of his *sub rosa* involvement with others in the firm. He unloaded on my performance, giving himself plenty of credit for all the work he had once done and was supposedly doing again as acting administrator. He claimed to have been "instrumental" in bringing my new billing system in-house. It had all been done much earlier, according to Charlie, and whatever I may have done later was done improperly.

The incident that most angered me was Charlie's testimony about the November day I asked him to take care of welcoming the Gaston & Snow people into our trust department since I had to fly to Florida to be with my father, who was in the throes of his death.

Charlie testified that I was "away on vacation or something." That he did all the work (after I'd stayed until the last possible flight to be sure all was in order), and that he reported to Jack Clymer how "disappointed" he was with the "lack of organization" and how I had handled the transition. "Alan," he had told Clymer, "just can't get the puck in the net."

I physically recoiled at these noxious words, remembering how I had arrived too late to say goodbye to my father. At the time, I had consoled myself with the thought, "That's what my father would have wanted me to do. To be responsible to my employer and do a thorough job, just as he always did." I sat in wonderment at the depth of Charlie's distortions. I'd been suspicious, but had no real idea of the reaches of his manipulations.

I picked up the next transcript, and found Margaret Hadley mostly neutral to vaguely hostile. She claimed I was not available a lot of the time. *When was that?* I wondered. And she was never comfortable with our relationship. On March 2nd, only days after I was fired, she returned to H & W for more money at the urging of Medaglia and Gaziano. It all seemed so pathetic. I had trusted her, encouraged her, offered to help train her, even groom her to replace me when I retired. But she just ran away from me, then came slinking back to be used by them.

Then, at last, I faced up to Eleanor Lanes' testimony. Right off, she found me wanting. My work hours, my leadership, even my demeanor "irked" her. Why hadn't I been double-checking her financial reports? I was a nice enough guy, didn't really bother her much, but I acted "foolish" at times clowning around and making jokes. This caricature of my efforts to ingratiate myself was too much. Of course she would never knife anybody in the back, but she had at last felt called upon to criticize me to Robins.

She certainly had plenty of opportunity. Though claiming to be overburdened with a heavy work load, she managed to meet "every single day" with Robins and did personal work for him at least eight to ten hours per month. Had I done anything well while working with her at H & W? "No." What's more, she had freely been telling other people, "I couldn't believe he was suing. For what little he did, he's collecting disability, and he should be very grateful."

I knew I must "forgive those who trespass against us." Yes, I could forgive them, even pray for them, but could I really—it hit me like cold water dashed in my face, far from holy—walk away from this lawsuit?

"These blockheads," I found myself snorting, "have got to see the handwriting on the wall." Exactly. They had to be made to understand they were responsible for harm done to my family. If they knew my livelihood was in jeopardy, they should have forewarned me. They were facing a lot of liability, and good judgment would surely prevail if we continued to press for a fair settlement.

I called David Rapaport, as I was truly upset. "I really don't want to get into a protracted court battle with these people. I need to get on with my life and put this dispute to rest. If you don't get a response to our initial offer in the near future, I want you to urge Mary Marshall to talk some sense into them."

Through my desire to forgive and forget, I was also seeing how vulnerable the other side was. "After all this discovery, she must have some understanding of the large risks to her client and the likely damages. They're a hell of a lot greater than what we're asking for."

"You're right, Alan." I could sense the determination and resolve in his voice. "These people are flirting with damages that are potentially very high—in the low seven figures, when you consider the impact of punitive damages, legal fees, and all the other court costs."

"She has an obligation to advise them of that," I stubbornly insisted.

"Tell you what," he counseled, "Let's finish up the discovery process and see where we go from there."

That meant Mary Marshall deposing my doctors. Dr. Peter Gross, my internist, quickly pointed out that he was no expert on MS, he would leave that to Dr. Wolpow as my neurologist. But he had spotted early symptoms of depression—my feeling overwhelmed, fogged in, plus my memory problems—and had sent me to Dr. Purcell. He believed my depression was a reaction to my illness, my growing worry that I could no longer live up to the "incredibly high standards" of professional performance I'd set for myself.

I really perked up when I read that Dr. Gross, after three months of treating me, had come to appreciate his patient's "style of having things very organized. He was doing a great job, I thought." He had encouraged me to keep working—my overall health and well being depended upon a sense of self-worth and self-esteem—but I should not do more than six hours of sedentary work per day. I needed to take breaks for rest and control my schedule (e.g. manage my own time) even take work home if needed.

Dr. Ed Wolpow's deposition was the only one I personally attended. I wanted to show him how important his testimony was to me, to bear living witness to his words. We met in a cramped conference room at Mt. Auburn Hospital, where I got squeezed in next to Mary Marshall.

This gave me the oddest feeling, like fraternizing with the enemy. As always, she was very professional, but overly formal, calculating and looking dead straight ahead. She gave me the creeps.

She questioned Dr. Wolpow closely about my symptoms compared to the usual MS case. How well had I been able to carry on as an administrator despite my handicapped condition? Dr. Wolpow summarized my medical history for her. Before I was fired, he said, my primary MS-related problems were physical, affecting the use of my right hand and my right leg. As for my mental acuity, he concluded I was then capable of functioning "at a very high level," provided that I was allowed to manage potential fatigue through work breaks, rest, exercise, and other palliatives.

But he found, over time that wasn't happening. By my January 16th visit to him in 1992, he could see I was "under a lot of stress and experiencing fatigue as a result of the heavy workload and long hours at H & W." He stated, "It was clear that he (Alan) was very close to the edge of his abilities in terms of emotionally and mentally managing what he could do."

Since then, and my sudden firing, it had been vital for me to keep going, stay active, seek "a job with flexibility." I was relieved, even tickled when he said that, with accommodations, I could still handle "any professional job with any sort of high intellectual requirements." And what was being done to treat my illness? In my situation, which was "relatively stable MS," he said, "the best treatment is no treatment."

On October 15th, Mary Marshall had her final go at me, a long, detailed interrogation about the record I'd prepared for David covering the personal financial losses I'd suffered at H & W's hands. She picked and pecked at each item, and I would face her lacerating queries before the jury, based on this final deposition. She also asked about the memo on Fred Grein's taking over my responsibilities as the new managing partner, and went on with last-ditch queries about projects I launched at H & W, including the abandoned self-insured health plan.

Her last effort was a fishing expedition. Why had Margaret Hadley left H & W? Was it anything to do with me? Our working relationship? Had Margaret ever *said* her decision to leave had anything to do with me? Had *anybody else* said it had anything to do with me? But I'd already read Margaret Hadley's deposition, and knew what shifting winds she followed.

So, by late autumn of 1993, all parties involved were on record, and in January, David drafted a letter, as we had agreed, urging her to press her client for a reasonable settlement.

I still hoped to recoup expenses incurred by our move to the Boston area, a just severance package, plus reimbursement for rising legal costs. These last outlays increased our price tag to upwards of $325,000.

"You know, Alan," David warned, as we reviewed the letter together, "time is running out. I can't wait much longer before I have to begin preparing for trial."

That meant an abrupt shift in his own mental attitude. It's really hard, as a lawyer, to keep up your role as a negotiator while getting ready to confront the same party as a litigator.

* * *

In late September, Lora called me at work and invited me out to dinner at a small bistro in Hingham. We split an order of fish and chips, and she smiled daintily over her napkin and handed me a check. Made out for $500 to Alan and Lora Labonte with a memo that read "Deposit on 815 Mandalay Avenue." It was her first real estate sale, even if it did have to be my family's house in Florida.

"I know you don't really want to sell the place," she soothed me. "I don't either."

"Yeah, I'm sorry we have to let it go," I admitted, with surprise, delight, and sadness. "I know how much my dad wanted it to be home for us after we retired." But mainstream life does not keep you trotting along one pleasant, always peaceful track. "I hope he's not angry with me."

"I'm certain that he's not." Lora touched my hand. "Look at the date on the check." The date was 9/22/93. My birthday, a few days ago, age 54.

I got a little misty and couldn't reply, but in my heart, I said my thanks. "Thanks for the birthday present, Dad, and for understanding."

* * *

So I was ready for some tough eventualities that might soon be upon us. "We'll need a response to this offer," David had previously figured on his letter to Mary Marshall, "within the next two, three weeks."

But once again, no response, until we received notice that H & W was filing a counterclaim against us.

To our astonishment, it was an action to recover legal fees suppos-edly due David Rosenthal for his brief assistance to Lora in helping her to settle a dispute with her original travel agency in Worcester. We'd long ago transferred that case to Rapaport & Rapaport, and David had already won her a settlement that contributed its early share to our small war chest for the Labonte Case. That H & W would now harass us for such payment was egregious harassment.

"I'm so frustrated and angry with these jerks," I complained, "but I don't know why. They're just trying to make us rich."

"That's right, Alan. These people have an exposure that could ap-proach one million dollars, and that doesn't include punitive damages. Believe me, we will have our day in court, and I am going to start pre-paring for it the minute I hang up the phone!" It was then that David and I agreed to go forward on a contingency fee basis.

* * *

Feeling the need to escape the frustrations of the legal battle, I jour-neyed once again to Bosnia to renew my religious resolves. On the way home, the lights went down in the airplane cabin, and the passengers pulled their shades shut, and the movie came on, like a rude awaken-ing. The in-flight movie that day happened to be *Philadelphia*. Its sto-ryline took firm hold of my surprised imagination, unrolling the actual world to which I was returning, full of premonitions.

It told the ugly story, based on fact, of Andrew Beckett, played by Tom Hanks, a young attorney in a stodgy Philadelphia law firm who is fired when he contracts the AIDS virus. Beckett sues, believing he has been dis-charged for being HIV positive. He is represented by a savvy lawyer played by Denzel Washington. Together, they fight an uphill legal battle against the law firm, which claims to have fired Beckett for incompetence.

I sat riveted by every turn of the plot, and when the lights and shades went up again—after Beckett had won a multi-million-dollar jury award, including substantial punitive damages—I kept shaking my head over the bristling parallels. At long last, I was beginning to ask the hard questions, maybe the right questions. Just like these manipulative "Philadelphia lawyers," had some of the partners of H & W actually colluded to fire me for my disability? Had I been set up in the same sly way as Andrew Beckett had been deceived in the movie?

The credits flickered on the sun-struck monitor, and I caught the name of the conniving senior partner, played by Jason Robards.

Charles, for starts. So right on, but better yet, Charles—Wheeler!

It was all so providential, one series of coincidences after another, whether in the days of wrath and love in Bosnia, or during my own struggles ahead in court. But as Mark Twain said, "Coincidence is God's way of remaining anonymous."

Around me, passengers were scurrying back and forth in the cabin of the 747, the way any audience jams and hubbubs the lit-up aisle after a good movie. But they soon settled down, many slipping off to sleep for the last hours of our flight. I found myself gazing out the scratched plastic window at the wide blue sky, through studs of clouds, down to the open sea below us, and mulling over the spiritual conflicts that so preoccupied me. Into which abruptly cut the captain's voice over the intercom, and the "Fasten Seat Belts" sign, announcing we would soon be landing at Kennedy Airport in twenty minutes, the weather clear, wind out of the southwest.

I checked my seat belt, and pressed the aluminum button that knocked my seat straight back up, with a sharp impact on my reveries.

I was right back coming out of the movie again, facing the looming dispute with H & W. If I was going to live the messages of Medjugorje and follow the passion of Christ, how could I justify proceeding with any legal action against even these money-changers, these Pharisees in the temple of the law?

Wasn't I being hypocritical? Wouldn't I just be using the law myself to extort money from them?

I closed my eyes and prayed. "Oh Lord, if this is wrong, please tell me. I am so frightened of the future, both physically and financially. I have to consider my family and their needs, don't I?" Then I murmured, "It will be hard, but if it is Your Will, I will abandon the lawsuit."

I ended my petitions and listened hard, but heard only the long whine of the jet engines as we began our descent into Kennedy. I wondered at the silence in my soul, and cast about in my mind for an answer, and kept searching, over the many days ahead, for some sign.

None came, but my words were not mocked. Instead, I now know, they were put on mock trial.

That is how I resolved my dilemma. Through that mock trial, I was at last able to see that seeking justice in Suffolk County Superior Court was facing up to a deep wrong that was not only being done to me but would continue to be done to others if I did not act. I did not know this truth at that moment, as the 747 lumbered its landing gear down into place, but somehow, almost gently, a pervasive and reassuring sense of rightness came over me.

"Everything is going to be okay," I told myself, as the giant tires thudded along the runway. "Yes, it's all going to be okay."

Chapter Six

Igt was time to go to court.

I knew I had to be at my best, always, and I took to heart the advice of that mock jury on my "sartorial appearance," as Tony would call it. That first Tuesday, August 16th, and everyday of the trial, I wore a very conservative, light grey or dark blue suit, and a white shirt with my gold tie pin that slipped through two holes, one in each collar tab. It supported my dark blue tie, flecked with red dots. Very trim, neat, executive-style deportment. And I sported the same wingtips I'd always worn at Hutchins & Wheeler. Cordovans polished to the same dark color I used to spit-shine my boots as a Marine.

I also wore my leg brace, and even a tad conspicuously, carried my cane.

But I still had this sinking sense, too much of the time, "If I'm the plaintiff, how come I kept feeling like the defendant?"

We'd been up Beacon Hill to the courthouse earlier on July 22nd, before Justice Catherine White, when H & W moved for summary judgment to dismiss the case; it was denied. David then asked for a jury trial. Justice White said she would wait on his motion until the *Dalis Case* was decided by the Massachusetts Supreme Judicial Court. The Court decided a few days later that persons suing for discrimination in Massachusetts had a right to a jury trial. "Alan, great news," he told me. "It will be the first case on handicapped discrimination to be decided by a jury in the State of Massachusetts." Three weeks later, we went to trial in Judge White's court, under those coffered ceilings, with the high, sun-striped windows streaming light into the tabled bay beneath her bench, like the flood of clarity the judicial process is always supposed to bring any cause for action.

I still felt keyed-up, nervous, and yes, awed, even though we only had jury selection that first day. I'd already made my one contribution to our trial strategy in the weeks prior to trial. Tony Medaglia had asked to testify on videotape, and David had at first been inclined to go along with Tony's request. "No way!" I said immediately. I was really adamant, which I know surprised David.

"You've got to put him on the stand," I insisted. "And once he gets up there, I guarantee you, he'll erupt." I'd noted his behavior at too many management committee meetings and knew how he reacted when under fire. And wasn't it brilliant strategy on their part to try to put Tony into a non-stressful, controlled environment when offering his testimony? David bowed to my inside knowledge on this one. Otherwise, he had his entire courtroom strategy laid out, in a series of trial notebooks, arranged in a mobile file, one devoted to each witness. These pages were filled with the answers he wanted to elicit through testimony.

"Never the questions," he told me. "I think of those on my feet."

But who among my Bay State peers were going to judge me on the merits of this suit we had brought for handicapped discrimination?

It turns out, as David explained, you aren't given much choice by the Commonwealth. The attorneys are not permitted to question the prospective jurors. When you consider how important the composition of a jury is to any final outcome, that's scary. As a litigator, you are often looking for the simplest, most elementary human values in support of your case from a jury.

But using his few preemptive challenges, David managed to have empanelled an exceedingly strong jury. I can see how Mary Marshall might have also agreed, since many of the jurors were well educated and would comprehend her lawyerly defense of H &W's survival instincts and their right to hire and fire. The forewoman was Dana Larkin, a financial consultant and daughter of a local Milford judge herself. There was an insurance actuary from Chubb and a doctor from MGH, along with a graduate student, a research analyst, a dietary assistant in a Boston hospital, and somebody from the mayor's office. There were also two firefighters (Boston and Chelsea), a limo driver, a sales person, two housewives, and someone who worked at the betting window of a dog track.

Fourteen potential jurors altogether, but significantly, eight of them were women. We had a jury composed of the gender majority that our own mock jurors had suggested we seek. A verdict in a civil case must be reached in Massachusetts by at least ten of twelve jurors, with two sitting only as alternates, on a preponderance of the evidence. Our prospects from the demographics of those initially put into the jury box looked promising.

The next morning came opening statements by both attorneys. David covered familiar ground, but emphasized H & W's utter failure to accommodate my disability. He speculated on their motives behind my January 27th firing. "If the reasons were the reasons they gave him at that meeting, then it was a direct result of their not accommodating his multiple sclerosis. If they come in and say, oh, well, we never liked Alan, he did a bad job the first year, that is a pretext for discrimination. There is no credible evidence they were so unhappy with Alan's performance that they were going to terminate him [for] poor performance."

And he would be asking for punitive damages, "so that they don't do to anybody else who has a handicap what they did to Alan Labonte."

Then Mary Marshall got up and first offered a few wan compliments. "Alan Labonte made a lot of friends at Hutchins and Wheeler. He is a good man. He is a kind man, and people at Hutchins & Wheeler are also good and kind people." Then she took off after me like a tigress.

In 1990, the firm decided it needed "a sophisticated, experienced, high-powered law firm administrator who would take charge of them, go head to head with the tough, aggressive partners of that firm and tell those partners what they had to do to make the firm more successful."

Instead, they hired Poor Little Inadequate Me, who was warned the job was tough. "You need to be able to handle an angry, difficult group of attorneys," she argued, and I simply wasn't up to the mark when it became clear "that Mr. Labonte's disease was preventing him from performing [his] stressful, demanding [duties] without burdening other employees who at that particular time were working an average of fourteen hours a day."

Worse luck, the firm had run "right into the 1990 recession." Management had to take "severe and drastic steps" to keep from "closing their doors and throwing two hundred employees on the street." After firing staff, renegotiating their expensive lease, even terminating some partners, the remaining partners chose to drastically cut their own compensation. "Each partner of Hutchins & Wheeler took a salary of $75,000 in 1991," she claimed, "the same year that Mr. Labonte received $120,000 in salary."

She then read my major duties, five in all, at each of which I had totally failed, never justifying my high salary. She was again covering familiar ground, but with her own one-sided spin on my travails.

"You will meet Eleanor Lanes because she is going to testify. Eleanor Lanes is, herself, a disabled person. She has a number of disabilities and, over the years, Hutchins & Wheeler has accommodated all those disabilities," Ms. Marshall claimed. "The firm has always granted her leaves of absence, has always allowed her to do whatever was necessary to take care of her condition." So Eleanor Lanes was now their poster girl.

Then came her version of how up front with me Tony had always been. "You heard that Mr. Labonte was not warned. The evidence will be that Tony Medaglia spoke with him on several occasions, repeatedly telling Mr. Labonte that his performance was inadequate, that things were not getting done. He was asked to provide financial information for the firm's lease negotiations with their landlord. That information was never provided by Mr. Labonte. He simply did not do anything."

She continued. "Sometimes lawyers like their problems solved yesterday. As you will hear from the doctors who will testify, multiple sclerosis is a disease with which people can work and hold full-time jobs, but not full-time stressful, demanding jobs that are unpredictable, and do not allow a person to rest whenever they feel tired."

Besides, as much as H & W sought to accommodate my MS, such as letting me leave work "early in the afternoon. Mr. Labonte never identified any other accommodation that he needed to this law firm." She listed all the people to whom I had not complained, nor ever asked for help, then added, "He never said anything about needing any accommodation whatsoever until after he left the employment of Hutchins & Wheeler and started this lawsuit."

Taking me aside, David confided, "They're attacking your competence." He was surprised at that approach, as he knew we could defeat such an attack. David has total concentration inside the courtroom. He is *always* thinking about the jury while he sits alone at the plaintiff counsel's table. I never sat up there, next to him, during the whole trial. Fred Grein could often be seen conferring with Mary Marshall at the defendant counsel's table, but I stayed seated back in the gallery. David wants the jury to know he has their every interest, as well as maximum comfort, at heart. "David won't drink a glass of water in front of the jury," says Diane, "because some jurors might be thirsty too, and they don't have water in the jury box.

That's why David was frowning over Ms. Marshall's opening statement. Tactically, her attack just made the jury uncomfortable. Why would anybody deliberately choose to go that hard after a nice guy like Alan Labonte?

So he put me straight into the witness box. That was more of David's strategy—to send me right out front, let the jurors get to know me, and what was, so to speak, bothering me. And I still recall what Judge White told the jury, just before I was sworn in.

They had all been given notebooks, to write things down whenever they wished. But she warned that one of their most important jobs was "to determine credibility, what witness is telling the truth, what are you going to believe, what are you not going to believe. I just caution you, you can't spend all of your time writing everything down because part of your job is to observe demeanor."

David had me run through my life and career. He also helped me emphasize my personal commitment to the job at H & W.

How many hours did I work per day during that first year?

"I got in around 8:30, and I worked very long hours those first few months, usually until six or seven at night, sometimes much later." A quick dinner at my Devonshire apartment, then "back to the firm."

Did I ever take a full lunch hour during that first year?

"No. The firm had a cafeteria just down the hall from my office. A good opportunity to get to meet people. I had to resist the temptation to talk about myself because I was still sort of interviewing for the job, if you will. I needed to hear about them, not tell them about me."

What accomplishments were made that first year?

"I prepared a major presentation for the partners on cash flow." I'd already testified how a law firm operated on cash for services, but H & W had twice as much money tied up in uncollected accounts as other firms. "Four or five million dollars. If the partners really rolled up their sleeves, they could bring in a lot of cash and, on a short-term basis, have a very, very profitable year."

How did that presentation go over?

"They were impressed."

Mary Marshall objected for the first time. Judge White overruled, adding, "This is his understanding of how it was received." We had our first indication Judge White was going to let me have my say.

We rolled along through my salvaging the telephone system, trying to turn away my Christmas bonus, keeping after tenants—and our landlord—at One Boston Place. "I had to act as a policeman," until we got to my working relationship with Charles Robins.

Did he ever criticize me?

"Yes," I answered, once back in March of 1991. "He said, 'You were five minutes late, and you came to the management committee meeting with your coat on, and you took your coat off in the room with us.'"

We brought this up to show the strict decorum at H & W. I was wearing my raincoat, since it was raining cats and dogs, and I was late because I'd been up the night before till one o'clock, preparing.

What did I actually do with the raincoat?

"I put it aside, on one of the other chairs."

And after the meeting, what was it that Robins said about the raincoat?

"He said I shouldn't take off my coat in the room."

Did he say why?

"No."

Petty stuff, but it showed how uptight Robins could be.

Then we took up Robins' annual review of my job performance. I said he told me "lots of positive things. They were particularly happy with the new financial reporting package that I had put together."

Did he give me any criticism?

"Yes, he did." About my seeking salary increases for employees. "You can bring us your recommendation, but when we say no, that means no. We don't want you to negotiate for higher increases for them."

Any salary increase for myself?

A raise of "forty-six hundred dollars," the highest that year.

Then we went straight to Dr. Wolpow's diagnosis of my MS, and the problems I had walking the four floors of corridors around H & W.

"Mr. Robins was particularly keen on having me visit with all the partners, all the attorneys who did billing and collections, at least once, sometimes twice a week, to encourage them to do all they needed to do." I wanted to make the physical demands of the job clear. "He preferred that I do this person-to-person, and not over the phone."

That got us into the chart of the H & W floor plan, showing how far I had to trek to reach either the elevator or the staircase, both of which I used to make these visits to four different floors.

What happened after I informed the management committee of my MS?

I said, "Robins and Tony Medaglia went to see Dr. Wepsic—Tony's client—in July, 1991. Then Tony came to see me in my office."

For how long?

"Fifteen minutes."

And the substance of what he said to me?

"I had nothing to worry about. They were bringing along Mr. Grein, intended to make him the managing partner, so he would be able to take some of the load away from me. He wanted me to go home if I got tired. Leave before I got so fatigued that I was ineffective. He drew a little curve in the air. Before you get to the top of this curve, your peak performance for the day, you should consider going home, getting rest."

Did he say anything about moving my office?

"No."

Did he ask me any questions about my office?

"No."

Did Mr. Grein begin to help you with your work load?

"No."

When was Mr. Grein appointed managing partner?

"January 1, 1992."

When was I terminated?

"January 27, 1992."

David turned back to my own work schedule. *From the summer of 1991 through the end of that year, did daily demands on my working life change over what they had been the previous year?*

"Yes."

How did things change?

"Well, burdens began to increase."

And from here on out, I calendared the heavier work load and personal setback caused by Margaret Hadley's resignation right on up through the traumas current on the day they fired me. Again, I've already chronicled these miserable six months, but I was now a lot sharper at setting forth just the facts, ma'am. David's questions brought me closer to the nub of matters, so that I was much clearer explaining what I'd done.

"We introduced a new life insurance plan for all the employees that significantly increased their amount of coverage. We were able to do this without people having to go for a physical or anything. All prior conditions were excluded, so people who previously couldn't get life insurance, now not only got life insurance, but *more* life insurance. The partners were able to get up to a half million dollars of coverage, and the cost was very minimal."

Then David asked, *Did I notice any change in the way I was treated by members of the management committee during these six months?* Ms. Marshall objected. Overruled, and I let loose with both barrels.

"After Mr. Medaglia came to my office, I was expecting we would be working more closely together, but just the opposite happened. They really avoided me. Where I had been meeting with the chairman of the management committee almost daily up to that point"—who was then Charles Robins—"I didn't get to see the new chairman"—now Tony—"hardly at all. Hardly ever. He never came to my office, so they just sort of ostracized me."

From that time on, did any member of the management committee come up and ask how you were feeling?

"No."

Did they ask what they could do for me that would make my job more tolerable?

"No."

Finally, David took me through the gruesome details of my termination, also covered already, and asked if I'd ever been fired before.

"No."

How did this firing make me feel?

"I just felt totally demoralized," I said. "I felt I was an invalid, couldn't do anything, couldn't think, couldn't walk right, couldn't be a manager, couldn't be anything but a liability."

I really thought I'd come up with a cool, thorough self-analysis, which shows how little I knew. But David kept after their further petty cruelties to me, finally asking if H & W had opposed my application for unemployment.

Objection by Ms. Marshall, so she and David went for a sidebar with Judge White. Ms. Marshall argued that the law prohibits the use of any documentation or responses to a claim for unemployment in a court proceeding. David conceded you can't use the transcript, but Margaret Hadley signed a form that charged me with unsatisfactory performance, and she says in her deposition she did so on instructions from Mr. Grein.

"Your Honor," argued David, "they said they cared so much for him, claim they accommodated him, but here they wouldn't let him have unemployment comp."

"It's also hearsay," said Ms. Marshall, "an out-of-court statement."

"It's simply whether or not H & W opposed Mr. Labonte's application," Judge White decided. "Overruled."

That put it right out there for the jury to ponder, my six bitter weeks of unemployment comp, before I managed to network my way into consulting work, and a dim, distant future as a researcher-teacher at BU.

The rest of that second day, till we broke at one o'clock, was devoted to such subsequent endeavors, ever onward and upward, as I've tried to show. I also began a close accounting, based on a "damages chart" I'd drawn up, of the moneys we were claiming H & W owed me in actual damages, both back pay and front pay. But Ms. Marshall, besides challenging my lack of "expertise" on my own future, would have none of any front pay for future damages since I'd opted out of the work world.

Another sidebar. "Mr. Labonte, had he elected to work rather than attend a Ph.D. program, would be mitigating his circumstances," she argued, or putting it more bluntly, "would be making money. He has elected voluntarily to remove himself from the regular work force and instead pursue a Ph.D. candidacy." Everything I was doing fit into that program, and "his own chart" shows I wouldn't be back up to speed financially until I completed my doctoral training, likely in 1997. "Essentially we are being asked to finance his decision to do something else with his life."

Both attorneys cited cases, and Judge White said she would have to reflect overnight on these cases, so we took the last ten minutes to show my past versus my present income, without the chart—$120,000 per year at H & W, plus twelve percent in various benefits, against considerably less from South Shore Hospital and BU. "Last month," I said, because of July shortfalls in the BU grant, "I received $800." But I would complete the doctoral program by 1997, and then be eligible to work as "a principal investigator on a highly complex research project" and "a full time member of the BU faculty."

How much?

"I believe the starting salary for faculty is $55,000 to $56,000 a year."

After Judge White adjourned the court, David immediately got me off in private, and to my great surprise, lectured me sternly. "Alan, you're not getting across to the jury on how it really felt to be fired like that."

Flustered, I asked, "How do you mean?"

"How it felt to you *emotionally*. If you don't tell them, they're never going to know. And if they don't know your feelings, that getting dumped by those guys really did to your insides, that jury is never going to see any reason to punish anybody."

He looked at me, very seriously. "I'm going to ask you again, tomorrow, what it felt like, over the whole aftermath. And this time, you tell them."

That sent me home to Cohasset, to do some reflecting of my own past emotional state. What I picked up on, finally, was that sense of being disgraced, which I'd probed at, so often, in my psyche. That weakened all the emotional reserve I'd set up to keep myself protected, and I just sort of fell through my own floor . . . into what I knew I had to say to the jury, that next day in court.

Back in her court lobby Thursday at 9:25 A.M., Judge White had finished reflecting on what Ms. Marshall and her associate had argued, and didn't like their memorandum on cases one bit.

"I look at these cases, and they *don't* say what *you* say, so right away I think, well, they're not being straight with me at all."

"It was a really stern rebuke," David reported back to me. She was going to let the jury decide "the factual question whether [Mr. Labonte] stopped looking for work," and all other moot points about my choice of a future career after H & W effectively dumped me from the Boston legal community. "I'm going to let him talk about his own damages, and estimate what he has lost." Over the entire period through 1997, Judge White ruled that we could use our "damages chart." She told us, "If you want to do it by means of a blackboard, fine."

That was a big win for us. *But*, and a big but, there was still "the seventy-one thousand dollars," my annual disability compensation from UNUM.

In the judge's chamber, Judge White asked, "How, in fairness can I let him put in everything that he has lost by reason of the defendants' actions, and then not let the jury know the defendants purchased a disability insurance policy for him, which he is still getting?"

"We agree that you can treat that sum, as mitigation," David said. "You've ruled they are entitled to an offset, so there is no way Mr. Labonte is going to get a double recovery." But that doesn't mean you have to tell the jury about the $71,000 he receives annually, because that just throws the jury entirely off the track. The Supreme Judicial Court has grasped this problem with jury deliberations, and so ruled. David continued, "When a jury hears that somebody is getting disability insurance payments, there is a tendency to say, 'Oh, well, he's getting enough, why should he get more?'" Especially Massachusetts juries who are notoriously conservative with monetary awards. "It's why they always keep this evidence out."

"But you're here asking for *punitive* damages," responded Judge White, "for discriminating against him under Statute, Chapter 151b. You've got to paint the defendants as having violated this statute, show that they've done nothing to effectuate the intent of the statute. But here they buy disability insurance for this man to provide for the possibility that he does become disabled. Which is, in itself, it seems to me, an effectuation of the purposes of the statute."

"The purpose of the statute," David rejoined, "is to prohibit discrimination, and you can't purchase discrimination insurance. Disability insurance is not a license to throw out [the rights of] the handicapped. The defendants can't buy disability insurance to pay people who are the victims of their own discrimination."

"That's a great argument, I agree with you," Judge White told David, "but how can I say the jury is not entitled to hear anything about it *at all?*" *That* was her problem, since the defendants were saying they purchased "something in the event that someone became disabled," and "that's their whole case, that this guy became disabled, not that they discriminated against him. Whether they did or not, I'm not making a judgment"—that was up to the jury—"but that's what they're saying, so I'm letting it come in."

This in camera lobby debate had both immediate and long-term repercussions. Immediately, my $71,000 annually went up on the blackboard as part of the recalculated "damage chart." In dull white chalk for the jurors to contemplate. Long-term, a crucial constitutional issue had been re-raised in the Commonwealth of Massachusetts in a utterly new context because there never had been a jury in a 151b trial for handicapped discrimination, to whom such guarded facts could be, by the judge's ruling, revealed.

He recouped by putting me back in the witness box for a thorough grilling.

As promised, David asked me to talk once more about my emotional state "from the time of the termination right up to the present. *During that week after you were fired, how did I feel at that point?"*

"Like a third wheel," I started in. "Sort of the uninvited guest who came to dinner. They didn't want me there, clearly, so I just came to work, maintained a low profile. Well, I was demoralized," I tried harder. "My confidence was pretty low. And my self-esteem. I felt lousy."

David added, *And the last day you were there, knowing that you weren't coming back anymore?*

"I don't remember honestly," I lapsed back, "how I felt."

So David moved along to my applying for unemployment. *How did that make you feel?*

"Worse." I had no problem getting into this agony. "I had no cane, so standing in line was physically very difficult, one line after another for hours. And then at the end of three weeks, or whatever it was when I was supposed to get my check, I was told I'd get no check because my former employer had opposed my claim."

Ms. Marshall moved to strike, but Judge White ruled this was "being offered simply for the state of mind of the witness," nothing more.

"So I felt slapped down once again by the firm," I continued. "And now it looked like I had to go through this whole appeal process to get my unemployment benefits." I actually gulped before I spoke the next words. "I had to do some begging. I felt as if I had to go in now and beg for the money, so I felt crummy." More words came. "I felt lousy. I felt like scum. What can I tell you? I felt lower than the lowest. I felt like crap, dog crap. Okay?"

I realize this is difficult, Mr. Labonte, I heard David saying, *but we need to get through it.*

Did he realize what I had stopped just short of saying, that "I felt like dog shit"? I just didn't want to say "shit," didn't want to stoop to that level, have it on public record.

Had you been getting proper medical attention? David asked this by way of eliciting my frightened testimony about my own mental health.

"Well, I had lots of doubts about my ability to do things," I began. "I knew I had multiple lesions in my brain from Dr. Wolpow's diagnosis, and I wondered if the disease was taking away my mind." That really got me launched. "Because I felt I had done a good job at Hutchins & Wheeler. I felt I had done extraordinary things. Yet people I had respected, people I admired, people I felt a loyalty to, at Hutchins &

Wheeler, felt I had done a terrible job. So bad a job that I needed to be terminated, fired, summarily dismissed.

"The conflict for me was to figure out, why can't I do things right? Am I losing my mind? Are these cells that are destroying my myelin tissue, are they eventually going to make me into an imbecile? All because I'd been fired, yet I don't really know why I had been fired. And so I was trying to figure out, 'What can I do? Can I do anything? Or am I just going to become progressively snowed in, and eventually useless?'"

Quite a mouthful for a repressed guy like me. I happened to glance over and saw Dr. Wolpow, waiting there in court, and he looked horrified. But David wasn't going to leave me at those dreary depths. *Had it later done me any good, picking up a few A's in my courses at BU?*

"Yes, because it proved I can still think. I still have some intellectual ability. It was a confidence builder."

David then asked, *And what about when I got offered the full-time job as project director at BU last summer?*

"Great." I finally had to tell them I had MS, we'd have to work out a flexible schedule, but Dr. Restuccia still wanted to hire me. He was willing to make an accommodation. "'Let's get on with it. We want to appoint you to the faculty. We have confidence in you and your work, and we need you on this project.' So I accepted."

How many hours a week did you devote to this job and your graduate courses?

"I averaged about fifty-five hours a week."

As of today, how are you feeling about yourself?

"Much better. I still have doubts," I admitted, "but I feel as if I've have made a lot of progress. I know I work with people I can trust, and that's important."

With that, I stepped down for Dr. Wolpow to take the stand. With busy doctors, you take their medical testimony whenever they're available to give it. He testified as my neurologist who had seen me over ten visits, emphasizing how distressed he'd found me during the winter of 1991.

"The sixty or so hours a week which I understood to be his work load was taking him over the edge, both mentally and physically," Dr. Wolpow said. My limping right leg, as well as some difficulties with my left leg, plus the fatigue I was experiencing, should have been accommodated. "I would speculate that a forty-hour work week instead of a sixty-hour work week would be something he could have accomplished."

Ms. Marshall then got into the record several detrimental medical notes on my visits, including my own words complaining about "loss of short term memory and mental acuity and difficulty organizing work, difficulty in developing a list of projects, decreased ability to focus clearly and concisely." But then she asked him for his "present assessment" of my "mental acuity".

"I'd say it was excellent," and he came forth with the best personal anecdote about my revived capacities we could have put before the jury.

In October of 1993, Dr. Wolpow had chaired a committee at Mount Auburn Hospital to decide on a study proposal from the BU School of Management—actually, the research project I'd been hired to manage—so I was sent along with Dr. Heineke as a representative of the BU team, to defend our proposal, amidst what Dr. Wolpow termed "a good deal of controversy."

I withstood "about an hour's worth of very intense cross-examination and scrutiny," he recalled, "frequently with three or four people talking at once." Well did I remember, including the fact that Dr. Wolpow, though obliged as co-chair to remain neutral, was clearly opposed to our proposal? But he now presented the debate as a happy experience since "I had the opportunity to actually see my patient in action."

It was a "stressful situation where several members of our board were rather antagonistic," Dr. Wolpow said, "and Mr. Labonte carried out his function extraordinarily well. He gave very good answers to our questions. He had a very gentle style, and didn't inflame things which were already quite inflamed." Maybe since we eventually won the committee's approval over his opposition, Dr. Wolpow had "no qualms in saying that Alan Labonte definitely can function at a very high professional level."

After that, I went back into the witness box to describe how I had developed the estimates in the "damages chart," now up on the blackboard, to arrive at our claims for back pay and front pay. I summarized my pitch with my figures for the final year, 1997, which is how long I projected my career might have lasted at H & W.

Over Ms. Marshall's objection, David elicited this culminating answer: "I told the management committee that I intended this to be my last job, that I intended to work at Hutchins & Wheeler until I retired." Now I wouldn't be retiring in 1997 but instead, both through necessity and choice, hoped to take up a full time faculty position at BU.

At which juncture, Ms. Marshall began her intense cross-examination, with a snippy give-and-take that went slightly awry. *Do you have any children?*

"I have no natural children."

Do you live with your wife?

"Yes."

During your employment at Hutchins & Wheeler, you lived alone with your wife or you lived alone at the Devonshire, is that correct?

"No."

What's not correct, sir?

"That I lived with my wife alone."

Okay, who else lived with you?

"My wife's brother lived with us in Greenfield."

When you moved to the Boston area, did your brother-in-law move with you?

"Yes."

So it was your wife, your brother-in-law, and yourself?

"Yes."

Yesterday there was a woman with a young child here in the courtroom. Were they related to you?

David realized that she was referring to Diane and his daughter Cary. He jumped up, faced the court, and said with a smile at the jury: "They were *my* wife and child, Your Honor."

Diane was almost always in court, since she knew this case was something special. She was the best strategic legal thinker David said he knew, and he depended upon her constant watch in the courtroom to tell him how any case was going. She had been bringing their five-year old daughter Cary to court every day. But Sloan, my brother-in-law's son, had been there too, and of course Lora, who was often in court, very much for me. Judge White couldn't say anything officially from the bench, but the jury surely noticed how tied together our two families were. The children became friends and would quietly play with toy dinosaurs in the last row of the courtroom.

From Ms. Marshall came a half-grudging admission, "Just wondered." It showed how determined she was to dig into any situation that looked questionable to her, even if she went off half-cocked. She was suspicious I was bringing my supposed cute kids to court to gain sympathy. That was dead wrong, but produced a far more heart-warming scene for the jurors to witness out of her wrong-headedness.

On cross, she was ruthlessly determined to dig into my own job situation, with an equal intensity and the same propensity for error. She was out to show how difficult an assignment I'd taken on, always beyond my abilities to handle, but especially so, once I'd begun suffering from MS.

I countered by mostly clamming up, simply replying in the negative until she asked the question correctly.

She then asked, *Early on, did you understand from the job recruiter and the H & W attorneys that the job 'required an individual who was going to operate essentially as the CEO of Hutchins & Wheeler'?*

This was absurd, so I just said, "No."

As the top level administrator of the firm?

This was closer, so I replied, "As the chief operating officer." That, after all, was my title, if she knew what a COO was, or did.

Reporting directly to the management committee of the firm, is that correct?

Finally. "Yes."

She badgered and harassed me for the rest of the day about my duties—or really, my supposed neglect thereof—but I kept my composure. Testifying under oath had made me nervous at first, but now it was starting to be kind of enjoyable.

I realized she was carrying most of the pressure. All I had to do was tell the truth, when and if she managed to put the question right.

We established that while Charles Robins, as chair of the management committee, was very involved in decisions regarding day-to-day operations, Tony Medaglia avoided them. I mentioned also that Tony could be rude, but did I have any criticism of his overseeing my performance? "He wasn't a good communicator. He didn't keep in touch. He didn't tell me what I was doing right or wrong. I felt we had very, very poor communication between the two of us."

She went after me with repeated questions about whether it was my job to get the lawyers to collect from their clients. *Was it necessary for someone at H & W "to encourage, prod or cajole" the partners into sending out bills?*

"Yes."

Whose responsibility was that?

"The management committee and the executive director," I kept dually answering.

Did they occasionally become impatient or rude when you asked them to do so on multiple occasions? Implying, I suppose, that a "nice guy" like me wasn't up to taking the heat.

"Not often," I said, "but sometimes."

She went nowhere, until she later asked if I expected Fred Grein *to take over the job of going from partner to partner and convincing them to bill clients and collect for those bills?*

"I thought he could do a lot of the running around and the face-to-face contact better than I could."

By then, I was admitting to some of my losses.

You experienced periods of time when you felt fogged in mentally, is that a fair description?

"Yes."

And if you were involved in intense work covering a significant period of time, you would feel overwhelmed mentally, is that correct?

"Could she rephrase that?"

You experienced periods where you felt simply overwhelmed by your workload, is that correct, sir?

"Yes."

Sir, is it fair to say that in 1991, your mental fatigue increased, the times at which you felt tired, mentally fogged in, overwhelmed, increased as the year wore on?

"No."

When did you feel most fatigued mentally?

"At the end of the day," I said.

And when did you feel most fogged in mentally?

"At the end of the day."

After working throughout the day?

"After work."

And during the day?

"No." I wasn't going to let her entrap me. "During the day I toughed it out, but at the end of the day, I was exhausted."

You found that you could work possibly four to seven hours predictably before you had to take a break?

"I think that's fair, yes."

She was representing a group of people who had done me harm, and I was not going to do anything that would make it easy for her. But I finally had to admit that I was expecting Fred Grein to pick up some of my responsibilities; John Thomson to take over managing One Boston Place, and other partners to lessen my workload.

Still, her most crucial question was the same one that had flum-
moxed me back at the mock trial. *In fact, except for telling Tony Medaglia and Charles Robins to speak to your doctors, you gave Hutchins &
Wheeler no information whatsoever about what accommodations you felt
you needed, is that correct?*

"I thought the doctors would do that." I wouldn't admit that I had
to ask outright for any accommodation, putting all the weight on their
failure to act on what so obviously needed to be done in order to ease
my physical distress and mental fatigue. I could see that my negative
responses threw her off stride, the same kind of thing a pitcher experiences after starting his wind-up when the batter suddenly calls for time
and steps out of the box.

Toward the end of that third day, I saw one of the jurors smile after
Ms. Marshall and I got into another such set-to on cross-examination.
He was one of the two firemen, and seemed to understand what was
really going on. Every night, another juror—the limo driver—always tipped
me a wink, exiting past me as I stood near the railing of the jury box.

Thankfully, I was excused from further interrogation until the mor-
row, but on Friday morning, David first called Dr. Peter Gross, my internist, who happened to be available that morning between appoint-
ments. David had previously interviewed Dr. Gross at his office, the
first time David heard of my trips to Medjugorje. When he passed me
on his way to his solitary seat at plaintiff counsel's table, he whispered,
with a grin, "You haven't been telling me all that you've been up to,
lately."

He went right after Dr. Gross's notation that when I first came to
him, I was feeling "despondent and hopeless." David asked, *What do
those words mean in a medical sense?*

Dr. Gross said they were "shorthand" to indicate when a patient
might be "suicidal." Dr. Gross had all along believed that depression
had as much to do with my mental fogginess as MS. He testified along
lines familiar from his deposition, but noted one new change in my
steadily improving mental state, under psychiatric care from Dr. John
Purcell. He'd witnessed "a lifting of my spirits," then added, "On a
personal level, I have developed enormous admiration for a man who is
struggling with his disease and able at the same time to give himself to
humanitarian causes. Twice Mr. Labonte has traveled—"

The jury perked right up, and Ms. Marshall objected. "That's sustained," said Judge White. "I think the question has been answered."

But I was the one who was really relieved, also chagrined. I had said nothing to David about my trips to Medjugorje—all along I'd considered my journeys of faith to be a private matter—but I also knew just exactly why, and how, Dr. Gross knew all about them.

I suppressed a sigh of relief, but counted on David to take another tack to reach the answer he still wanted. He asked Dr. Gross if my "physical ability to walk and move around has improved since you first saw him?" Yes, it had. I was swimming in the ocean, walking goodly distances with my brace and cane. *Were there "any activities in connection with traveling that Mr. Labonte has undertaken?"*

Dr. Gross nodded. "He has traveled twice to Bosnia, on personal humanitarian missions."

The jury perked up again, and Ms. Marshall could not stuff the cat back in the bag, since David asked, *Do you know how long those trips took?*

"I believe they were at least a week, but most importantly, they took a lot of pre-activity. Of which I am aware because of the need to bring medical supplies to Yugoslavia that we assisted with, in our office."

There it was, a very large cat taking very big jumps that had everybody in the courtroom fascinated. I felt even more chagrined, but couldn't really complain about the reactions David was getting from the jurors. He gave it one more twist. *Dr. Gross, how did this bear "on your observations about his ability to think and organize?"*

"I was amazed at the amount of energy he put into the humanitarian activity," Dr. Gross concluded, "and how much organization it must have taken."

Mary Marshall did gain a significant admission from Dr. Gross, under thorough grilling: *And assuming that those accommodations which you have identified had been provided to him, was Mr. Labonte able to perform the material functions of the job of executive director at Hutchins & Wheeler?*

"Not in January, 1992, when I met him."

Then there was another witness taken out of order, this time by Ms. Marshall. When David conceded that this judicial exception was acceptable to us, Judge White wryly commented, "Ladies and Gentlemen, you are seeing two very agreeable lawyers here." It was my old Worcester nemesis David Rosenthal, the litigation partner. He testified he had supported hiring me as executive director, which hardly fit with the dismissive reception he had given me when I first interviewed with him. Then he revealed the phone conversation he had with Lora and me, right after my firing, in which he'd played the friend, full of sympathy, what "a terrible scary thing" to have this disease. But that hadn't kept him from asking me whether or not this had really been affecting my ability to do the job at the office. "Alan said it had," then "I remember him saying that the follow-through just isn't there, he was dropping the ball from time to time," et cetera. I'd seen Rosenthal earlier that day before he testified, coming into the men's room. We'd shaken hands, and I recall his saying apologetically, "This is just business."

I couldn't see his smarmy testimony having much impact on the jury, but then I was soon back before them again, with Mary Marshall hard on my case. She led off with the UNUM documents, asking me to please read aloud my own answers to various queries. They were not helpful to my cause. "'Unable to work long hours in a stressful job, need flexible work schedule.' For several months prior to my disability, I was unable to meet the mental and physical requirements of my position." This was in contrast to my own job description, which read: "'Chief Operating Officer, overseeing financial systems and operations involving eighty attorneys and two hundred plus support staff.'" *Demands of the job?* "'Unusual mental and/or physical requirements: an extremely stressful position, heavy work load, demanding and erratic schedule.'"

Now she questioned me about the spread sheets I had drawn up with David to show shortfalls in my income since leaving H & W. This was her chance to throw me off stride with rapid-fire petty points, make me look uncomfortable, even incompetent before the jury. And she did it with a vengeance. *Had I consulted the Price Waterhouse survey of salaries for law firm administrators that covers New England, to determine my projected salary increases?*

"No, I didn't." Nor had I gone back to actual salary increases at H & W for '93 and '94.

So where did this idea of a six percent annual increase originate?

I'd previously testified that I'd taken a low point on the spread between four and ten percent in average national salary increases, but wasn't that just my own guesstimate?

On benefits, did I increase the FICA even though after reaching a certain salary, such as my own, nobody paid more into Social Security? How much of my $350 monthly payment for health insurance from BU did I actually pay myself?

One hundred and fifty dollars, as best I could recall. I was soon fumbling with hard copies of the supporting documents I'd used to prepare the damage chart. And it was if she'd caught a schoolboy cheating on his multiplication tables.

Sir, I'm sorry. What are you looking at?

"I'm looking at my pay stub from Boston University."

Could I see that, sir?

There was a pause, an impasse, while I waited for David to object, but he said nothing. I didn't want to give up my reference material, all stapled together in a neat package, but it seemed I had no choice.

"Certainly," I had to agree.

Then she started quizzing me from my own pay stub in rapid fire, until she said, "Your Honor, this is the first time I've seen this document, so if I could have just a few minutes with this."

Judge White suggested she move on to other questions, then come back to it. Ms. Marshall agreed, with her own clever spin. *Mr. Labonte, I'm going to take your pay stub with me, and then next week, using the figures which you used, but which unfortunately I do not have, I will ask you questions about that next week. All right?*

"Okay," I gulped. "If you will give me back the rest of that package. You have more than my pay stub."

"At the end of the day," allowed Judge White, "Ms. Marshall can take what she needs and return the rest." It was a glaring heist, but nothing I could do about it.

Ms. Marshall launched blithely into my deposed loving characterization of Eleanor Lanes, though I was starting to see how I was digging myself deeper into an eventual trap. Then she tried to make out my doctoral candidacy to be a case of deliberate malingering. *Hadn't I applied to enter the Ph.D. program at U. Mass. before I took the job with H & W? What other efforts had I made to find regular, full time employment or consulting work before I decided to go back to school at BU? If I was supposed to be paid $33,000 annually to lead the research project at BU, why had I settled for $800 per month over this summer and the upcoming fall?* I tried to explain the sudden shortfall in our federal funding, but she just kept pressing me.

How much total had I been paid by South Shore Hospital for all the consulting work I did for them?

"Around twenty-seven or eight thousand dollars."

Then how had I managed to run up $6,000 in business expenses on that consultancy?

I did my best to explain that my tax accountant expensed out a new computer, a new phone line, other office outlays, travel, parking, publications, paper, and paperclips. Besides I had cut off the whole arrangement at the end of August because my employment contract began at BU on September 1, 1993.

But her questions subtly implied that I was simply failing to mitigate losses, thereby increasing my wrongfully sought-after compensation from H & W, and she would surely be back on Monday, to finger me to agents of the IRS.

I was emotionally crushed, and full of foreboding that she might take the entire weekend to review my pay stubs, plus other worksheets and notes—a cache of back-of-the-envelope calculations—come in Monday prepared to crucify me in front of the jury. And that is precisely what she did.

On Monday morning, she announced: *Now, sir, I'm going to give you back a number of documents which you used last week to form the basis of your testimony.*

David objected to her assuming how I had used those worksheets, and Judge White sustained. "Simply ask questions, please."

That marked a momentary pause before Ms. Marshall began inundating me with confusing numbers. I spotted an error in the BU tuition remission, but she plunged implacably ahead, rattling out her final total of $93,713. *Is that correct, sir?*

"You're going much too fast over these numbers," I admitted, "and I haven't looked at these papers in a long time."

"Sir, I'm just basing these on the papers which you provided me."

"No, Ms. Marshall," Judge White warned again, "a question, please."

Do you have any reason to doubt that these figures comprised your 1993 income? And she popped off a series of numbers like a string of firecrackers. Each made a familiar pop, but together their sum was just one long rippling bang.

"I can't do that arithmetic in my head. I'm sorry."

Would you like a machine, sir? And she reached her hand calculator toward me.

"Sure," I managed to answer, but in utter disbelief. "I mean, I will add the numbers up for you if you want me to."

Are you ready? Why wasn't David objecting? This was humiliating, yet he was letting her freely make a monkey out of me.

She started reading off the same numbers, all over again. I repeated them aloud as I entered them. A monkey with a calculator. Again I balked at the tuition remission, as she was treating it as if it were a financial benefit I was receiving. "It's not the right number but I will put it in."

Sir, it's the number on your document.

"That is a worksheet, counselor."

Four thousand three hundred forty-four dollars, she repeated.

"Yes," I acquiesced.

And disability benefits of $71,760.

I looked up from the calculator, a quick glance at the jury, and was aghast to see one of them glaring in my direction, sullen with what had to be very near to loathing.

And I had failed, she noted again, from my dismissal until today, to apply for work *to any corporation or organization other than the one owned by you and/or family members, is that correct?*

David did object to this canard, but Judge White said, "I'll allow it one more time and then I'd like to move on."

It got worse. Ms. Marshall began delving edgily into my calculating twelve percent as the increase in my fringe benefits. *And you can feel free to use the adding machine again, okay?* Should all these benefits really have been included? After another whirligig of numbers, she asked, *If "worker's compensation, unemployment compensation, dues and education" were removed from the damages chart, wouldn't that lower the figure below twelve percent?*

"Yes," I had to say, and when I glanced over again at the jury, I felt certain that they might be looking at me in real disgust, as if I'd tried to overstate or lie about my financial situation.

She started on a question that seemed to be leading to a properly reduced figure for my 1993 income (with my salary raised only four percent, not six), in contrast to the amount shown at the bottom of the blackboard, but her numbers just wound around and around on themselves.

"Objection," David said, "What is the question?"

"There doesn't seem to be a question," Judge White frowned.

Ms. Marshall still kept asking if these numbers were my numbers.

David objected again, and Judge White asked her to rephrase, and she still insisted that *the summation of the total of those income figures appears on the bottom half of that blackboard, is that correct, sir?*

"You're talking about the numbers that we just went through?"

That's correct, sir.

"I'm not sure, really." At this point, I couldn't be certain what my own name was. Her last series of questions had thrown me totally off stride, and I was sure everybody in the room could see it.

Sir, should we go through the calculations again?

By now, the jury was visibly angry, and that broke it for Judge White. "No," she snapped, "we're not going to go through it again."

"Can we have a stipulation," Ms. Marshall asked, "that these are the numbers that Mr. Labonte just testified to?"

"We will let the jury decide what it is," Judge White ruled imperiously. And there was no mistaking she wanted an end to this badgering, now. "All right. Let's move on."

I was at a real low point, psychologically, and it didn't help when Ms. Marshall moved on, immediately, to my five days of depositions. She asked me, *And each day was three hours long at my request?* David objected, but she got me to read back her question after the first three hours of the deposition. She had asked, *Are you able to go on?*

And I had answered, "I have to say no." Among other deposed answers I had to repeat with regard to my MS, reading aloud, were "clearly I was feeling mentally and physically fatigued throughout the day," plus all the adverse symptoms I had described to Dr. Wolpow, also that I was ready to give over my larger responsibilities to other partners, mainly Fred Grein, who "could perhaps take over regular attendance at the management committee meetings—as more logically the person who could deal with the policy issues, particularly as they applied to the attorneys—and that I could report to him" as Chief Operating Officer.

In a nutshell, where I saw myself asking H & W to accommodate my disability, H & W saw me attempting to abdicate my responsibilities. My last reading aloud was her question: "Is it fair to say that absent the changes in your job, you could not have continued to perform the work of firm administrator in 1991?" And my answer: "Absent the accommodations that we have discussed, I couldn't have done, continued to do the job properly."

David then got up to salvage whatever we could on redirect, helping me clarify a lot of Ms. Marshall's misleading points. *On the damages chart, hadn't I really used a modest six percent increase for health insurance?*

Yes, and that would have been $360 per year, but "the H & W family health insurance actually rose twenty-three percent between 1992 and 1993, an increase of $1300 per year."

Why hadn't I insisted on more of my $33,000 salary at BU?

The federal grant has only so much money left, and "I'm one of the few people who continue to be paid."

Ms. Marshall suggests a four percent increase in salary, why did I say six?

"Salary increases range from four to ten percent, and I had taken the lower part of that range, and I know that Union Mutual uses a figure of seven percent in their projections."

Why hadn't I discussed my MS with my fellow Boston law administrators?

"Because I had asked the management committee not to tell anybody I had MS. I felt that it would inhibit my relationships—"

Ms. Marshall moved to strike, but the question was allowed.

So I continued, "And I didn't want to be discussing it with people I barely knew at other law firms."

At the management committee, did they discuss whether billing and collecting "could be more effectively done by a lawyer versus a non-lawyer?"

Yes, and "everybody agreed" that other attorneys would be "much more responsive" to a managing partner than "a salaried executive director."

Did I, or did I not, have to make a turn in the corridor to get to the elevator?

Yes, the diagram is confusing since it indicates "EL" right next to my office. That stands for Eleanor Lanes. The elevator is actually well down the corridor and to the left, off the diagram.

We set other matters to rights. I didn't learn to use the Wang computer at H & W because I didn't need to waste my time on it. I already had plenty of IT expertise. Dr. Wepsic isn't my doctor. Dr. Wolpow is, so any consultations Charles Robins or Tony Medaglia had with Dr. Wepsic on accommodating my disability were peripheral at best. But David also read into the record a statement from Dr. Wepsic that stipulated what he had told Tony and Robins about MS and how they could help me do my job. Significantly, Dr. Wepsic said that Alan should be provided with some relief from walking long distances, such as relocating his office.

Yes, I did favor Fred Grein taking over H & W in the role of chief executive officer, and as COO, I saw myself doing "all the work down in the trenches, so it's a kind of partnership, if you will." And I was seeking an accommodation with Mr. Grein on billing and collection responsibilities. "I just thought the one-on-one stuff could be done better by him, but I was going to give him all the information, so he could have a quick conversation either in person or over the phone."

David asked me, *After you told them you had MS and had this one conversation with Tony Medaglia, for the rest of your tenure at the firm, did any member of the management committee ever come to your office and ask you how you were doing physically in terms of the work load and your multiple sclerosis?*

"No."

I left the witness box, after the better part of three days spent testifying on-and-off between appearances by my two good doctors, feeling I badly needed their immediate care. I was utterly exhausted, and ashamed of myself, in agony over much of my last fumbling, witless performance.

I had to admit that Mary Marshall had done a masterful job of exposing my weaknesses. She had succeeded in throwing me off guard on my worksheets, and once she started drilling me on all those numbers, everything grew more stressful. That was my constant trouble with the mental underminings of MS. As the stress grew, my confusion increased, and my ability to reason intelligently and function capably became impaired.

I sat back down in the gallery, convinced I'd probably lost the case for us.

I couldn't look at the jury, couldn't face remembering how angry I thought they'd become at me. I could feel their emanations of sullen disapproval.

Why hadn't David stepped in, objected right from the start to Ms. Marshall's mauling tactics, and stopped the whole debacle from ever occurring? Why did he wait so long, until the judge ultimately had to take it on herself to rule this form of mental torture out of order? I felt like marching right up to his table to ask where he'd been hiding himself, but David, with his fierce focus on whatever is coming next, was already getting up to question our next witness.

In fact, he didn't really come clean until long after the trial.

"Honestly, Alan, I'm sorry I had to leave you up there for so long," he confessed, a little sheepishly. "I could see how you were suffering."

Then he hugged me around the shoulders.

"But the jury wasn't angry at you," he explained. "They were mad as hell at *her*, for what she was *doing* to you. It was clear to both Diane and me that they hated it."

Chapter Seven

"**P**laintiff calls Mary Ellen O'Mara," David announced, and I almost didn't recognize her.

I was so used to her very prim and trim appearance around H & W, always proper and stylish in her dress, that her sudden dowdiness was a numbing surprise. She came into court in a drab outfit, clumping along in low heels. Halfway through her testimony, David asked, could she recall a single thing that I'd done well at H & W after July of 1991?

"Alan is a very nice person," she replied, *non compis mentis.*

Excuse me, please, David said. *Just tell me if you recall a single thing that he did well after July of 1991?*

"I can't recall off-hand."

These mental lapses were what David wanted the jury to assess—for basic credibility—after I stepped down from the witness box just before noon on Monday. He had abruptly shifted his tactics, turning around one hundred and eighty degrees, to mount an aggressive confrontation with those who might cast doubt on my three days' testimony. He immediately began calling the defendant's witnesses to the stand—questioning, as if on cross, those who had every reason to know I was speaking the truth, such as Ms. O'Mara.

How could this obviously intelligent woman, whose daily practice was, she said herself, "public offerings and private placement of stock, tender offers, mergers and acquisitions," have such failure of memory when it came to recalling my work product? Or of my very presence alongside her at meetings of the management committee?

Ms. Marshall, on direct, managed to elicit Ms. O'Mara's confession: "I was only peripherally involved in all of this because my mother was very seriously ill in Pennsylvania." She said she had spent "a great deal of time, running back and forth," trying to help her ailing parent, so that it was, in an ironic echo of my situation with my own father, "a very stressful period for me."

But she carried her denials too far. She refused to acknowledge that I might need to walk around the four floors of the firm, seeing lawyers about their overdue clients' payments.

Did you ever notice Alan Labonte limping while he was Executive Director of the firm?

"I have a recollection from time to time that he limped."

Did you ever ask him why he was limping?

"No."

Did you ever wonder why he was limping?

"I didn't really think anything of it."

Too callous, or too evasive to be believed. "Fairly early on," she had decided I was "not going to work out on a long term basis," since I just "wasn't a self-starter."

For David's parting shot, he asked, *And is it your view that his limping in no way hindered his ability to do his job as Executive Director?*

This question got an affirmative and self-damning, "Yes."

Charles Robins, always so impeccable, also came attired for Dress-Down Day at the office. His testimony was more circumspect, but just as know-nothing and deceitful. This is hard for me to say, since I once felt that I'd shared a good working relationship with him. But that was rapidly fraying away into nothing by his denials. And during his two days on the stand, it came apart with a sickening snap when David, on cross, caught him in a particularly outrageous statement.

He began by not acknowledging that I'd taken over Eleanor Lanes' daily meetings with him during her medical leave, then not recalling "any dialogue" with me about my wanting to refuse that 1990 Christmas bonus. He did remember my "integrating smoothly on a personal basis within the firm," but other areas of my performance were "not remarkable."

Is that why they gave me a raise after my first year?

"No," Robins hastened to say, they wanted to protect their "significant investment" in me, wanted to encourage me to see if my performance "would rise to the level that we hoped it would."

Didn't they intend the raise—the largest given to any non-legal staff—"to be a signal to Mr. Labonte that he was doing a good job?"

"We intended to encourage him," repeated Robins. "I think my word, encourage, speaks for itself."

That was the worst of his testimony at the tag end of Monday, though his thoughts on how to accommodate my MS after he and Tony Medaglia visited Dr. Wepsic were pretty ludicrous. Primarily they were told I would need rest. "We described the fact that Mr. Labonte was already evidencing a symptom in the form of a limp," so Dr. Wepsic "told us that he should avoid using the stairs, and we encouraged—"

More encouragement.

"Alan to avoid the stairs."

Next morning, Tuesday, brought another slew of mental lapses from Robins about anything I'd ever accomplished at the firm. These amounted to never denying I might have had something to do with any given project, but "who actually did the work?" Robins' best dodge was his answer to David about my concerted campaign to get clients to pay their legal fees up front. *Did Robins "recall a collection of $20,000 by Mr. Labonte's efforts?"*

"I'm sure he must have collected a dollar or two," he testified, "but I recall the collection efforts that he undertook generally to be unsuccessful."

Did he recall lecturing me about being five minutes late to a management committee meeting and plopping down my wet raincoat?

"No." After David somewhat refreshed his memory, Robins allowed he might have done so. "Punctuality is important for meetings, but I don't recall the incident you describe with particularity."

Had it ever occurred to Robins, in the summer of 1991, "to warn Alan Labonte not to sell his house in Greenfield and buy a house in Boston?"

They had hired me "as a sophisticated executive director to run our business," so Robins opined that I was "fully capable of making personal business decisions about when to move," et cetera, that I didn't need his advice "to assess that."

Would it have helped Alan Labonte "to assess the situation if you warned him there were performance concerns?"

"I never thought of that at the time."

Robins "believed" that H & W had done whatever the firm could to accommodate my disability. He had "a general notion that there was some effort made to lessen the stress and moderate the hours."

David asked, *So I am to believe that you believe that it was done?"*

Robins thought long before he answered, "I am speculating."

Now Ms. Marshall took over, on direct, and covered familiar ground, largely having to do, as she put it, with how Robins made sure he was keeping his finger "on the pulse of the firm." He usually walked in on a very easy basis and said to anybody, "Good morning, how's it going?"

Did he generally stop by and see Alan Labonte?

"If he was there. Sometimes he was, sometimes he wasn't." But he definitely saw Eleanor Lanes daily, let her air her complaints. She might say to him, "You know, the billing crunch we have. I don't know how I'm going to get all this stuff done." And he'd suggest how "we could deal with it by doing this or doing that." He had the same easy dealings with Margaret Hadley before she left, in fact, with everybody including Charlie Gaziano, who came to him, after Eleanor complained about my not telling her about Fred Grein's canceling of the 1991 stub period, "with essentially the same story" he was hearing everywhere.

"All the executive functions were being pushed down on other people's shoulders," Gaziano told him. "People simply couldn't get the work done and do their own jobs."

So he knew from taking the pulse of the firm that I had to go, especially with all the pressures on the partners, and forthwith came a lugubrious tale of the recent fiscal woes of Hutchins & Wheeler. 1991 had been "a difficult year," Robins lamented, but "1992 was even a worse year for us."

Why?

They faced a terrible recession after the firm's too rapid expansion in the 80s, so that now they had all that "excess capacity, excess space" at 101 Federal. There was also a spate of bankruptcies around Boston. "We had banks failing, and these were our clients."

Did that impact the firm?

"Well, yes, our own principal bank started to give us a hard time." I perked right up at this oblique mention of State Street Bank. "They like to lend money when the sun shines, but when it gets cloudy, they worry about it, and want their money back." Or at least, I ruefully recalled, some show of responsible fiscal discipline.

"We said, 'Look, we're going to move our line of credit to a different bank (Tony's client, Olympic Bank), a bank that we felt would be easier to deal with' at the time. That was all well and good—except that bank actually failed, and was taken over by the FDIC, and we were in the unenviable situation of running a small business without a credit line." And what came next was not too good. "And with a large debt to the FDIC that the FDIC wrote us letters they wanted the debt repaid right away."

And after that prissy rundown, he explained how the whole firm nearly hemorrhaged. With 88,000 feet of space sublet "on adverse terms" at One Boston Place, plus 18,000 too many more feet right where they were elegantly stuck at 101 Federal, excess capacity was "really choking the business." All that saved them over the next three months were negotiations with the landlord, with lenders, with the FDIC, then with another law firm almost their same size, about a possible merger. At the very last, the merger fell through. "But a group of twenty-nine lawyers from another firm joined us."

Whence came Hutchins, Wheeler, & Dittmar.

These twenty-nine lawyers brought along forty support staff, and it took the development of innumerable computer models to fit everybody into the new arrangement. More computers were needed, more telephones, new systems to keep track of their time and billing, desks, lamps, pencils, pens, and stuff. "In retrospect, it was a monumental undertaking." And they had to turn to "outside consultants" because they weren't able themselves to do that analysis in-house. "We're lawyers, and are trained to deal with legal issues." They had fired the guy that could have helped them through these difficult transitional times.

"You know," Robins added sheepishly, "I have trouble getting the switch right on my computer to bring up my calendar on it."

I was bursting to talk to David about all these revelations, but he was already approaching the bench for another sidebar.

"Your Honor," he said, "Mr. Robins has clearly brought out the financial status of the firm as an issue. At this point it would be unfair not to permit me to bring out the actual financial status of the firm during the years in question."

Mary Marshall wanted none of that. Robins had raised a lot of issues, talked about a lot of negotiations, she argued, "but he never said there was any impact on the bottom line."

"He raised enough of a question about banks and lines of credit and financial problems," Judge ruled, "that I'm going to let Mr. Rapaport inquire."

David offered Exhibits B, C, and D, the firm's three tax returns for 1991, 1992, and 1993. Records that David had fought tooth-and-nail to get. Ms. Marshall objected, but in they came. I realized we were about to see the upshot of H & W's belt-tightening that supposedly had every partner limiting himself to a $75,000 "draw" in 1991.

David honed in on Robins' worries over "running a small business without a credit line." *Had he not "characterized Hutchins & Wheeler as a small business?"*

"I did."

What were the annual revenues of Hutchins & Wheeler in 1991, sir?

"Twenty-one million dollars."

And in 1992?

"Twenty-two million dollars."

And in 1993?

Robins didn't know, didn't have that information, but David had hard enough numbers to keep pressing.

Did Robins feel that a business generating $22 million is a small business?

"Compared to General Motors," Robins riposted. "Very small, compared to Digital Equipment."

Most of the people in the courtroom laughed, including the jurors.

David went on. *In the year 1991, is it true that "you were the highest paid partner at Hutchins & Wheeler?"*

"It's possible." He was getting brittle. "I'd have to look to be sure, but I think so."

David handed him the documents, and asked him to take ample time to refresh his recollection.

"I think I was," Robins allowed.

And was he also the highest compensated partner in 1992?

"Yes, I was."

And in 1993?

"I believe so."

Now David gave this gradual grilling a last, damning twist. He was after a particular figure. *And what was his 1993 compensation?*

I held my breath, listening intently for those next words from Robins, who was white with anger.

"It was $880,000 and change."

You would not believe the thumping impact of the hush that hit that courtroom. The magnitude of Robins' deception stopped the proceedings in a silence that made the truth crystal-clear after all that poor-mouthing.

David repeated the figure, *Eight hundred and eighty thousand dollars?*

"Yes."

For you?

"Yes."

By that afternoon, Robins' laconic reply was all over the Boston Bar. David had his one money figure that we so desperately wanted, first, to prove their collusion and use of half-truths, but second, to show they could, and should, suffer the consequences. What did the trick was Robins' arrogant tag—"and change." That little fillip rendered this well-deserved bit of come-uppance extra outrageous, and twice as quotable.

On further cross, David got other admissions out of Robins, that Eleanor Lanes kept his personal checkbook, did his taxes, and most especially, that I'd told him the reason I didn't tell Eleanor about the elimination of the stub period because Fred Grein had instructed me not to. *That faced Robins with a conflict in terms of whom to believe, correct?*

"Yes."

And you chose to believe your partner, Fred Grein, correct?

"I certainly did."

But who was now going to believe any H & W partner, after Robins' forked-tongue duplicity about his earnings before the court? I kept cool until David and I could find a quiet spot off to one side in the courtroom, later in the day, for a private conversation.

"Now I think that I know what they did," I whispered. "Remember my saying something was wrong during the close of 1991? Partners on the management committee *in particular* were just not getting the billing out. They weren't pushing their clients for payment before the year's end. Robins and Medaglia went off to Florida as usual, and then they eliminated the stub period *secretly*. To prevent any new money from accumulating for 1991. I think that it was all part of a master plan to make the financial situation look worse than it actually was, so they could negotiate a new concession on the rent with the landlord at 101 Federal. This also might have been the justification for getting rid of Ken May and five other partners, and to put some other partners on salary. This way they wouldn't have to share the profits with as many people in the future! The end result would be a windfall after 1992, and that would explain why guys like Robins got such astronomical pay packets."

David gave me a very serious, questioning look. "Are you sure that's what really happened?"

"Of course I can't be positive, but it certainly presents a plausible explanation for the numbers we're hearing today."

David, keeping to his attack strategy, next called Charlie Gaziano. He freely admitted he'd opposed my being hired, had later gone behind my back to complain about me to Tony Medaglia, Jack Clymer, John Thomson, who knows who else? But he also had to admit that since he had replaced me, the managing partner Fred Grein had helped him with billing and collection. He tried to claim he did "ninety-nine percent" and Grein a "very small minority" of the work.

"They said they couldn't have made an accommodation for me," I whispered to David, "but they did it for Gaziano!"

David asked, *If, around the time I was fired, he recalled telling Alan Labonte he shouldn't try to apply for any other jobs as a law firm administrator.*

"Absolutely not."

Sure that never happened?

"Absolutely."

Gaziano was followed by James Westra, among all the partners who served on the management committee, the most sympathetic toward me. David quizzed him carefully, asking, *Whether, once he had developed "concerns" about my job performance, he had ever thought "to warn Alan Labonte to think twice before he sold his home in Greenfield and move to Boston?"*

"No," Westra said, he was unaware I'd even made any such move.

With a slightly raised eyebrow, David set up a record on this strange ignorance. *Within H & W, did Westra recall receiving "a conflict of interest memo from Kenneth May about his proposing to represent Alan Labonte in the house transaction?"*

"No, I do not," Westra said, since "probably forty or fifty of those circulated a week." He stayed noncommittal, almost friendly, until Ms. Marshall took over, on direct.

She soon got into criticism of my effort to convert the H & W health plan, and Westra said, "There had been a number of false starts." A date had been set for conversion, as I too well remembered to my chagrin, "and we had to change it on one or more occasions." Westra made it quite clear he had kindly volunteered to take over and straighten the whole mess out.

How would he assess my role?

Issues came up "which should have been perceived in advance," causing "some false starts and stops," he said. "It was a job which I felt was not well performed."

Polite as he was, he was right on the same denigrating page as his partners. He reprised their fiscal woes, at Ms. Marshall's prompting, repeating their $75,000 draw in 1991, "from which all medical benefits, everything else, had to be funded." He then struck a note of personal sympathy, since "My brother-in-law had contracted multiple sclerosis several years before that." He understood "the illness is a very difficult one, very unpredictable, and that it's often aggravated by stress and fatigue. And unfortunately, 1991 was an extremely stressful time for all of us." He'd come round to see me when he first learned I had multiple sclerosis—"and simply expressed my sorrow at having heard it"—but he didn't keep inquiring after Alan's medical condition, since that would have been "an invasion of his privacy." And he agreed I had to leave, since "Alan was really not performing the job that we hired him for. There was a real sense of drift at the administrative level."

David came right back at him on cross, *Let's talk, Mr. Westra, about the $75,000 in 1991.*

He got Westra to "tell the jury how much money" he actually earned as a partner over those three years. Specifically, $134,355.80 in 1991, $265,437.99 in 1992, and $443,088.14 in 1993. No mention now of "and change."

David then allowed Westra to "explain" these large sums. Then he asked, *Who was actually responsible for the "false start" on the healthcare conversion, namely two H & W attorneys with whom I'd consulted, Carol Brown, who handled ERISA matters, and Michael Gengler. Did Westra know whether or not Brown and Gengler, working with Alan Labonte, had spotted the tax problem?*

"Yes, they did."

Did they spot it before it was submitted to the partners?

"No, after."

Afterwards, David repeated. *In your view, should they have spotted it before it was submitted to the partners?*

"In my view, the entire effort should have been coordinated in such a way that they would have," Westra totally fudged, affirming his judgment with a softly reassuring "Yes."

David quickly moved on, toward the close of Tuesday's session, to Fred Grein, the managing partner, who then made it a perfect day for total denial by likewise not being able to think of "any job at Hutchins & Wheeler, any task that Alan Labonte performed well during his first year."

"No, I cannot."

More than that, he didn't think it important to let the management committee know how low he rated my financial planning abilities.

"No, I didn't."

What a jerk, I had to conclude. He was treasurer of the partnership when I was hired. I still remembered his terse dismissal of my talents when he first interviewed me with the management committee. That alone obliged him to report his supposed doubts about my financial competence. Did he really think anybody was going to buy all his malarkey?

He was busy running down every well-known accomplishment within H & W that I hadn't achieved when Judge White ended court for the day. "Ladies and Gentlemen," she forewarned, "I'm asking you to make arrangements tomorrow to go all day. Be prepared to go from nine or 9:15 is what usually happens here, to one and then two to 2:30 and maybe even four." Was she clearing the decks for what she sensed might be a real battle royale?

* * *

It was another hot August morning on that Wednesday. Workers outside the courthouse were busy removing a noxious industrial coating from the facade—deemed environmentally dangerous, and certainly odiferous, so that tension was on the rise inside the courtroom. Judge White spoke out for calm, reassuring everybody that there was no health hazard, and David resumed questioning Fred Grein.

He only got more adamant denials than the day before. Grein testified he ceased being treasurer, once I was hired, had nothing further or good to say about my work through to my termination. But this go-round, David brought up the H & W Christmas party. *Hadn't it been planned by Alan's wife, Lora?*

"Yes, that's true."

David then asked Grein to read from his deposition, and they got as far as the party's being held at the Park Plaza Hotel when Ms. Marshall objected "to the remainder of this."

At the sidebar, she argued, "I just don't see the relevance."

David said, "There was dissatisfaction with the way the Christmas party was managed," part of why I was fired.

Judge White asked, "This was organized by his wife?"

David said he would show that Mr. Labonte had responsibility for the Christmas party, "and he sort of delegated it to his wife."

Judge White agreed to that, and it turned out very much in our favor since Grein had to admit that Margaret Hadley had suddenly resigned, leaving me with her responsibility for the office party.

David read the question from Grein's deposition, *"Did you have any dissatisfaction with the manner in which the party was organized?"*

And in came "the remainder," which Ms. Marshall had so primly sought to forestall.

"Well, it had fallen through the cracks," Grein read out his very own words, "so it had to be scrambled together at the last minute. It was not of the caliber, if you will, of our prior parties. I know there was some dissatisfaction about the location, both in terms of geographically where it was, and the Park Plaza Hotel is a little bit seedy, if you will."

To this soupçon of snobbery, David then added a deft inquiry into the firm's having "sometimes had Christmas parties at the Meridien?"

And Grein obligingly completed the list of socially acceptable venues for H & W's wassail. "At the Meridien, the Long Wharf Marriott, and the Four Seasons." Nothing could have made it clearer—to the jury, and yes, to me—where the Labontes humbly ranked on the H & W social ladder.

David also got him to admit to helping Gaziano with laggard lawyers who delayed billing their clients. "Very infrequently on my part," he said, but then admitted they did meet with a procrastinating attorney whenever Gaziano advised him of a problem. "The two of us go together, yes."

But we got little help from Grein on whether he had instructed me not to tell Eleanor Lanes about the elimination of the stub period. *Did he recall any such conversation?*

"No, I do not."

Any recollection one way or the other—that you did or didn't have such a conversation?

"I have no recollection at all."

But then, said David, *When Robins indicated to you that Alan had said you'd told him not to tell Eleanor, you specifically denied it.*

"I denied that to Mr. Robins," Grein affirmed.

And David dug in. *But do I understand that, in fact, you have no recollection of that. Or any such conversation. One way or the other?*

To which, Grein replied, "I have no recollection. I wouldn't have said that. It doesn't make any sense."

That ended whatever ordeal it may have so far been for Fred Grein, and Ms. Marshall deferred her own questioning until later. David called our first friendly witness, Kenneth May, my real estate lawyer and a former partner at H & W. Since Ken happened to have occupied the office next to mine on the 31st floor, he was able to testify to my regular attendance to my duties, and the long hours I had devoted to H & W. "I saw when he was there," he told the jury, "and saw when he wasn't there." Ken's main contribution came from his direct dealings with my real estate sale in Greenfield and purchase in Cohasset. While at H & W, he had distributed a conflict memo on the transactions that left no member of the firm unwitting about my moving to the Boston area, on the basis of my believing I still had a future with H & W.

If May was a friendly witness, John Thomson, with whom I'd worked so long and hard on renting that unused floor at One Boston Place, was an almost friendly witness. He didn't stray very far from the page his partners were on, but he was not so blankly unknowing as his deposition. Once Ms. Marshall got over objecting, he declared that my termination was totally "unexpected to me because I hadn't realized there was dissatisfaction with him from the management committee. We had a good relationship."

And that brings us around to Anthony Medaglia.

In sharp contrast to Ms. O'Mara and Charles Robins, Tony came into court unusually well-dressed, with a nice tan and his nails manicured, ever the dapper one. Along with him arrived Alan Miller, a very senior partner in Ms. Marshall's firm, who came to see how Tony and Mary would comport themselves before judge and jury.

Tony had been an obstructionist, while being deposed, so David began by asking him to read his answers back to the jury, as David reposed the original questions. Very soon, it became patently obvious how uncooperative Tony had been. The effect was cumulative.

Tony began to read from the depostion:

*Question: Do you recall any other conversation with Mr. Labonte
prior to April 27, 1990, other than the one you already told us?*
Answer: What do you mean by conversation?
*Q: I mean, speaking with Mr. Labonte either by telephone or in
person.*
*A: I expect that I met him in the hall and said hello, shook his hand
or something of that nature. I have no specific recollection of any
specific time that we had a detailed discussion. That doesn't mean
that it didn't happen.*
*Q: After the interview that you did have with Mr. Labonte, did you
form any impression as to whether he would be a good candidate
for the executive director position?*
A: What do you mean by good?
*Q: Well, after you interviewed Alan Labonte, what did you think of
him as a candidate?*
A: What do you mean, what did I think of him as a candidate?

There was much more of this stonewalling, and one sidebar at which
Ms. Marshall got Judge White to rule that Tony's plea "I'd like to talk
to Mary" need not be read aloud to the jury. But the weird thing was
how quickly Tony actually slipped into his innate arrogance, replaying
his role to the hilt. One of the court clerks had to hide his laughter
from the jury behind a document he raised over his mouth. But the jury
caught on, started reacting to his nasty and uncooperative responses.
As David closed down the demonstration, Tony turned to Judge White
and asked, "Do you mind if I stand? I've got a back problem." She declared a half hour break. After the break, Tony still remained standing,
as if taking command of the courtroom. Judge White promptly ordered,
"You will sit like all the other witnesses."

Somebody, maybe Alan Miller must have talked to Tony during the
break, because he calmed down, actually got kind of "folksy." He didn't
give up an inch he wasn't forced to yield, but he was more jovial and
less caustic in his denials that I'd ever saved the firm a single penny on
rent, upfront fees, overtime, collections, life insurance, health care, or
even parking spaces. He didn't have any "direct recollection of those
parking spaces," he claimed, which was a real stretch since his own son
had been using one of them.

Did he recall my fixing problems with the phone system?

"We always have problems with the phone system. I'm sure that we had one then. We've got one now."

Did he recall my preparing a financial presentation for the partners, early on, about billing and accounts receivable?

"This was done on a regular basis. I have no recollection of a specific one."

What about my consolidating and reorganizing various financial reports for the management committee?

"My understanding is that Eleanor did that."

So he didn't think Alan Labonte did any of it?

"I think Alan was a participant in it but Eleanor took credit for it later."

Then, is it true that during Alan Labonte's first year at H & W you weren't pleased with the way he handled any functions?

"That's not true."

So David read aloud again from Tony's own deposition, *Did he recall ever being pleased, etc.*

Then his answer was, "Not at this time. I didn't say no," Tony countered stubbornly, and started a wrangling argument that didn't stop until Judge White glowered, "Let's have Mr. Rapaport ask the questions, please."

David repeated the Q & A, and demanded, *Did that happen?*

Ms. Marshall signaled, "Your Honor, may the witness—"

But Tony was up wrangling again, until Judge White interrupted, "Excuse me, Mr. Medaglia, but your lawyer has a statement to make."

"May the witness read his entire statement?"

David, jumping in ahead of Tony, picked right up on that reading again. *Question: Do you recall being pleased with the way Alan Labonte handled any particular projects, etc. Answer: Not at this time do I recall any.*

But Ms. Marshall kept hard after it. "Excuse me again. May he read the entire answer? Continue with the next line."

At long last, Tony bore further witness. "Within the first year there was a reconfiguration of our financial reports which I believe Alan participated in. That was an improvement."

David then said, "Your Honor, I think the record should reflect that that answer followed a conference with counsel, Ms. Marshall."

Mary Marshall said, "I object."

"Sustained," agreed Judge White. "That is stricken."

But everybody in the courtroom was getting a pretty savvy read on Tony, especially the jury.

David was now asking, *Were you dissatisfied with Mr. Labonte's performance during his first year?*

"Yes."

Not the right person for the job unless he improved substantially?

"Yes."

When you learned he was contemplating a move to the South Shore, did you have serious concerns about his performance?

"I had concerns."

And were they serious?

"Not as serious as they became later in the year."

By which time I'd learned I had MS, and informed the management committee. David began another reading aloud from Tony's deposition.

Question: Did you have any information about the nature of multiple sclerosis?
Answer: Yes.
Q: What did you know as of that time?
A: It wasn't a good thing.
Q: Did you know anything more specific?
A: They sent me a card to raise money.

David knew that Tony and Robins together went around to see Dr. Wepsic for "about an hour" over lunchtime. They brought along sandwiches, and learned what they could about MS. So David asked, *Anything about what sort of accommodations the firm could provide Alan Labonte?*

"No."

Anything about changing the location of his office so he wouldn't have to walk so much?

"No."

Anything about the fatigue Alan might be feeling?

"Yes."

On my fatigue, Tony was eloquent, "If you're tired, leave early," he testified that he'd told me. "It's more important for you to be here at the top of your game. You want to rest, leave, and, you know, don't worry about it." If only such words, I reflected again, had ever been translated into some real help.

Did Tony ever consider relocating my office so I could be closer to the elevators?

"Nope."

Shifting some of my work to Fred Grein?

"No."

To any other attorney at the firm?

"No."

Or to any other support staff?

"No."

Then David brought up my father's "passing away." *Hadn't I requested some vacation time during December so that I could resettle my mother in Florida, and hadn't Tony told me December was a busy time, take as little time as possible?*

"Yes."

And did I end up taking three days?

"He took some time. I told him he could go in January, it would be fine."

David pressed, *But isn't it true that you, yourself, took some vacation time off in December of 1991?*

"Four days," Tony snapped back.

You were down in Key Largo, Florida?

"Four days," Tony said again.

Now David began raising larger questions about Tony's knowledge and treatment—and the firm's—of my illness. *Did he recall any discussion with Alan Labonte about what effect multiple sclerosis might have been having on my work before my termination?*

"I never discussed the disease as such. I asked him about how he was doing. Was everything okay, you feeling any pain? But I never used the words, multiple sclerosis, no."

By then, since I was visibly limping around the firm, *couldn't the management committee have done something to lessen my working hours?*

"We could have said, Stay home!" Tony bridled. "I don't understand the question. Sure, we could have lessened his hours by saying, 'Don't do your job, go do something else,' but, I don't understand what you're driving at."

David politely suggested they might have lessened my hours by "having a partner help with the billing and collection effort."

"No," said Tony.

That was impossible?

"That was his job."

Wouldn't consider having a partner go around and do some of that?

"That's what he was hired for."

David began bearing down on the real nexus of power within the firm. *Would it be your view, Mr. Medaglia, that if a partner wasn't getting out his bills as quickly as he ought, it would be more effective to have Mr. Labonte speak to him than for you to speak to him?*

They got into another real wrangle over this. Best to have an administrator do it, Tony insisted, "because you don't get into the lawyering-back-and-forth with all the excuses." Tony got tough. "Alan was running the books. He's the guy to come in and say, 'Look, you've got 'X' amount of stuff, you should get it out.'"

But Alan ran into resistance, didn't he?

"Absolutely."

In dealing with such resistance, "do you think you would be less effective than Alan Labonte?"

In the case of continued resistance, Tony propounded, "You send in the chairman of the compensation committee. But that's a dire thing, to tell somebody we're going to cut your pay if you don't send your bill out."

How about taking measures short of that?

"I don't understand. What are you driving at?"

How about if Fred Grein goes and talks to the resistant lawyer as managing partner?

"Fred doesn't," Tony said. "The executive director does that. We hired the executive director because lawyers do that poorly."

David moved that last answer be stricken, "as unresponsive." The motion was allowed.

Mr. Medaglia, there was no attorney, no partner at H & W who could have been equally or more effective than Mr. Labonte at approaching the partners to bill and collect?

"Not consistent with good operations."

But it was going on, wasn't it? People other than Mr. Labonte were actually doing that while he was there?

Tony shifted uneasily, and out it came. "Robins would beat up on me because he was across the hall every now and then, but it wasn't an organized thing."

David asked again, *It was done, wasn't it?*

"Yes."

There was further corroboration from Tony's deposition, read aloud, and then David asked Tony, *If his office was "located right across the hall from Charles Robins?"*

"Yes, it is."

Did they speak to each other every morning and afternoon, have lunch together often?

"Generally true."

Don't you call him "The Robin," share a close professional relationship?

"Very."

After that, nobody could have doubted who had the real power to deal with problem lawyers at H & W. David made that doubly clear by asking who were the terminators at my own termination. "Charlie Robins, myself," said Tony, "and Freddie Grein."

But neither "The Robin" nor Grein were then on the management committee, were they?

"No."

Do you recall Mr. Labonte asking whether he could stay on somehow in his job? "It didn't make sense."

All that remained was to get into the record, out of Tony's own mouth, his true income for those three critical years. Which came to $188,402.69 in 1991, $342,960.60 in 1992, and $470,828.54 in 1993.

Ms. Marshall reserved her direct for later, and Tony stepped down, slightly bloodied but still unbowed, and suddenly we were very close to resting our case. "I have Lora," David told Judge White, "but she will only be ten minutes."

Not if Ms. Marshall had her druthers. At a sidebar, she raised two objections. First was spousal disqualification, which in Massachusetts forbids either spouse to testify about any communications between them. Second, if Lora was going to testify that I'd "expressed unhappiness or emotional discomfort, that's also hearsay." But David was well up on the spousal disqualification. He wasn't going to ask about any conversations with me. Only about my leaving and returning home, to prove the long hours I worked, then Lora's own observations on my later emotional distress. "Those are the only two purposes." Ms. Marshall renewed her objection, but Judge White asked, did she have any cases about it? "I haven't brought any with me." So her objection was noted but overruled, and Lora took the stand as our final witness.

She looked lovely. She was dressed in a conservative pink skirt, with a blouse and jacket, her graying hair carefully done, squared away in a neck-length curl. A no-nonsense woman, used to being all business, but I could tell she was hiding her nerves. David asked if she was married to Alan Labonte. Yes, since 1964.

David got her safely through the working-long-hours part. I'd been "getting up at five and leaving usually at six" from Cohasset, while it was still dark. I liked to take the boat, but often had to drive in, since the last boat back was at 7:30, and sometimes I couldn't leave for home until later. "Nine o'clock was not unusual."

Then David turned to the day I was fired. *Did she recollect seeing me that day or over the next day or so?*

Lora froze. I caught it, even before David, who quietly urged her, *You have to respond verbally.*

"Just give me—" was all she could utter, and Judge White said, "All right. We will take a short break. Five minutes."

It lasted fifteen, from five of noon to ten after. Lora managed to get back on the stand again, and David asked for "any observations" of me.

"I observed someone I thought might be dying. All his color was gone—"

Objection from Ms. Marshall. Judge White agreed. "The conclusion is stricken. Just confine yourself to what you observed."

I watched Lora struggling for the right words.

"Just ashen, sallow, almost like an empty person."

Where did Alan go when he came home that night?

"The bedroom next to our bedroom we had made into an office for him, and he often, when he wasn't at work, he was working in that office."

Objection, move to strike, overruled. "Please continue."

"And that's where he was. Just sitting there."

Could she describe my behavior the next couple of days, please?

"Yes. He walked from his office to the bed and to the office." She was trying so hard to stay calm. "He told me what had happened."

Somehow Lora took hold. "He was depressed. He had no resilience like he had had. Even when his father died, he came back faster. And when he found out he had multiple sclerosis, he came back faster. But this blow was so great, he took a long time to come back. He wanted to—"

"Objection."

"All right," nodded Judge White, but no need to rule.

For the first time in my life, I saw my wife unable to carry on. At her lowest ebb in the hospital with a collapsed lung, she had carried on, but not now, she just had to give up. If you looked hard, she was in tears, but it was like watching a stone cry through its tiniest cracks. And then I started to cry. David said no further questions. Ms. Marshall said no to any cross. David escorted Lora slowly back to a seat in the gallery next to me. I took her hand in mine.

Somewhere in all this turmoil, David said, "I have no more witnesses, Your Honor," then got into a fuss over those tax documents with Ms. Marshall before Judge White. It took a while for the emotional tension to ease off in that courtroom, before David could say, "The plaintiff rests his case," and Ms. Marshall called her first witness.

"Tony Medaglia."

I could not believe my ears.

I actually signaled to David and leaned over to whisper. "Why? Why would Mary want to bring on this guy again? Lora's sitting right here, the jury can see she's still upset. Talk about lousy timing, what is her strategy?"

David cupped his hand over my ear. "I agree, but who's complaining?"

He was back, this time to tell his own Tony version, at Ms. Marshall's prompting, of the H & W saga. He'd seen H & W go from "about a fifteen to twenty person law firm" in the 60s—not even a Xerox, only carbons, file cards, with rubber bands—through rapid growth during the Massachusetts Miracle into near bust in the 90s. So they decided to hire somebody "to come in and be the chief executive officer of everything except running the professional side, which was what the lawyers do."

So now I at least knew where the screwy idea came from that I was the CEO. Whoever they hired "would be a full participant," said Tony. "Be there and discuss things," and tell them "how we should run the ship." Tell Tony, the ex-Navy officer, how to run a ship?

How did I fare, asked Ms. Marshall, *during that first year?*

"Alan is an extremely pleasant, cordial person," Tony carefully replied, "who fit into the culture of Hutchins & Wheeler very well." But Tony soon realized that "Alan didn't have the command of the skills that he needed to bring the value added." I was "less participatory than reporting." Alan had to keep calling in the staff, since he "wasn't able to answer the tough questions on the stuff he brought to us."

When Tony took over the management committee, did he take over supervising Alan Labonte?

"More so than before, yes." He had this "seminal conversation" with me, all about how I had to "make sure everything was going right. You're running this ship. You're it. You're the skipper." And the nautical images kept on coming, "You've got to be on deck, you've got to show the flag."Though once piped aboard, I don't remember his ever quite turning the ship over to me. Instead, he made it clear that I had the responsibility for billable hours. "That's our inventory, the hours." And my big job was "to go around and make sure the lawyers get the bills out the door because you can't get the money until you send somebody a bill. That's the livelihood of the law firm." Still, he recalled having much larger expectations of me. "Most important job you have is to think," he said he told me. "You're here to give us strategic guidance." And he emphasized how key I was to the agenda of H & W. "Alan took the reports from administration, from human resources, from finance, from word processing, from everyone, brought them together and presented them to the management committee, which was like the board of directors. He was the focal point. He was the CEO."

I've truncated a lot of Tony's florid speechifying, and needless to say, hardly care to vouch for the bona fides of any of it. I've covered this same territory too many times already, to accept my oddball elevation here to CEO along side his chairmanship of the board. Under Ms. Marshall's guidance, Tony followed up with a more sympathetic rendering of his concerns for my welfare after I'd been diagnosed with MS.

He offered his own scribbled note to show he had reached a better understanding of the disease beyond its being "like a frontal lobe thing."

"A person can become less focused," Tony interpolated his scribblings, "so that there would be more of a requirement to focus on things. Judgment calls are not going to be a problem, but there could be a lack of involvement on things that are important."

It struck me how loquacious he was, and David even objected once, "Excuse me, Your Honor. Can we proceed to question and answer instead of narratives?"

Then Ms. Marshall asked him to *describe for the jury the first performance-related situation that you had an opportunity to assess, i.e. my long effort to restructure their health care insurance.*

"I remember being especially unhappy with the way that was handled," Tony boomed. "A memo would come into the management committee on this, and you'd start asking Alan questions about it, and he'd have to call in Margaret Hadley to answer the questions. Here was someone who should have been expert in the field, and he was deferring to somebody else. He just was not taking responsibility. He wasn't running with the ball. He wasn't bringing value added from what the troops were doing. He was more messenger than processor."

How did Alan's health reform play out?

"It totally disrupted the firm because, without asking the people at the firm and ascertaining what made sense to them on a very important issue—"

Totally untrue.

"Alan trotted us down the path of the Tufts plan, and actually got us all cards for the Tufts plan." Then he gave his real reason. "I told him I couldn't deal with the Tufts plan because I have a child who, since he was born, each of the first fourteen years of his life, spent the summer in the hospital having reconstructive surgery. Tufts plan doctors were not going to be his doctors from Children's Hospital. I can't flip Chris out, so I said I will pay the extra for my own kid." Then others complained they had medical ties that couldn't be "pushed into the Tufts mold. 'Why can't we have our own doctor, is there another way?' That's what bothered me. It was disruptive."

Did the health insurance conversion finally get done?

"Yes. We ended up with Bay State." Through my own concerted action, by the way, still at large savings. "It was a long arduous process."

With a deliberately leading question, Ms. Marshall then asked, *Did any member of the management committee help?*

At which point, Tony blanked. He made a few stabs at answering, but he didn't have a clue, even though the jury already did. Ms. Marshall gave him a broad hint. *Did he know if Jim Westra became involved?*

And Tony responded. "I don't have any specific remembrance of Jimmy—"

She cut him off instantly. *At some point in 1991 was the firm involved in negotiations with its landlord?*

A whole new subject. Because it had to have been pretty obvious to everybody in the courtroom, as it was to me, that Tony didn't have his facts straight on how the health care insurance conversion had been managed.

He picked up fast on Ms. Marshall's new line of inquiry, about his negotiations to get concessions on the rent for their four floors at 101 Federal. I'd taken enough of his abuse during those dealings, so I was dying to hear his latest excuses.

The day before, he'd asked me for "the stuff" on H & W expenses. "Two hours before we go downstairs to meet, Alan gave me some materials which were just not what I asked for, not something that was credible to go down with to the landlord. We needed a cut in the rent, and asking the landlord to take money off his table and leave it on our table is not an easy thing. You have to have real data to convince him this was serious, and I just didn't have it.

"So I blew up and told him it was unsatisfactory and stepped upstairs to Eleanor's office." She told him that Alan "didn't ask her for the stuff that I am now asking her for, but she would see what she could do in an hour, and she gave me some jury-rigged kind of presentation."

What happened with the landlord?

"They threw us out, basically. I mean, we just did not have a convincing case."

That's maybe because in an hour even Eleanor can't prepare a full set of amended statements.

For which he ended up blaming me. "I said, Alan, this is totally unsatisfactory. We have got our butts against the wall. We're working for our survival. We've got three hundred people working here, and if we don't pull this off, we're going to be *meh-hu-get* like Gaston & Snow."

Tony had dropped right back into character, and even Ms. Marshall was stumped by what he's saying. She asked, *You're going to be* what?

"*Meh-hu-get*, bankrupt, out of business, gone."

So a week later, did another partner ask Alan Labonte for this expense information?

"The Robin had to go down and meet with the landlord. I was going to be out of town."

Results?

"I gather when I got back, it was a replay—"

What did you say to Alan about his performance in getting financial information for Mr. Robins?

"That it was unsatisfactory because Charles was unhappy, and he didn't get the information he needed."

Did you tell him what you expected him to do in the future?

"A better job, yes."

We took a lunch break at this point.

After lunch, I noticed that Alan Miller, Ms. Marshall's boss, was not there. No longer a restraining presence. Ms. Marshall brought Tony slowly around to the integration of the Gaston & Snow partners into H & W. "There were just no plans laid out or made for this team of about ten people to join us," Tony complained, though he said he had restrained his criticism of me because of my father's recent death. But "the specter of Gaston & Snow just closing haunted him, what with our credit line frozen, our revenue flattened, so that we were in a cash squeeze, with the lawyers screaming for money." On December 11th, the management committee met, and "we had to come up with a bogey of going to the partners and saying—"

Ms. Marshall asked, *What's a bogey?* Speaking for the entire court-room.

"A target, you know, this is our goal. Alan had all the financial projections in front of him, and we are sitting there, and I remember it vividly, saying, 'What's the bogey?'" Tony had the bogey figured. "I said, 'It seems to me now it's probably about $2 million.' But I'm a conceptual person. I'm not a strict numbers guy. Alan looked up and said, 'Yup, that's just right,' and somebody else said, 'So our bogey is going to be $2 million. We'll put that out in a memo, and if we get it, we can make a distribution.'

"But I said, 'Let's make sure.' Because I'm thinking back to the problems I had with Alan and the landlord situation. We spread out the stuff, and looked at the expenses, and looked at what the cash requirements were. And it was clear that we needed at least $2.7 million to get to a point where we could make a distribution.

"I said, 'Alan, we just can't do this! We have got our butts against the wall, and people are screaming. If we put out a number, and they make it, and we don't give them cash, we are in deep yogurt. If people don't get paid, the best leave, and we'll be in a self-fulfilling prophecy of what happened to Gaston & Snow.'"

What did Alan say to your concerns about his accuracy?

"He was kind of indifferent. Alan seemed detached."

David objected. "The question is, what did he say?"

"He said nothing."

I was shocked by this assault, and so was the jury—especially his crude language—but then it hit me that Tony was working off his scribblings about my MS. He was attacking me as a gross incompetent, as expected, but he was describing my actions—or supposed lack of action—as the symptoms of multiple sclerosis. A whole nasty new stratagem.

But my memory of the meeting was quite different from Tony's. I'd reacted calmly because I was perfectly satisfied to have Tony raise the bogey on his own say. If they put out a figure of $2.7 million, I figured, maybe they'd work all that much harder to bring in the bills due. If they fell short, we'd still be okay at about $2 million. If they achieved the $2.7 million goal we'd be even better off. That was all to the good. So I quietly nodded as Tony set his own bogey.

"That was a Wednesday," Tony kept on. "On Saturday morning, we had another management committee meeting, and Robins is at it too, as a key player, because this was going to be a disastrous year. We had to find some place out there where we could say to the partners, 'It's worth sticking in here rather than putting your resumes out on the street and doing a dixie.' We went over the projections that Alan had, and I was terribly disappointed, as were the other people.

"What Alan had done was a pure economic computer-driven model. He got the number of lawyers, the number of hours they should work, put in their billing rates, multiplied them together, came out with a number. 'This is what our revenue's going to be.' Then he just carried forward our expenses from the prior year. 'This is what our expenses are going to be.'"

What was wrong with that? asked Ms. Marshall.

"You can't say every lawyer in the office was going to have enough business to keep him going," Tony said. "You can't just say, we sold fifty popsicles last year, we'll sell fifty popsicles this year, because you have to make sure people are going to eat popsicles."

Did Tony say anything to Alan Labonte about the disappointment?

"I said, 'This is cockamamie. I can tell you that two of the banks that I know of, that we have been getting big bucks from, ain't going to be here. A million dollars worth of billable income that isn't coming in.'"

Actually, I'd taken my projections to Mary Ellen O'Mara; she had made adjustments for each attorney based on her own "inside information," then we developed the final figures.

Ms. Marshall asked how I'd taken his criticism.

"He said, 'Well, I'm sorry.' Kind of shrugged his shoulders." Then that same slur on my MS. "He was indifferent."

Drastically, they decided that "a number of lawyers would have to be let go," even partners, along with their staff, "and that we would have to go to the landlord and give up a floor." Tony justified these draconic measures by telling the jury, "As they say on *Star Trek*, sometimes you have to sacrifice the few for the many. Either we had to lighten ship, or the ship would sink. But nobody was to breathe one word about the coming layoff, outside that room."

Was that made clear to everybody?

"Absolutely, in spades."

Then he found out from Robins, at next Wednesday's management committee meeting, that I had called in my key people to forewarn them of another layoff. Quite true. How else were we going to face up to the coming devastation unless we prepared to take steps in advance? But I unhappily had to talk, among my key people, to Charlie Gaziano. And Charlie didn't hesitate to rat me out.

"I was absolutely, positively livid," Tony roared. "It was also in the newspapers. I concluded that Alan Labonte was more of a hindrance and a detriment to the management and success and actual viability of Hutchins & Wheeler than he was an asset. That we could no longer afford to have him stay there, that he was a liability, that this, *this* blew my mind!"

Tony's passionate speech continued, "We had no other choice. Based upon his lack of performance and his leaking this information, he had to go." When I was fired in late January, Tony further claimed I had admitted to my mistakes. "Alan said that he agreed he was not focused, that he was not crisp in his decisions, that he was having problems." Once again, hinting at likely MS symptoms.

"He said he wasn't able to do the job, which caused him to be angry and to take it out on me. He looked at me and said, 'I'm sorry,' and I said, 'No problem.'" But Tony was adamant that he would never have me back on any conditions that I tried later to offer. "Because Alan had shown me that he could not keep a confidence, he was incapable of doing what had to be done, and we could not have him in the inner circle of what was happening."

Tony was not going over at all well as a witness. All his slang about bogeys and deep yogurt and popsicles seemed out of place in a court of law.

As Tony continued, there were huge contradictions between his deposition and his present testimony. Early on, David inquired about my responsibility for renting One Boston Place. Tony said it was "an essential part of Alan Labonte's job," but David interjected, *You didn't even remember that it was part of his job when I deposed you a year ago, did you?*

Tony responded, "I didn't know whether it was or it wasn't."

David continued, *Has your memory about the facts of this case improved since the time of your deposition, Mr. Medaglia?*

"Yes." And a few people chuckled at this classic blunder, particularly from a trained attorney.

Did it improve as the trial got closer?

"No."

David kept after him, *Why couldn't they provide me help "for, say, ten percent of the time" I was spending on billing and collection?*

"It's a unified job. How could you split the salami?"

Mr. Gaziano and Mr. Grein apparently are splitting the salami, aren't they?

"No, no, they're not," Tony insisted. "You don't split. You have got to have somebody with the mantle of authority do it. That was part and parcel of the job." He simply would not admit that Freddie was helping Charlie these days, as both of them had already partially admitted in court.

When the management committee decided to terminate Alan Labonte, did they discuss any ways in which they could accommodate his MS?

Again Tony retorted. "His termination had nothing to do with his multiple sclerosis."

David said that was not his question, moved to strike Tony's response, which was granted, and offered to repeat the question.

"You're asking a trick question," Tony snapped.

"No, Mr. Medaglia," Judge White interrupted. "He asks the questions. You either say yes, no, or I can't answer the question."

And Tony reluctantly answered "No," they hadn't discussed accommodating my MS.

David got other damaging admissions out of him. Or at least pretty strong indications that he wasn't exactly being forthright.

At the time of those negotiations to reduce the rent, had he tried to make the financial position of H & W look worse than it actually was?

"No."

Aware of anybody else at the partnership who did that?

"No."

But you didn't include Alan Labonte in those talks with the landlord?

"No."

Did Tony recall any demands made on Mr. Labonte's time that might have been at all inconsistent with his telling Alan to get needed rest?

"No."

Did you ever ask him if he was overworked?

"No."

Ever warn him that he was in danger of being fired?

"No, not in those words."

Hadn't Tony told Alan that his most important job was to think?

"That's the most important job that any of us have, yes."

And during their interview, when Tony asked him if he was tough enough for the job, hadn't Alan said, 'I think I'm smart enough'?

"Yes."

And on this thinking issue, hadn't even Dr. Wepsic told both Tony and Charles Robins that he didn't find any problem with Alan's ability to think?

"Yes."

How many attorneys were in the firm at that time, roughly?

"Ninety-seven."

Some of them not fully occupied?

"As lawyers."

None of them could have assisted Alan Labonte?

"They were the wrong people."

Not one of these ninety-seven lawyers was "the right people?"

"This was not a lawyer's function. I've tried to make that clear to you."

Please, please, Mr. Medaglia, David wound up. *You're saying none of these ninety-seven busy lawyers had any hours to spare? If these lawyers had spent any time helping Alan Labonte, that would have impacted on their revenue?*

"Precisely." Then he changed that to "Probably."

Ms. Marshall then asked, *Was he aware of any conversations between individuals on the management committee that took place outside the confines of an established meeting?*

"Absolutely not."

Did he have a habit of letting people know how he really felt about their work performance?

"Yes, I do. I don't hold back."

But David came at him again, with "Just one more question, Your

Honor," on recross. *Wasn't it the purpose of Tony's candor to give people feedback as to how they are doing?*

"Yes."

So he would certainly tell somebody if they were in danger of losing their job, wouldn't he?

"You don't tell someone—"

Would you, Mr. Medaglia, or wouldn't you?

"No."

Tony stepped down after what I believed had been his most atrocious, crude, and devious display of uncontrollable ego ever. He had blown up in front of the jury repeatedly during the hot, late afternoon. He had constantly contradicted himself, yet stubbornly held onto untenable positions, until he burst under David's pressure. I felt mischievously like applauding at the end of his testimony. What a performance!

Judge White dismissed the jury for the day and then called both attorneys into her chambers. An unusual move, as David told me afterwards. She leaned forward and stated that: "Mr. Medaglia has not done himself, nor his partners, any favors today. In light of his testimony and the fact that you have a sympathetic witness here in Alan Labonte, I strongly recommend that you enter into settlement discussions."

Chapter Eight

Judge White's surprising pronouncement sent David and me hurrying out of the courthouse—or as fast as I could go with my cane and brace—and back to his office. It was a prime opportunity for us, but also a worry to David, who hates to get caught in the lone lawyer's bind of simultaneously seeking a settlement and pressing his case at the same critical moment of trial. "Usually it happens just before a trial starts," he tells me. "Just as you're getting all charged up for the adversary process, along comes the offer to negotiate, and you're running in two different directions at once."

But this time it was the judge urging the parties to seek agreement, already more than halfway through the trial, after a long afternoon of Tony Medaglia. We started drawing up terms for a settlement, and it gradually dawned on me, this late in the day, as David scrawled away at his yellow legal pad, how alone and flying solo he was. He did have Diane to keep courtroom watch and advise him on trial strategy, but all the nitty gritty—searching out the cases and drafting memoranda on the day's disputed legal points—he had to do on his own. All this, *after* a full day's unrelenting court action as my counsel.

He got right down to the sharpest terms he could sketch out, a proposal for a payout of $750,000. We deliberately set this sum higher than we ever expected to recover. If we got anything in the $500,000 range, we then believed, we'd have died, in my words, and gone to heaven. David faxed our proposal over to Mary Marshall.

He didn't need to worry. There was no court session on Thursday, and when he showed up Friday in Judge White's lobby, before court opened, Ms. Marshall reported that her client might move closer to $100,000, but that wasn't a certainty. David dismissed that as far too low. It didn't even open up the possibility of reaching a settlement. Judge White nodded, and ordered the clerk to call in the jury.

So David's stretch of unease was, in his words, "mercifully brief." We were right smack back in the trial again, but a mystery remains how H & W could come up with such a ridiculously lowball counter to our offer. Ms. Marshall, by her demeanor, was giving nothing away, but we had to wonder if, as a young woman lawyer, she enjoyed any real clout with this difficult client.

She called Charlie Gaziano to the stand.

His testimony was about integrating the four Gaston & Snow lawyers into H & W back in November of 1991 when my father suddenly died down in Florida. David had just objected to going over this same ground again with Gaziano. "This is getting repetitious." So Judge White asked Ms. Marshall, "Could we speed this up a little bit?" Charlie promptly came on strong about how he had taken over in my absence and managed the whole transition, really despite me.

"I expected there would be some sort of a file, or a folder, or something," he complained, foxy as ever. "There was nothing, so I really had to scramble around and put this thing together."

"Nobody had thought it through," Charlie charged, meaning me—how to fit these four new lawyers, their secretaries, and two paralegals into the right chairs and desks, keep proper time-keeping and billing, and be integrated into the computer system.

Did he ask anyone to help "who had formerly been an employee of Hutchins & Wheeler?"

"Yes," he said. "Margaret Hadley."

Another intra-office revelation. "I was just up to my eyeballs," Charlie pleaded, so he brought "Margaret back three or four evenings to interview these secretaries and paralegals, just to take the strain off me." Without ever telling his supervisor—me—at a time when I was desperately trying to get the management committee to let me hire a replacement for Margaret Hadley.

Then merging two hundred Gaston & Snow trust files into the H & W trust accounting system proved to be "a mountain of work" for Charlie. Nights, weekends. Of course, that was Charlie's basic expertise and job assignment, so perhaps that's why he had never said word one about these Herculean labors to me. Instead, he went to Jack Clymer, his boss in trusts and estates, to bemoan his burdens. And eventually to Tony.

He stated that he said to Tony, "What's going on in this place? It's getting out of control. Administrative managers coming to me, day in, day out. I have people crying. I'm a little bit tired of it. What is Labonte doing here?"

What did Mr. Medaglia say?

"He said, 'I need to make an accommodation for Alan.' And that's all he would say to me."

Both David and I perked up at that. Gaziano had done his worst by me, and David would press him hard on cross about his working only thirty-five to forty hours per week, with help from Fred Grein, as interim administrator, but the trenchant legal point came out of that recollected shot from Tony.

David confronted Charlie on cross. *You testified that Mr. Medaglia said to you, 'I need to make an accommodation for Alan'?*

"'I need to make accommoda*tions* for Alan' is what he said," Charlie answered, changing to the plural.

Did he actually use the word "accommodation"?

"'Accommoda*tions*,'" Charlie re-emphasized the plural.

He did?

"Yes, he did."

There it was, sworn testimony that the managing partner uttered the word "accommodations" with reference to me—raising an inference that Tony understood his legal obligations.

The next witness to be called was Margaret Hadley herself. I hadn't seen her since she suddenly quit on me, and she came to the stand, poised as ever, tastefully dressed. Somehow she always reminded me of a high school cheerleader. But in her prim and proper way, she proceeded to discredit my work on every possible score. Her office was "right next door" to mine, our doors "abutted," and we shared a secretary, so she claimed to have had a close-up view of my daily comings and goings, my curtailed work schedule.

She testified that during my first year, she spent all of "five minutes" with me daily. Mary Marshall asked, *Was that enough?*

"I would say, not really." My door was "closed or ajar most of the time," and when she did hesitantly knock to enter, our exchanges were curt. "I felt he was impatient for me to leave. Just from his body language, his demeanor, I could tell he didn't want to prolong the conversation." Later, as our working relationship developed, I did become "a little more accessible," but she soon found that I wasn't up to speed on handling H & W affairs. "He spent half his day on personal matters," she had the nerve to say, "and a portion of his day on business matters."

This slander continued through her testimony on my struggles to convert H & W's health insurance to a single, self-funded plan. She criticized me, just as Medaglia had, for signing off on a plan that forced new medical providers on many employees, even though they could opt to pay more and stay with their present doctors. We'd arranged to grandfather all prior members into the Harvard plan, requiring only future employees to join the Tufts plan. But she went further and charged me with misleading Michael Gengler and Carol Brown, the two ERISA attorneys, when it was they who had failed to forewarn me of the tax problems involved.

It was the same story with everything else I had done. The decrease in overtime came from nothing I did. It was the economy, and "we were included in that down turned economy."

"He spent eighty percent of his day in his office," she claimed, offering her own close-at-hand observations on my exact working hours. "Approximately 9:15 to just about five o'clock."

And what were her own hours?

"8:30 to 6:30, most of the time."

After too much of this mistreatment, she decided to leave in the fall of 1991 and take a similar job with a small patent law firm. "They never had a personnel director before," she had explained to me, "and I thought it was a good opportunity."

But were there other reasons for your leaving that you did not share with Alan?

"Yes. I was uncomfortable with Alan's style of management. He didn't seem to provide any leadership. There was no longer a strong team feeling among the managers. There was anxiety among the staff, and I felt I had an opportunity to leave, so I took it."

And why didn't she tell me her real reasons?

"I didn't want to offer any complaints to him because I didn't want to burn my bridges. If my new position didn't work out, I was going to turn to Alan Labonte for a reference."

Instead, she returned soon enough to H & W after I left, in time to respond in writing to my application for unemployment benefits.

She had written that I'd been discharged, and she testified, "and the remarks section allows you to explain that," where she had typed in, "Unsatisfactory performance."

But later, when an official called her, "I said that the firm would not oppose Alan Labonte's claim." That was her contribution to H & W's beneficence.

David, however, was having none of this, and on cross, immediately demanded, *Ms. Hadley, when you spoke to Alan Labonte about the reasons why you were resigning from Hutchins & Wheeler, you were not truthful with him about those reasons, were you?*

Ms. Marshall sharply objected, but David snapped, "Cross-examination, Your Honor."

"Overruled."

David continued, *You were not truthful with Alan Labonte on that occasion, were you, Ms. Hadley?*

"Not completely."

David pounced on that. *You told part of the truth?* She ah-hummed, then said, "Yes, I did," and David kept after her for so dissembling, because maybe she was thinking she might want to return one day to H & W. She denied that, but her denial didn't hold much water, since there she was, right back at H & W.

You did testify a few moments ago in this courtroom that you didn't want to burn any bridges, that was why you didn't tell Alan the whole truth?

"That's correct. But I also said—"

David stopped her cold, and then, over Ms. Marshall's objections, got her to admit that her salary had since jumped from sixty-five to seventy thousand dollars.

Now, hadn't she also testified that I was spending half of my day on personal matters?

"Yes."

And how many hours, from her close-up observations, constituted an entire day for Alan Labonte?

"Seven."

So I was then spending an average of three and a half hours each day on personal matters as distinct from my work as executive director?

"Yes."

And did Alan Labonte have his door closed a lot of the time?

"Yes."

So how could she know, clearly she didn't know what he was really doing when he had his door closed, did she?

"No."

You're guessing, aren't you?

"Yes."

Is there some reason, Ms. Hadley, why you want to try to minimize the amount of time Alan Labonte spent on his official duties as executive director?

"No."

Soon enough, she was getting flustered. Her face flushed in embarrassment, and she began to reveal a distinct animus toward me. David brought up the complaints of employees about having to leave the Harvard plan and change doctors. *Hadn't I recommended that these H & W employees be grandfathered into the new plan, meaning they could keep their rights under the old plan?*

"Yes," she said, "but only after there was a disapproval at the firm meeting, against our dissolving the Harvard Community Health Plan."

Okay, David said. *So he reacted to this disapproval by coming up with a solution, correct?*

"Yes," she had to admit, as she began to backtrack on other accusations she had no way of showing, or sometimes even knowing, were true.

David left her a hardly credible witness to what little she faultily recalled, and Ms. Marshall's redirect didn't do much to rehabilitate her. Over David's objection, Margaret Hadley reiterated her charge that I isolated myself from the staff. "He wasn't visible. They didn't know him. Secretaries would not go up to his office and ask him questions. They would come into my office."

On recross, David got her to admit this was exactly as it should be. *Because when a secretary had a problem, she was supposed to come to you, wasn't she?*

"That's right."

A problem, say with overtime, you weren't suppose to bang on Alan's door, were you?

"No, and I never did."

But she had gone into Alan, at the last, to discuss her own problems before resigning from the firm, though not quite all of them. *The reason you didn't tell him the whole truth about why you were leaving was be-*

cause you thought you might need a reference from him someday, is that true?

"Yes."

So in order to obtain some kind of a benefit for yourself, you were willing to tell less than the truth, is that correct?

"Yes." She spoke this last yes like a penitent, into an ominous silence.

David thanked her, as well he might, and then came over to me, and whispered, "Stick a fork in her, she's done."

To a toasty T, but the last member of the firm, up next on the stand, was another proposition altogether.

Eleanor Lanes had to be H & W's star witness. She has been loyally with the firm since 1979, a spinster, the source of support for her sick mother and ailing father in Marblehead, Massachusetts, and an avid Boston Red Sox fan. She was a small woman, dressed in a stylish grey suit, bravely playing her own disability to the hilt. When called by Ms. Marshall, she walked slowly and deliberately to the witness box. She stumbled and a court officer came forward and offered his arm, which she gratefully accepted, as he helped her up the one step into her seat.

She came across as a rock-ribbed Yankee hard luck case. She'd done two years of business college, then went nights to BU, but never did get her accounting degree. "I had a sick mother," she told the jury, "and there were numerous bills, and I just went to work." In brokerage houses for twenty-five years, until she was hired by H & W for "the bookkeeping job." She'd worked on their financials with pencil and paper, on long green sheets with neat numbers, for over a decade, until she had "a very cordial relationship" with Mr. Robins. "I saw him every day. He'd always stop by to ask me how much money came in the day before."

She was out on medical leave when I came to the firm, with an array of ailments that she summarized for Ms. Marshall.

Has the firm made accommodations for your medical condition?

"They have always been very accommodating," she extolled her bosses. "Any time I have had to go to the doctor for anything, they have never given me a hard time. They never asked me to make up the time."

Here was an entirely new view of H & W as an institution with a heart, from someone who was eliciting a lot more sympathy than the two prior witnesses. Even I had trouble keeping it straight who was supposed to be the Neediest Case here.

Eleanor had assisted me from her home in Marblehead until she returned to work, when I shifted her office closer to mine and Margaret's, from her niche near the accounting department, six doors away. "He said, 'Please, I want you closer to where I'm located.'" But she was worried about being that far away from her own department.

Did she tell him that she had difficulty walking?

"He knew I had difficulty in walking, so—"

David objected, "Did she *tell* him?"

"No, I didn't."

The management committee had raised questions about her being paid full salary over a three-months absence, not me. I reminded myself I was the one who saved her job. But other rude surprises lay ahead.

Actually, according to Eleanor, I'd only redesigned one of the financials. "The balance sheet. He condensed it." From two pages to one. She'd made all the other changes. Nor would I stay late, past six o'clock, to approve the monthly billing.

Then there was the abrupt departure of Margaret Hadley. To my astonishment, Eleanor said I hadn't wanted to replace her—hard as I kept trying, in the face of Tony's resistance—"because it wouldn't look good on the budget." So, when I divided up Ms. Hadley's tasks among the three of us, Eleanor felt overburdened with the extra work.

"I'm not a human resources person. I never went to school for it. Sometimes I'm very shy with people." Then she unloaded a bitter series of complaints about straightening out the health insurance payments, disability payments, life insurance payments, and having to call people about excessive overtime charges.

"They came up there, and they were yelling at me and screaming at me, and they demanded their money," so she sent them "to Alan Labonte, who said, 'Pay them, we'll deal with it later after the first of the year.'" When she told Mr. Robins, just before I was terminated, "He was aghast."

There was worse, but it is all best exemplified by her testimony about my returning my mother to Florida over those three days in early December. It was too busy a time for me to leave, Eleanor insisted, and claimed I told her, "'I don't do anything. What difference does it make whether I'm here or not? You run the show.'"

Was he right?

"Yes."

David was worried about her effect on the jurors, who were greatly charmed by her—another of H & W's walking wounded. I knew she was killing me up there, but somehow I still couldn't bring myself to feel she was being malicious. She was simply, once again, showing her full loyalty to Mr. Robins and the firm.

Back on the stand, after her break, she said she still hesitated to complain about me to any partner. "Alan is a nice person. Very kind, very quiet. But I don't think he had any concept when he said, 'Do this, do that'—how long and hard it was to do." She finally did go to Mr. Robins. "I can't handle it all, I just can't. I can't do my job, Alan's job, and Margaret's job. It's just too much. I'm going to get sick."

Now came new charges from the witness that I was growing forgetful.

And finally there was the cancelled stub. She had been doing "a mammoth amount of work because it's like keeping two sets of records." As I've already painfully described myself.

When did Alan say anything to her about that stub period?

About the middle of January. "'Oh, we did away with the stub,' he said. 'We're not going to have a stub period this year.'"

"I was very upset. 'Alan, you knew I was coming in weekends. Why didn't you tell me? It would have eliminated a lot of my work.' He said he was told not to tell me."

"I was very, very upset. Basically, that was the straw that broke the camel's back. I went charging down to Mr. Robins' office, stood outside his door, and I said, 'I want to talk to you.' I just let it all hang out. I started in by saying how much work I was doing, and they were going to kill me out there! Then, this is ridiculous, you didn't tell me about the firm meeting, you didn't tell me about the stub period. No job is worth it!"

That tirade put Robins into a panic, and he promised he would take care of everything.

Then Fred Grein came to her with a generous offer—an accommodation, if you will—to help her do the financials. "He really thought it would be much easier for me if I learned Lotus 1-2-3. He was going to give me an incentive. If I learned how within a year—and they would provide schooling if I needed it, or anything else—they would not only set up a Lotus system in my house, so I could be with my dad who is now eighty-six-and-a-half with cancer and a heart condition, but I could work at home if I had to, in the winter when I wasn't mobile. He would also give me a $10,000 bonus if I learned how to do it within the year."

Ms. Marshall let Eleanor end her testimony on a note of triumph. *Did she get her bonus?*

"Yes, I did. Boy, I was determined to get that."

And the jury loved her. Adored her. David got up, set on seeing her pass from their further view as soon as possible. He began by inquiring, *First, Ms. Lanes, do you feel good enough for me to ask you a few questions?*

"Can we go about fifteen minutes," she replied, "and then I will stand up, if you don't mind." David told Judge White he would only be fifteen minutes. The judge informed the witness, "We don't want to make you have to come back on Monday, so—" Indeed we did not, so everybody was ready to proceed with her polite and expeditious dispatch.

David quizzed her carefully on the private work she did for Robins on his P.C., his two checkbooks, and his taxes. She said it took her all of "maybe five hours a month," for which Robins paid her.

Was she loyal to Robins? Did she like him?

"I think he's very, very nice." All of which might have gone some way toward establishing her bias, but she shrewdly added, "In fact, Mr. Labonte used to always say Mr. Robins was like a brother to him."

David kept trying. *About an unwelcome errand I had sent her on, had she said to Alan, I don't want to go?*

"No, because I'm the type of person, if somebody asks me to do something, I do it. I have done that all my working days."

But if there was some reason she couldn't do it, she'd tell Mr. Labonte, wouldn't she?

"No, I would just do it. I'd keep my mouth shut and do it."

She wouldn't tell Mr. Labonte, 'Gee, I don't really want to do that'?

"No, I wouldn't."

There was simply no shaking her stubborn, canny loyalty to the firm, though perhaps the jury might be brought to see how obliged to H & W she really was. David brought out how much the firm had lately done to ease her difficulties between office and home. More agreeable hours. "Now that I have the system at home," she said, "I try to get there by five because I have got to make sure my father is taken care of." How well she was compensated—$95,000, including "the $10,000 Lotus learning bonus"—and her plans to remain at Hutchins & Wheeler, forever.

We were glad to see this court day end. David's cross-examination of Margaret Hadley had been devastating, but he hadn't been able to do much with Eleanor. She even described me tactically bowing to her long experience. "He used to always say I was the boss," she half boasted. We could only hope the jury—after the weekend to reflect, then hearing my rebuttal testimony on Monday—would recover from their brief infatuation with Eleanor. It wasn't a question of how good or accommodating the firm had been to her, but rather the serious question of whether they had made any accommodations for me.

* * *

Ms. Marshall started off that Monday with an expert witness—an executive recruiter from Isaacs and Miller named Alan Wichley. Appropriately pronounced "wishly" since Mr. "Wishly" believed I had a "reasonable chance" of obtaining a job in the health care field in the Boston area for a salary of $80,000-135,000. On cross by David, Mr. Wichley continued optimistic about my chances, but, *Had he ever placed an executive who'd been terminated and also had MS?*

"No."

And would having been fired by H & W for poor performance affect how an employer might view any job application from Alan Labonte?

"Yes."

That left us feeling much relieved during the brief recess. "Why would she bring in a guy to say I could have gotten a better job?" I pondered aloud. "Sounds like damage control to me. They're thinking we might just win this thing, so they're trying to impact the amount of money the jury could award for back pay." If so, they now sent out their last remaining officer, Fred Grein.

Grein had been in court every day of the trial, and he looked really tired and worn out. Usually he sat alone, back in a chair located near the exit where the jury always had to file close by him. Sometimes he moved up at the defense table to talk animatedly with Mary Marshall and her assistant about some legal point. He was civil, even bland, but he was definitely the point man for H & W.

"I did interview Alan, yes," Grein testified about my hiring. "I remember him saying one of his strengths was very strong financial skills." And I remembered how Grein seemed dubious at the time. One morning, soon after I'd started, Grein said Robins came to him and "basically said, 'Thank you for what you've done as treasurer.

You don't have to come to meetings anymore. You're relieved of those duties.'"

There it was, still smoldering—his resentment—though he'd soon enough caught up with my shortcomings, since I kept coming to him with questions that indicated I wasn't "really getting a grasp of the firm's finances."

Then, one more time, I had to hear how I'd screwed up their health insurance. At least Grein had enough compunction to say he was first concerned, as a member of the Harvard plan, "that my premiums were going to go up." But his real complaint was the usual one. "In February I spent three weeks in the hospital and a week and a half at home recuperating from a major medical problem, and now I'm being told, two months later, I've got to change my doctors whom I've been working with. Alan never asked me about this, never talked to anybody about it. I was irate at the firm meeting, and I let my views be known rather strongly."

In October of 1991, the management committee voted and the partners agreed to Grein becoming managing partner on January 1. They told him about my MS and their wish to see that I didn't get too fatigued. We had something of a meeting of the minds on future shared responsibilities, but Grein insisted he never agreed to assume any of my functions or duties, decrease my work load, or take over responsibility for encouraging attorneys to bill and collect.

In fact, closer contact only led him to conclude that I "hadn't really learned how the firm operated from a financial standpoint." He also backed up Margaret Hadley's and Eleanor Lanes' complaints against me.

It all came out so pat, and damning. Amazing how many of my staff and compeers had long been keeping a close weather eye out for my problems! "Alan hadn't really learned anything in a year and a half, didn't know enough about the firm's finances and was relying exclusively on Eleanor Lanes."

On another crucial matter, he now spoke right up. Ms. Marshall asked him, *Mr. Grein, did you tell Mr. Labonte not to inform Eleanor Lanes that the firm was eliminating the stub period?*

"No, I did not."

That denial, made under oath, really astonished me. On cross, David pressed him harder. *Had Grein ever told anybody on the management committee about his doubts concerning my financial skills, or said anything critical to me?*

"No, I did not."

Wasn't he somewhat concerned that the executive director didn't have any grasp of the firm's finances?

"I thought it was catastrophic."

It was catastrophic, but you didn't bring that danger to Alan Labonte's attention, did you?

"No, I did not."

He still denied he'd helped Gaziano on billing and collection in ways nobody had ever been willing to help me. All Grein would admit, "I walk around very late in the afternoon of the last day of the month with Charlie to make sure that we," and he caught himself. "That *he's* kicked all the doors, and nobody's left any bill that should have gone up to accounting." Until David refuted him with his own deposition.

So the truth is, Mr. Grein, David asked, *you do walk around to get the lawyers to bill and collect, don't you?*

"Very infrequently."

But David still kept after him. *Mr. Gaziano does ask for help with a difficult partner who's having trouble billing and collecting, doesn't he?*

"He'll ask for advice on how to approach a particular person."

Sometimes *"you actually approach that person, don't you?"*

"Very rarely."

But sometimes Mr. Gaziano has to bring in the heavy artillery, doesn't he?

"*He's* the heavy artillery," Grein had the nerve to say. "I'm not."

Ludicrous. And everybody in the courtroom, especially the jurors, knew it. And things only got more ludicrous when Ms. Marshall called her final witness, Jonathan Bashein, who had my job at Peabody & Brown, another law firm in our same building.

I knew Jon well enough, as a colleague who often walked with me to meetings of the Association of Law Firm Administrators. We'd discussed mutual problems, even arranged for our two firms to share storage space. Jon's tenure went back much farther than mine, so he'd long known Hutchins & Wheeler. "They've always been right on top of us, both at One Boston Place and 101 Federal." But what upset me was how he used and twisted this knowledge to zap me.

Jon was there, as a paid expert witness, to show how much better he could have done my job than I ever did. "I'm not aware of any law firm of any size in Boston," he first testified, "where lawyers take a strong hand in the billing and collection process." He himself used cajolery, effrontery, and badgering. "I'm not a lawyer, and therefore I have the freedom and ability and guts, and it takes a lot of guts, to go after these men and women and force them to do the job that is most difficult for them to do."

Bashein also readily admitted to his success in gaining a consensus within Peabody & Brown to change one of their health insurance carriers. "And it's a real hot button for lawyers in particular to change an insurance carrier." He stood up to members of the executive committee as "the odd man out"—"I have to stare them down"—and made a point of keeping constantly in touch with all staff and attorneys over 60,000 square feet of office space. "I will walk around the firm rather than send anything interoffice. I always walk around the firm."

There was more of this effusive devotion to duty, "I'm a pretty good forest fire fighter. Lawyers start the fires, and I put them out." But I didn't stay around for it. I was frankly revolted by his smugness and conceit, a thin veneer over his dirty work on my competence. I couldn't stand to listen anymore. I got up and walked out of the courtroom.

I slumped down on the bench outside the courtroom, at a loss to explain why I was feeling such revulsion. And weariness. Listening to somebody that I had considered a friend and colleague, someone of my own status in the Boston legal community. Someone who understood the edgy, ragged crises within a law office, and hearing him testify, if only by indirection, against his fellow professional, just disgusted me.

I only caught up with everything Bashein had to say later by reading the trial transcript, but the worst of it was his "opinion to a reasonable degree of professional certainty" that I couldn't possibly do the administrative job with my MS, no matter what accommodations were made.

But I was out in the hall, hunched over the bench, and looking pretty ashen. Lora came out to get me an ice-cold drink, always an elixir for my MS. Then Diane came out, along with daughter Cary, who was carrying her plastic dinosaurs. Diane, I later learned, was greatly worried. She knew David wasn't aware of my absence—this was the only time I had skipped out on the trial— and she saw right away I wasn't "the capable and vigorous" specimen we were determined to project to the jury.

"Was he even going to be able to testify?" Diane wondered, since David had plans to call me next for rebuttal.

So they went to work on me, all three of them. Lora arrived back with a cold drink that had deliciously soothing slushed ice in it, and Diane gave me gentle but strong encouragement to return to court.

So I rallied. "He pulled himself together," Diane says, "and somehow got ready to give his best testimony of the whole trial."

I returned to my back row seat, just in time to catch David on cross. David pressed Bashein to admit there were no set standards for how law firms assigned duties to an administrator. David asked, *They can do what they want to do, can't they?*

"They're lawyers," Bashein shrugged. "They always do what they want to do."

At his close, David managed a retort. Jon had been defending his native abilities to get his attorneys to bill and collect. "The only hammer I have is embarrassing these people," he argued. "Authority has nothing to do with it." They had once tried using other lawyers for two years. Pointless. "The lawyers don't want to tell other lawyers what they have to do."

David asked, *No lawyers want to tell other lawyers what they have to do?*

"Very few."

Have you ever met Anthony Medaglia?

"No."

Mary Marshall quickly objected, but the whole courtroom exploded in laughter.

After Jon Bashein's testimony, Judge White, in an unexpected move, announced that she was going to release the jury early, that she had another matter that required her attention.

This provided me with a welcome, necessary and blessed reprieve. I returned the next day, fully refreshed, to take the stand one last time myself.

David hit every hot button, and his questions came at me, staccato. *Did the management committee ever take steps to get delinquent attorneys to bill and collect?*

"Yes. We would sort of divide the list up, and Mr. Medaglia would take some of the attorneys on the list, and Mr. Robins would take some and then—"

How was it decided who took which attorneys?

"The person was selected who would have the most influence over the lawyer who was delinquent. For example, Mr. Robins would talk to Mr. Westra or one of the other attorneys who was working on matters related to Mr. Robins' clients."

How frequently did this happen?

"When Mr. Robins was chairman, it happened practically every month."

It felt so good to get that off my chest, and on the record!

Now, there has been testimony from Mr. Grein that in the fall of 1991, early winter, in his view, "you weren't doing much of anything." How about that, what hours was I working?

"I worked long hours, every day. And every Saturday. I was also doing a lot of the work Margaret Hadley had done before. It was just constant. We were going through our year-end closing. A very demanding time."

Did I do work at home?

"Yes."

In the evening?

"Yes."

When Mr. Medaglia set out to negotiate with the landlord in the fall of 1991, was I involved in those negotiations?

"No." But they are saying I didn't get information to Mr. Medaglia until the day before his meeting with the landlord.

When did he first request that information from you?

"I believe he requested it the day before the meeting."

How much information?

"Quite a bit."

And what did I do to comply?

"I went to Eleanor and asked her to run the necessary reports. But I didn't present the reports that Eleanor prepared. I gathered information from her computer reports, created my own summary, and presented that to Mr. Medaglia."

And what happened?

"Basically, he looked at the report and said, 'This is no good.'"

Did he say why?

"He said, 'It makes us look too good.'"

What did I say?

"Those are the numbers. That's our financial position at this moment. This is where we are today."

What did he say?

"He made one of his bread-on-the-table speeches. He basically said, 'Look, we are going to the landlord. We are going to ask them to take bread off their table and put it on our table. And they aren't going to do that unless we show them that we are starving up here.'"

Did the numbers show that the firm was starving?

"No."

There is far more to this humiliating run-in with Tony, as I've already described, but at least I'd gotten that much out in the open including his parting salvo, "I'll get my own numbers," for the jury to weigh.

Once Tony became chairman, David then asked, *Did I ever have difficulty locating him when I needed him?*

"Yes. Tony was constantly either not in his office, or in his office but—you know, sealed off. Most of the time his secretary would say, 'He's not seeing anybody right now.' Or you couldn't find him. I would track him down, but when I posed a question that I had, he wouldn't want to respond. 'Don't bother me with that, Alan. I'm busy with other things.'"

David brought up the transfer of the Gaston & Snow attorneys.

"I met with all of them. I traveled over to their offices. I reviewed the benefit plans we had. I brought them forms which they needed to fill out, and I processed the forms, and gave them to Eleanor so she could enter them into the payroll system."

Did I give any instructions to Mike Dunham to help get these lawyers settled?

"We determined the office locations, where the support staff would be going, how many boxes they would be bringing over. What kind of desks and furniture needed to be moved, what we needed to acquire, those kind of things."

And what did I ask Charlie Gaziano to do when I suddenly had to fly to Florida?

"I asked him to work with Mike. Mike knew what he had to do, but I needed Charlie to be available because things never go off quite the way you planned."

Apropos of those complaints about my "closed door," would I explain to the jury what my practice was when I was in my office?

And I was quick to reply that keeping my door ajar—never really closed—originated from dire warnings given to me by Charlie Gaziano.

"When I came to the firm, Charlie said, 'You have got to be real careful about the way you handle confidential stuff. You need to lock those files when you go home at night. In fact, you need to lock those files whenever you leave your office.'" I kept my door swung almost shut to screen my desk, when I was working on these confidential records. "I left it open a little bit so that someone could poke their head in, if they needed to."

Did they ever do that?

"Sure."

Did you see them if you could?

"Sure." And David took me through the many ways—knocking, voice mail, notes on a spindle—in which I made myself readily available to staff.

Now, Margaret Hadley testified you worked from 9:15 to 5:00 roughly. Were those your hours, Mr. Labonte?

"No."

Did I recall occasions when I was there longer than Ms. Hadley?

"Yes. Margaret generally caught her train to Braintree from South Station at 5:40 or 5:45. And every afternoon she would change her shoes and put on some 'flats.' Then I would hear her run down the corridor to catch her train."

Any nights when I was there longer than Eleanor Lanes?

"Yes."

What were my working hours, in the fall of 1991?

Between 8:30 and 9:00 until after 5:00, the average was 6:00 to 6:30. But many, many nights—I worked until my work was organized for the next day."

Did I recall Eleanor Lanes testifying that I didn't stick around late in the evening at the end of the billing month, when she was still getting out the bills?

"I usually stuck around for as long as I could be useful."

Eleanor Lanes testified that when she got back from her medical leave, she found all her vacation time had been used up.

Did I have anything to do with that?

"No."

Who was responsible for docking vacation time if someone was out for too long a stretch?

"Margaret Hadley."

Excuse me?

"Margaret Hadley."

Did Eleanor Lanes ever complain to you about somebody taking away her vacation time?

"No. She didn't."

Then I explained how I had helped her further free up vacation time for the Boston Red Sox spring training camp in Florida by my learning to do the payroll entries, which were considered so confidential. "It involved sitting with Eleanor, by her side at the computer terminal, for an hour to two hours, over a week to ten days."

There were still three Big Ticket items yet to deal with.

First, there had been testimony—Mr. Grein, for one, lately criticized my work—that I did my financial projections by just taking the attorneys' going rates, and the number of hours they billed last year, then multiplying—and doing nothing else.

Had I done anything further to prepare those projections for the December 14th meeting?

"Yes, I worked with a member of the management committee."

With whom?

"Mary Ellen O'Mara."

What did the two of you add to those financial projections?

"One by one we went through the eighty plus attorneys. Some she added hours on, others she took 'em off. Some she changed the billing rates, some she didn't. And then I reran the report."

Had I spoken earlier to these partners whose projections I was doing?

"As many as I could."

How did the management committee receive my report?

"They seemed to be receptive to the whole financial package."

Did I recall Mr. Medaglia yelling at me about the report?

"I don't."

Second, there is testimony that at that meeting, cutting staff was discussed, and all present were pledged to secrecy. But I spoke later to Mr. Gaziano and Mr. Dunham, and that was a breach of confidentiality.

What was I asked to do by the management committee that led me to speak to these two managers?

"They were pressuring me to make more cuts. And I said, 'Wait a second. I have cut twenty-three people out of the non-legal staff, and you guys have only cut seven attorneys. How about you guys talking about reducing some professional staff before you ask me to cut more people that I can't cut?'"

That's when they got brutal. They would discuss cutting attorneys privately. And they said, "'And you're not going to be here. That's our business. We want you to look at Gaziano's area. He's a fat cat down there. Lots of people. He hasn't given up anybody. We want you to talk to him. Dunham's got a lot of people working for him in mail and messenger. You can cut two or three people there. And next time we sit down, this coming Wednesday, we want you here, front and center, telling us where you are going to cut.'"

Would I ever consider coming up with names of people to cut from Mr. Gaziano's staff without talking with Charlie Gaziano?

"No."

Why?

"Because I felt he ran a tight ship, and I knew Mike did. If they are going to have to bleed, I'm going to give them an opportunity to have input prior to making my decisions. And if they can't do it, I'm just going to the management committee and say, 'No, we can't make any cuts.' So I sat down with them, and we talked about it."

And third, with regard to Eleanor Lanes not being told the stub had been cancelled, did I have any conversations with Mr. Grein about informing Eleanor that the stub had been eliminated?

"Yes. I did."

Where did they take place?

"Either in Fred's office or just outside his office."

Was it one conversation, or more than one?

"More than one."

Substance of the first conversation?

"I said, 'Fred, we have got to tell her because she is doing all this work, and it's all going to be for nothing.'"

What did he say?

"'Not yet.'"

How long after that first conversation did I have a second conversation with Mr. Grein?

"About two days later."

And what did I say?

"I said, 'Fred, we have got to tell Eleanor what's going on.'"

What did he do or say?

"He didn't say anything."

That last statement gave me a deep sense of satisfaction. The jury will ultimately have to figure out whom to believe. But, at least I've had my chance to tell my side of the story. "It could have been so different," I said at the last, over Ms. Marshall's objections. I was relieved when Tony Medaglia said, after learning about my MS, "It's a good thing we are bringing Freddie along." After Fred Grein was named managing partner, I went to him to discuss "how we could begin to work together as partners. He would become the CEO of the firm, and I would be able to concentrate fully on the operations as COO, the job I was hired to do."

With my testimony, gratefully, out of the way, now, at last, we were approaching the end of this ten-day court battle, with the two counsels ready to give their closing remarks to the jury.

Mary Marshall spoke first for the defendants, and she stuck to the guns she had already leveled at me. Once I contracted MS —if not even before, but certainly afterwards—I simply couldn't hack it. The jury needed to consider "only two facts." One, she began, "Alan Labonte was not able to do the job of firm administrator as of January 1992," and two, "nothing Hutchins & Wheeler could have done would have enabled him to do the job."

She was sternly medical on her first point, maybe overly technical in arguing I couldn't physically or mentally do this "stressful, demanding job." But she went on to ask, why didn't I ever go to those people I knew so well at the firm and say, "I can't do this, I need some help"? Because, she said curtly, "What he needed the firm to do, as he has testified, is remove his job responsibilities."

If relieved of these "essential job functions," I claimed that I could still have supervised my department heads. But they have all come in and testified, "and every single one of them said that he did not supervise him. They worked around him." Especially Eleanor Lanes, a handicapped person for whom H & W has done many things to enable her to work. But Mr. Labonte doesn't ask that here. "He wants you essentially to rip his job to shreds. He wants you to take away this responsibility, take away that responsibility, and what is left is a part-time job."

She then hit on a last analogy for the jury to ponder. Her whole emotional tone changed. Earlier that summer, her son had tried out for a Little League baseball team. "He didn't get on it, so we went to the coach because he wanted to know why he hadn't made the team. And my son, who is going to be in fifth grade, said, 'Coach, I think I should have gotten on the team. I'm really a good hitter, and I'm really a good runner.'

"And the coach said, 'You're right. You're a good hitter, and you're a good runner. But you can't catch the ball, and you don't throw very well. If you want to be on the team, you've got to do everything that a baseball player has to do. Unless you can do those things, you can't be on the team.'

"And the coach was right. Unless you can do all the jobs that your position requires, you can't keep that position. And you can't maintain a law suit alleging that your employer terminated you wrongfully when, in fact, Mr. Labonte could not do the job."

It struck a strong chord, this chastening Little League story, sounding a human note in Ms. Marshall's appeal for the first time in all her trial presentation. David admitted he was impressed, and a tad worried. He stepped forward, without notes, taking up his midway position in front of the jury, but still well back from the rail. He had told me earlier, "You never want to invade their space." He then began a detailed chat about what he argued was handicap discrimination against Alan Labonte.

"Ladies and Gentlemen, this is a case about respect." Respect for the law, and respect for the people whom the law is designed to protect. "Hutchins & Wheeler did not obey the law, and they almost got away with it, but Alan Labonte decided to fight back." Yes, I could honestly admit as much, at long last. "And he is here before you seeking justice."

I had an abrupt sense of "How-Else-Could-It-Be?" as David laid out in simplest outline the scheme H & W had perpetrated. "Let's just step back and look at the timing. Alan Labonte goes to work for Hutchins & Wheeler as executive director. A year later he gets a good performance review and he gets a raise. Then he gets multiple sclerosis. Then he gets fired." David postulated "a relationship" among these events that he would substantiate as a plot to get rid of me, in guilty haste for fabricated reasons. I recalled how this echoed what one of the mock trial jurors had told us.

"No one questioned his integrity previously." Now they come forward with a crowd of witnesses who "would not give him credit for anything." But they have a big problem. "The problem is, Mr. Robins gave him a good review and a raise. What does Robins say? He tried to tell you that the reason Alan Labonte was given a raise was to, quote, protect our investment. Double talk! The man wouldn't even admit they gave Alan a raise to approve his performance."

Then they claim—Fred Grein, only yesterday—that Alan never had any "grasp of finances." Still, nobody including Fred ever voiced that criticism to Alan or the management committee, even though everybody, from all department heads to Tony Medaglia, apparently "knew."

But would anybody like Fred Grein, knowing how supposedly inept I was—how "catastrophic" for the firm—just "keep quiet about it? Of course not."

David closed the loop, into a dangling noose. "It was not true. These are reasons they made up after the fact to justify terminating a man with multiple sclerosis. They had to come up with reasons. They can't admit it was because of the multiple sclerosis. No, sir! Why, then? Well, because he did this, he did that . . . " And David plunged forward, still without notes, into the intricate details of their crude deceptions.

"You remember the only criticism Alan told you he recalled receiving from Mr. Robins at his annual review was that he was fighting too hard for his people. Trying to get them raises, and Robins said, 'We don't want to feel you are on the other side of the table.' He'd even offered to give his Christmas bonus to Mr. Gaziano and Eleanor Lanes! Is this the kind of man who has no decent relationship with his staff? And would they have given him that significant bonus if he was sitting all the time in his office with his door closed, refusing to meet people?"

They never warned me, either verbally or in writing. "You don't fire somebody like Alan Labonte who has just moved his family, sold his house in Greenfield, bought a house in Cohasset. He went out on a limb for them. Then what did they do? They sawed it off behind him and let him fall down." Is this because I proved a disappointment to them from the start, only got myself ever deeper into trouble? "The answer is, he wasn't in terrible trouble. They are making it all up after the fact."

Consider what happened when I told them to see my doctors about my MS. "Who do they go see? Dr. Wolpow? Not interested, no. They saw Dr. Wepsic, their client. And this is an extraordinary meeting, Ladies and Gentlemen, because there is a conflict in the testimony."

David reminded the jury of Dr. Wepsic's stipulation, which he had read aloud to them earlier, what Dr. Wepsic had actually said.

"*He* said that, if possible, Mr. Labonte should not have to walk too much, so it would be helpful if they could locate Mr. Labonte closer to people he had to see frequently. *They* indicated they did not feel that walking was important, and were more concerned about Mr. Labonte's mental ability and attention to the job. And now they *deny* that Dr. Wepsic ever told them to consider relocating Mr. Labonte's office."

David took that conflict straight to the heart of our case, reminding the jury that every defense witness "got on the stand and told you it was important for Alan Labonte to walk around the firm. They all believed it. Their expert, Mr. Bashein, believed it." Yet nothing was done to arrange for any accommodation, they never even considered it.

"They didn't care, Ladies and Gentlemen. They didn't care about him or his multiple sclerosis. Remember how he testified—and this is important, Ladies and Gentlemen—he perceived a change in their attitude after he told them he had multiple sclerosis. They started staying away from him, didn't come too close to him. He was like an outcast. You may conclude from that—that these people didn't want somebody with multiple sclerosis as their executive director."

Next, David addressed Ms. Marshall's full-bore attempt "to convince you he couldn't do the essential functions of the job." He drew attention to "Alan's increased workload, and their blaming him for not working harder," but concluded, "now, where is it carved in stone about the essential functions of the executive director?

"Remember Charles Gaziano? He was the acting executive director for a year before Alan was hired, and then he became the acting executive director again for two years after Alan left. His job duties were essentially very similar to Alan's. There were some things that Alan did that Mr. Gaziano didn't do, yet the firm survived, didn't they? They have done quite nicely with Mr. Gaziano spending about thirty-five to forty hours a week, both *before* Alan and *after* Alan, as executive director. In addition to his regular duties."

Then David hurled his deadly stone at this stumbling Goliath. "They were able to accommodate Mr. Gaziano's schedule. You can almost look at it as if Mr. Gaziano had a handicap. Mr. Gaziano was running the trust department, and he had to spend about thirty-five to forty hours a week doing that, so they accommodated the situation. Because they *wanted to*. They *wanted* to help him do it. They found some way to get it all done before and after Alan Labonte."

I could almost see him as the young prosecutor, back in New York City, whose sharp-edged rhetoric cut away the lies, and left their scheming exposed. "You are going to have to make many, many credibility determinations in this case, Ladies and Gentlemen," he warned. "They took Alan Labonte, and they didn't treat him the way they should have, the way the law required them to treat him.

"They kicked him around, and then they kicked him out."

On that last accusatory note, he turned to the Special Questions that Judge White would soon be submitting to the jury. Seven steps in inquiry that now tend to run together in my mind with David's pleas.

1. Was Alan Labonte a qualified handicapped person capable of performing the essential functions of the executive director position at Hutchins & Wheeler with reasonable accommodation to his multiple sclerosis? Yes___ No___

"If your answer is no, then that's the end of it," David said. "We have to prove he was capable of performing the essential functions with reasonable accommodations. I'm asking you to answer that question yes."

2. *Was the accommodation required to be made to Alan Labonte an undue hardship to Hutchins & Wheeler? Yes___ No___*

"There's been almost no believable argument made to you, at any time in the trial, that it would cost too much to accommodate Alan Labonte. If your answer is yes, that's the end. We ask you to answer no."

3. *Was Alan Labonte's termination by Hutchins & Wheeler a result of the failure by Hutchins & Wheeler to provide him with reasonable accommodation? Yes___ No___*

4. *Has Alan Labonte proved the reason given by Hutchins & Wheeler for his dismissal was not the real reason for his termination, and that he would not have been terminated but for his multiple sclerosis? Yes___ No___*

"We ask you to answer questions three and four yes." Though answering yes to *either* question would oblige the jury to take up the final three questions on damages.

5. *Please set forth the amount of money which will compensate Alan Labonte for the damages he has suffered as a result of his termination, in the following categories, and bearing in mind the definitions I have given you of each of these categories.*

    Back Pay
    Front Pay
    Emotional Distress

Judge White would soon instruct the jury on assessing these three types of damages. Back pay was salary I hadn't been paid since my firing under H & W's employment obligations to me, and front pay was salary I might reasonably have expected to receive in the future, both minus any compensation from UNUM. But emotional distress was more broadly defined. "Emotional distress can include mental anguish, embarrassment, anger or humiliation, or any other unpleasant mental or emotional state that you find resulted from any conduct by the defendant." But she warned the jury they may not award damages for emotional distress caused by my own "learning to live with MS," only that caused by provable suffering "sufficiently linked to an unlawful act committed by the defendants."

David had already argued the scope of the emotional distress I'd suffered. "They destroyed his chances of working as an executive. He lost his confidence. Probably the worst and most egregious failure to accommodate was when they fired him. He even asked them, 'Can I stay on in some capacity?' The man was practically begging for his job. No, it's too late. They testified they didn't even consider accommodating him at that time. That was absolutely an outrageous violation of Chapter 151b, the antidiscrimination act."

6. Have you determined that Hutchins & Wheeler should pay punitive damages for their conduct in this matter? Yes___ No___

David forewarned, "Judge White will tell you, the purpose is to punish the wrongdoer for violating antidiscrimination laws, to make sure that they don't do it again. You can consider the wealth of the defendant, the nature of their conduct, and what amount it will take to get the message through to them." Judge White instructed, "Punitive damages can only be awarded if you find Hutchins & Wheeler not only committed a discriminatory act but that their conduct was outrageous or extraordinary or characterized by reckless indifference to the rights of Mr. Labonte."

7. If your answer to question 6 is yes, please set forth the amount of punitive damages. $ _____

"There is only one language these people understand, and that's money," David began his peroration. "Remember how they talked about Alan as an asset or a liability, as if he were a stock or a bond. In this case, I would ask you, as you are assessing punitive damages, to send a message loud and clear. Send a message they will hear on the thirtieth floor of 101 Federal Street that this kind of treatment of a person with a handicap is absolutely unacceptable. Totally unacceptable. Don't do it. Don't ever do it again."

"So punitive damages are not required, they are permitted," Judge White further instructed. "You may consider what amount would sufficiently punish the defendant so as to prevent a repetition of the discrimination. One of the cases says that the award should be enough to smart or to hurt."

I am mixing together David's passionate appeals in the late morning with Judge White's sober instructions during the early afternoon, but they somehow did seem to flow into a haze of nervous conjecture as I found myself watching the jury depart the courtroom early that afternoon to begin their deliberations.

"In a civil case, you don't have to be unanimous in agreement," Judge White had told them. "You reach a verdict on a particular question when twelve out of the fourteen of you agree on an answer. Usually in a case where we impanel fourteen jurors, two of you are declared alternates. And that means you have to sit outside, and you don't have a chance to deliberate, and always, alternates are miserable. Counsels have agreed here, and I'm glad they did, that you can all deliberate."

Once more, all fourteen jurors filed by us. I stood at the rail with David at my side and faced each one of them knowing that the next time we saw each other would be when the verdict was to be announced. My stomach jumped a bit at this very sobering reality.

Now the waiting begins, I realized, feeling emptied, as if I'd been shifted at day's end to a parallel but silent universe.

That Tuesday afternoon, we left a courtroom still bustling with activity, rife with argument after two loud weeks of litigation. By Wednesday morning, that same forum had been struck dumb. In the abandoned gallery, there remained only four weary watchers. David and Diane Rapaport, and their daughter Cary—my own little "dream team"—along with myself. Not even Mary Marshall was there. We had begun that excruciating vigil that parties to any lawsuit must mount and endure. It would end when the jury returned to this courtroom. "You are all governed by the same oath," Judge White had charged the jurors, "and that is to reach a verdict. As you know from your Latin—*dictare veritas*—it means to speak the truth."

But none of us knew when the truth might be spoken. "This is always the worst time for me," David said, from long experience. "It's so hard to just wait and anticipate the jury's decision when there's nothing left you can do about it. I think I'll just go for a walk."

David got up and left in a tired rush—on the first of several long walks—and Diane said, "He did such a wonderful job, Alan. I'm very proud of him."

As well as she understood him as a wife, I knew Diane was speaking strictly as another lawyer. Rapaport of Rapaport & Rapaport was reading Rapaport's courtroom performance rightly.

Nothing was heard from the jury, all that Wednesday, and we showed up for further vigil on Thursday morning, again like out-of-work actors in this empty courtroom scene. After a couple of hours, I was restless and announced I was going to church. And I knew just where, at the Chapel of St. Anthony over on Arch Street, around the block from 101 Federal Street.

I had to take a taxi there, and got out beside the entrance to the church at the corner of Washington and Arch, which wasn't far from where I'd once gone to collect my unemployment checks.

I hurried—as best as I could, still working my cane—across the sidewalk, along the wall of the chapel. "All Are Welcome," the sign read over the chapel door.

Inside, it was quiet and shadowy, but the altar bright with the mosaic glitter of a mural—St. Anthony kneeling before the Blessed Mother. Masses were offered throughout the day allowing ample opportunity for those who worked in the City or resided nearby. I slipped in among the several people who were moving toward the empty seats—feeling the comfort and sense of home in the shared experience that is church.

As the Mass was offered by a Franciscan priest, I knelt and prayed, asking the Lord to give me the strength to bear the verdict. I did not ask for any specific verdict, though I admit I prayed that the jury "speak the truth." And I prayed hard for the Truth.

Reexperiencing the sacrifice of the Mass was wonderful as always, bringing me peace and the acceptance of whatever God's will might bring. I knew then, with all my heart, and felt then, with complete confidence, that all was well. In this church, I had found my rock and upon this awesome truth I would build my future.

I headed for the street, grabbed a quick bite to eat, then flagged down a taxi to hurry me back to the New Courthouse.

David and Diane were still waiting out the jury, and told me there had been a request from the jurors while I was at church.

"They wanted a large pad," said David, lifting his eyebrows.

To do their calculations, I sensed immediately, and sat down to wait myself, in nerve-tingling silence.

Some short while later, a court officer came in with a question from the jury. Judge White quickly reconvened, without Ms. Marshall. They wanted to know if a monetary award would reduce the amount of my disability benefits.

David shook his head. "No, Mr. Labonte's disability benefits would remain the same." Then he came back toward me, after the officer had left. "Alan, I'm so tired that I don't even know what day it is," he said.

I blinked. I just sat there, dumbstruck at the magnitude of what I was sure had just been revealed. I knew we had won the case. Why would the jury ask such a question if they hadn't already decided the first four questions in my favor and were right now determining the damages lawfully and equitably due me? That actuary on the jury must already be working on some figures.

So I leaned over to David. "I'll tell you what day it is," I whispered in his ear. "It's pay day!"

His face lit up, and he went over to tell Diane what I had said. We all laughed together in the eerie silence of that courtroom that lay like a misplaced pall on the Truth.

An hour later, Jimmy Kelly, the court clerk, came over to us. "The jury is ready to come down. Do you know where Mary Marshall is?" David didn't, nor did anybody, anywhere in the courtroom. Jimmy came back in a few minutes. "I've left a message at her office that we need her ASAP," he confided. "She's supposed to be in here, standing by. The judge is wild."

David shrugged. Not his worry.

When Mary entered, in an unaccustomedly flustered rush, Judge White was already on the bench. Mary stopped and stood erect, not far from where we were seated in the gallery. She apologized. Judge White, visibly upset at the inexcusable delay, muttered a weak acceptance.

Then Judge White ordered the court officer to bring in the jury. We all stood in respectful silence until they were seated. As they passed by me, I couldn't tell a thing from their controlled faces. "I wouldn't want to play poker with these people," I thought, even if they'd already given us a quick, half peek at their hand.

Ms. Larkin, the foreperson of the jury, stood up, handed the written verdict to Judge White, who read the two pages without expression, and handed them back. Ms. Larkin then proceeded to read aloud the jury's answers to those seven questions, as I stood erect, stone-facing my own nerves.

All fourteen jurors affirmed my claim of handicapped discrimination by answering the first four questions unanimously.

Yes, Alan Labonte could have done the job as executive director with reasonable accommodation to his MS. No, the accommodation required would not have caused undue hardship to H & W. Yes, my termination resulted from H & W's failure to provide reasonable accommodation. And Yes, the reason given for my termination was not the real reason, since I would not have been terminated except for my MS.

Then, she read out the jury's award of damages.

First came Back Pay. "One hundred, twenty-five thousand dollars." Just as we had asked.

Next came Front Pay. "One hundred, ten thousand dollars." Much as we might have expected.

Now she reached Emotional Distress. "Five hundred, fifty thousand dollars."

That large number broke into my artificial calm. We were stacking up almost three-quarters of a million dollars.

Then, Ms. Larkin simply said, "Yes." H & W should pay punitive damages for their extraordinary misconduct.

I was already in a near state of shock before I heard her read out the jury's final award.

"Two million, five hundred thousand dollars."

That hit me like a thunderclap.

I remember standing there in utter awe, almost floating, feeling as if I were back watching *Philadelphia* on that flight home from Bosnia. Only now I was caught up in its gripping final scene—the delivery of the jury verdict.

In addition, both the back and front pay were subject to 12% interest, retroactive to January 27, 1992. Another $55,000. Plus recovery of our legal fees of $172,000.

That brought the total award to $3,513,000. And change.

As the jury broke apart in happy relief and the courtroom turned into chaos, I stood at the rail, gripping it hard, trying to thank as many of them as I could reach, any juror whose eye I could catch.

"We just wanted to *hug* you and Lora," one of them said to me in an anonymous phone call the next day. I couldn't keep back the tears, feeling purged, at last, by a surge of emotion that lifted the burden of humiliation I had carried since the day I was fired.

Chapter Nine

Amild, fevered euphoria reigned in the courtroom, even as Mary Marshall took a firm grip on herself, and at last walked across the well toward David. She looked beaten, badly shaken by this harsh turn of events against her clients and their misfired schemes. Still, she gathered her courage and shook David's hand, offering him congratulations. But as she turned to leave, she stiffened and rallied herself, looking back toward him.

"This isn't over yet," she reminded him. "This case is going to put my kids through college!"

That valiant hail to the future, almost a taunt, caught my ear as I hurried to find a public phone outside the courtroom, to call Lora with the good news. She sounded very happy, but dropped immediately into a more serious tone. "I love you," she assured me. "Now, be safe on your way home. And don't spend it all before you get here."

I laughed, but soberly realized I hadn't seen any millions yet. Not even change for the phone.

David came over as I hung up, smiling proudly, asking if we wanted to set up a meeting with reporters from the two Boston papers, the *Globe* and the *Herald*. "I think we may have secured one of the largest awards in a handicap discrimination case in the Commonwealth," David said with enthusiasm. "The public has a right to know about this," I readily agreed. "But will you meet with them? I need some time to myself right now."

I was feeling awkward, and for me, surprisingly shy. We walked back into the courtroom together, and I hugged Diane, embraced them both. "Thank you for all your support over these past two years," I hesitated, caught up in the emotion of the moment. "I'm very grateful." But after all that baring of my soul over those past ten days of trial, I still couldn't face more questions from the media.

So I slipped out of the courtroom, took the elevator down to the first floor. This time, stepping off into the vaulted lobby, everything was different.

I no longer felt like the guilty party.

But it went far beyond judicial absolution. I realized the immensity of what had just happened as I came to the guards at the scanning station, whose brief but close acquaintance I couldn't help making over these past two trying weeks. One of them smiled and waved me by, and spontaneously I raised my arm and shook my fist over my head.

"We won."

That was it. "Hey, great," he replied. It was the *other guys* who were guilty, that whole Hutchins & Wheeler hallway roster back at 101 Federal, that long legal letterhead full of them.

I reached the pavilion steps outside the New Courthouse, already saying an internal goodbye. Like David earlier, communing with the building. "I got the justice I came here for," I thought to myself. And a memory from my youth so many decades ago flashed back, of my father walking me downtown past the Worcester Courthouse and pointing at the inscription carved across its entablature: OBEDIENCE TO LAW IS LIBERTY.

"Don't ever forget that!" he'd told me.

And I never have. Over the next two often agonizing years, it stood as a battle-torn banner of my faith in the law's path to justice. The problem from now on was to oblige H & W's working remnant to obey the law, to deliver on the large award levied against them by the jury. We had headlines in both Boston newspapers the next day, along with a later story in *Lawyers Weekly*. David began getting phone calls from lawyers he'd never known, becoming something of a sudden celebrity among the Boston Bar, many of whom were scathingly critical of H & W's impolitic conduct of the case.

But no cash was yet accruing to our benefit from this judgment—only that ticking twelve-percent interest.

David advised us that the hardest time in a long law suit really comes *after* trial, when the appeal process drags on and on, always threatening to take everything you've won away from you in one fell swoop of an adverse ruling. Psychologically, it was as insidious, I discovered, as my own MS.

Besides, I told David flat out, "These guys make me nervous."

I'd watched some of the H & W attorneys siphon off all their profits into their Professional Corporations, in part, using the PCs to protect themselves against this very kind of liability. I also knew that their PCs were generally maintained at a zero asset level, so that there might be little there to recover.

David started right after them, ready to force financial disclosure upon the individual partners and eventually got back to me with "great news." The present firm—Hutchins, Wheeler & Dittmar, a P.C. itself, formed in 1992—had assumed all the liabilities of the old partnership of Hutchins & Wheeler. Jim Dittmar, himself a litigator and a prime mover in the newly incorporated group, had taken over management of our case. And he was ready to retain Richard Renehan of Hill & Barlow—a top-notch lawyer in an excellent firm with lots of experience defending other law firms. "Mary says that Hill & Barlow is going to charge an enormous fee," David finished. Half a million dollars, we estimated. "That's why they want to discuss settlement at this time."

That *was* welcome news, and readily understandable. I knew from a business standpoint that the new group might have an end-of-year audit problem. To gain unqualified approval of their books from their auditors, they would be compelled to list a substantial liability—covered by funds in a separate bank account—to satisfy our judgment.

"And don't forget they will have to keep adding to this reserve as interest accrues on the debt they owe us," I added.

David laughed, "The next challenge for us will come when Mary presents her post-trial motions." But what could Mary possibly have up her sleeve to ask of Judge White at this juncture? David gave me what he called a "fairly standard" list. A motion for remittitur to reduce the amount of damages. A motion for a new trial on grounds of unfairness, and a motion for judgment notwithstanding the verdict, "Claiming there was not enough evidence to justify letting the jury decide the case."

"She's handling the post-trial motions," David said, "but Renehan will handle any appeal."

I shook my head. "So much for this case putting her kids through college. Mary is going to get canned just like I did. I don't think that this is a sound decision on their part, do you?"

David nodded and replied, "No one would fight harder for them in appeal."

"What's the basis of their appeal?"

"Mary says their main issue is insufficient evidence to justify the verdict." David said she kept harping stubbornly on the same point: I had never shown I was capable of performing the essential functions of my job, even if reasonable accommodation had been put in place, period. "She also says they think the awards for emotional distress and punitive damages are outside the bell curve," (i.e. out of line with past Massachusetts verdicts and previous judgments).

"Do you think the jury gave us too much?" I blurted out.

He assured me that "the punitives were only a few times the compensatories." That is, back pay, front pay, and emotional distress. "And the emotional distress award is largely within the jury's discretion." But he needed to analyze the issues and balance our chances of prevailing on appeal, especially over any challenge to the large amount of damages. I didn't hear from him for another two weeks, when he cautiously allowed he was ready to discuss a settlement.

"But let's not be the ones to start the bidding process." He would send a letter to Mary, summarizing our position—one of considerable strength, with that $3.5 million judgment hanging over them like the sword of Damocles—and suggest that they make an offer. Some few days later, he called me late at night, in utter exasperation.

"These people's attitude has not changed. Their recalcitrance is maddening. They refuse to make an offer!" he sputtered. "They want *us* to discount the judgment by some percentage, *then* they'll respond to it."

I saw their ploy immediately. "They're not serious. Look at the calendar. The end of year is coming, and they need some documentation as to the extent of their liability before they distribute the year's profits. That's why they want us to send it." I was angry. "If we remain silent, the only thing they have in writing is the jury's award of $3.5 million. Let them go fry ice."

"Maybe you're right." He sounded relieved. "If these guys ever do get serious about a settlement, they will give us a few sleepless nights."

"Right now I'm feeling very sleepy."

"I'll write Mary tomorrow," he said. "We're not going to give them a discounted number. We need them to propose a settlement figure."

"Have a good night," I wished him. "And David, sleep well."

Over the next few months, we both did, if sometimes restlessly. H & W successfully delayed any reappearance in court until after year's end through legal jiggery, but by January 26th we were back before Judge White for our own very good day in court. The verdict was finally entered, and David got our complaint amended to include "Hutchins, Wheeler & Dittmar, P.C." as the liable entity. He also obtained approval for attorney's fees and secured 12% interest on back pay and emotional distress from September 11, 1992, the date we filed suit. That came to $675,000 in additional moneys.

"Great job," I said. "Now, what's next?"

"Hey," he chuckled, "give me a minute or two to revel in this, okay?" Then he laid out the future, in legal time periods from ten to sometimes ninety to 120 days, when he would again be before Judge White to answer Mary's post-trial motions.

I sighed, said we'd already been at this for three years, was there no end in sight?

"Be patient, my friend," he said.

Two weeks later, Hill & Barlow sent a scathing response to David's brief that disgusted him. "I knew this was coming, but I had no idea it would contain so many outrageous statements. They've directed a personal attack on me. Dick Renehan has some other attorney working on our case, who's really stepped out of line. In my twenty-five years of practice, this reply is one of the most vicious I've ever seen."

"Demonstrates the desperate nature of their situation," I told him. "Reminiscent of a wild animal flailing around in a cage. You're finally getting to them."

But it put David into ripping overdrive to get his own answer out to their memo. Their attack on his motives and integrity had "no place in this litigation." Against all amity, "In addition to labeling counsel's arguments as absurd, nonsense, insulting to the court's intelligence, etc., they assert that Mr. Labonte's counsel is either unwilling to address, or determined to misrepresent, the law."

By way of rebuttal, David simply quoted what Judge White had said to the jury at my trial: "I just want you to realize that you have, in this case, two very competent lawyers representing their clients who, at all times, were civil, polite, but firm advocates. They really represent the best of what lawyering is about."

More portentously, Hill & Barlow had raised a new and disturbing argument in their latest submission to the court. It was based on *August versus Offices Unlimited, Inc.*, a federal case decided by the First Circuit Court of Appeals in Boston, which carried a legal implication that persons with disabilities who seek protection under the Americans with Disabilities Act (ADA) forfeit their rights under that law if they apply for disability insurance. How the Massachusetts courts interpreted the *August* Case was paramount to my case since I had applied for disability payments from UNUM prior to filing my complaint with the MCAD.

"What makes your case different from *August*," David explained, "is that Mr. August was never able to establish that he could perform the essential functions of his job, even with reasonable accommodation." He was not what the law calls a "qualified handicapped employee."

"That's a good point," I agreed. "So why am I still worried?"

Very quietly, he said, "I am too."

Lora and I drove into Boston on April 7th for argument on post-trial motions before Judge White. It was a bright spring day, one of those wonderful, balmy breaks out of a long, cold winter that bring you a quiet rush of hope. Lora, while driving, asked me, "How long has it been since H & W let you go?" She marveled when I said more than three years, but then she puzzled, "Somehow it seems like so much longer."

I agreed, and told her, "We were in a much different place then. I guess I felt that I was locked into this fast track, all wrapped up in my career, with less and less time and energy for anything else. Now, even though I'm busier than I've ever been, I'm doing real stuff. Like my education and singing in the Schola at Glastonbury Abbey, things that make me feel more complete as a person. And a lot happier." I reached over and touched her hand lightly on the steering wheel. "Not to worry, honey. Except for this damn litigation, I'm doing fine."

"How's our financial situation?"

Typical Lora. She was already out beating the bushes, and had obtained the first listing in her new career in real estate.

"It's strained," I hedged. "We've got all these legal expenses, and Cohasset is really more than we can afford. But every time we've needed money, there's been some kind of windfall—or deadfall, if we've had to go into our savings—to carry us through."

"So I guess God must be taking care of us. Right?"

"Right!"

"I *knew* you'd say that." For Lora, God is the guy who only takes care of the gal who takes care of herself. "But maybe I think so, too."

In court that day, Judge White was patient and judicious, ever gracious to both contentious sides of the battle. Her demeanor remained relaxed, until the obnoxious attorney from Hill & Barlow referred to the *August* case. She sat bolt upright in her chair. "Are you suggesting Mr. Labonte was disqualified from seeking relief under the anti-discrimination law when he applied for compensation under the firm's disability plan?"

The attorney, the same guy who had written so insultingly about David, flushed. "Why yes, Your Honor, I am."

"Well," she glowered, "that's an issue that will not be decided at this level!"

Her grave tone of judicial forbearance struck me as ominous and David thought that we might legally have a real bear on our hands if and when we reached the appellate level. But he was confident about today's proceedings. "I think it went well."

And during the weeks we would have to wait for the judge's decision, Lora and I were suddenly able, at long last, to get married in the Catholic Church.

Ever since I'd first gone to Medjugorje and been admonished by Father Kevin to ask a priest back home for help with my long-delayed wedding vows, I'd been trying to find an amenable father in the South Shore area. When I'd last seen Father Kevin, he had made me feel I was procrastinating, but that wasn't really true. I'd already found a likely priest in Hingham at the Resurrection Church, where I was then worshipping, and I was ready to approach Father Mooney when he suddenly retired. The new pastor was Father Arthur Calter, a former military chaplain, and I'd gone to him shortly after my second return from Medjugorje, still smarting from Father Kevin's apparent disappointment in me.

Father Calter took his time. He checked the matter out with the Worcester diocese, but there was no record, not even of Lora's petition from thirty years ago. He had recently called on the phone and said, "I've been giving a lot of thought to what you and Lora have shared with me. Why don't you come by and see me this morning." When I got there, he said. "I've only done this once before in my thirty-eight years as a priest, but I have the authority to marry you, and I'm willing to do it."

I sat there in a mild state of shock, which turned into a beamish grin. "Father, I don't know what to say." I flew out of there like a fool, drove straight home, to find Lora in her office. "You're not going to believe this. I just spoke with Father Calter, and he's willing to marry us."

"What's *this* going to cost?" she asked, right off.

"It's not going to cost us anything," I blurted, like a school boy caught with big news. "All we have to do is set the date."

"Okay," Lora allowed. "Let's look at the calendar."

We picked April 11th, Lora's first free day. I immediately phoned Father Calter to give him the date and inquired, "When can I go to confession?"

"I'm here all morning."

I jumped back in the car to rush to the rectory. When I had to stop at a traffic light, I got into an absurd theological dialogue with myself. "What if I don't make it back there for some reason? Now that I can go to confession. I've waited and hoped for this all these years. Finally it's within reach, and I'm stuck at a traffic light!"

Pure Graham Greene. But the light changed, I made it to Resurrection Church, and there I made my confession for the first time in over three decades. "Here I am Lord!" At long last.

We were married in that Hingham church four days after the arguments before Judge White. We stood before Father Calter as the whole wedding party. We both looked on this ceremony as a renewal of our vows, but there was no question that Lora was going through all this Catholic rigmarole for my sake. "I saw how important the Church's blessing was to Alan," she insists, always looking after my spiritual welfare.

And I felt truly blessed, and with spring blooming through our nuptials, I began thinking about another trip to Medjugorje. At Easter, I said to Lora, "Honey, would you like to come with me this time?"

My heart yearned for those mountains and the rock-solid faith of the people in Bosnia-Herzegovina now the home of old friends I hadn't seen for almost a year.

"I'd love to . . . " Lora hedged a bit. "But is it safe?"

Not altogether. The United States, acting through NATO, had imposed a "No Fly" zone over the area. The marauding Serbian Air Force could no longer wreak havoc, but unrest and some fighting still persisted. She wanted to talk to her brother Fred first to see what he thought.

"If he wants to come along," I said, "that's fine by me."

A couple of days later, Lora marched into my office. "Fred says that if I'm going, he's going, and if he's going, Sloan's going too." Still fine by me. "But Alan," she asked, as usual, "how are we going to pay for this?"

"We have to raise some cash to pay a slew of other bills," I stood my ground, "so I've arranged for a home equity loan of $30,000."

"Oh, I hate to do that!" Lora objected, as I knew she would. But I'd already done some financial forecasts of our future course, weighing what I believed to be the right actions against likely prospects from our $3.5 million judgment. Lora ultimately accepted my decision and we made our travel plans when we heard from another member of our extended family, Lora's son, Jonathan.

"Pops, listen, I'm really worried about Mom going to Bosnia with you." Jonathan was calling me from Fort Lauderdale where he now worked.

I wrote him a long letter that night, reassuring him that going to Bosnia was not "an insane idea." I laid it on the line:

To get to the point about my planned trip to Medjugorje with Mom and Fred and Sloan. I truly know only this, that we have another family in Bosnia. Their names are Vesna, Blanka, and Vedran. Vedran is the boy, our godchild, whom we adopted last year. His father was killed in June 1993 about two weeks before my first visit. As you are my son, he is also my son, and a son needs his father and family and the knowledge that he is loved. When I first held the refugees in my arms, I learned unmistakably what war truly means, what things evil hath wrought, and I took from that experience the spiritual strength that had been missing from my life.

That seemed to answer Jonathan's doubts, and we proceeded to rendezvous in Medjugorje, so that I sat again at that long table in the home of Marinko and Dragica Ivankovic, now with my own family. It was an enjoyable week for everybody, though Fred and Lora went off exploring on their own, while I stuck closer to town with my brace and cane. I set off on another visit, all by myself, to St. James Church, and found an old acquaintance still sitting on his same bench in the courtyard, under his familiar sign that said "English."

"Father Kevin, can we finish what we started three years ago?"

He squinted hard, half-recognizing me, but uncertain just where it was that we had left off. "And what might that be?"

"To have you hear my confession," I laughed.

Father Kevin was elated to learn of my stumbling return to the faith, and listened kindly to me as a welcome penitent, giving me the absolution he had once felt forced to withhold. After all, it was his advice—to seek out a parish priest, not to go through the hierarchy—that had gained the Church's blessing of Lora's and my union.

One of my fondest memories was our meeting with Vedran, accompanied by his mother Vesna and his sister Blanka. A young woman named Spomenka acted as our interpreter during the several hours we spent getting to know each other. Vedran was about the same age as Sloan. He had poise and dignity, and despite the loss of a father and the harsh uncertainty about his future, was still a resolutely self-assured kid.

I embraced him, then lifted him onto my lap for a few pictures. After we'd had some soda and cookies, the boys ran outside and, to our delight, kicked Sloan's soccer ball around.

* * *

We were back in Boston by July 1st, where I was still working on that research grant at BU, under a welcome twelve-month extension from the U.S. Public Health Service. I was learning tons of stuff about research in both my grant and course work. I loved what I was doing, and for all the limitations imposed by my MS, I got caught up in the exuberance of educating myself for the complicated tasks ahead.

On the day after the Fourth, David called me at home. "It's good news for us again. Judge White has denied all the post-trial motions. Our verdict and award for damages stand!"

David immediately filed for discovery of H & W assets with Judge White, hoping to keep the pressure on these cornered lawyers. "Who will not take kindly to having their personal assets attached," he explained. "That may encourage them to consider settlement." But Hill & Barlow filed their own notice of appeal at the end of July. Dick Renehan was now H & W's lead counsel, and Josh Davis had replaced the attorney who was so insulting to David. Mary Marshall was entirely gone, no longer to be copied with any future correspondence. Who will educate her kids now? I wondered. Had her youngest ever made it into the Little League? I held no bad feelings for Mary, and wished her well. She had done an outstanding job of defending her uncooperative clients.

"I could really use some help during the appeal process," David said. Despite having argued a large number of appeals, he had not been before the Supreme Judicial Court for several years. "Someone with a good deal of appellate experience, especially before the SJC, with whom I can discuss strategy. I'd like to approach Jerry Benezra."

"Is he very expensive?" I sounded like Lora.

David only knew Benezra by reputation, maybe $200 per hour. "But I'm willing to split the cost with you since this would not be a regular out-of-pocket expense." So we hired Benezra as a consultant, to make sure we submitted the very best brief possible to the SJC.

Benezra was helpful in drafting our briefs to suit the peculiarities of the appellate justices. "It's been tough," David said, "keeping up with all the stuff that Hill & Barlow was throwing at us."

I sat down to go over the Labonte finances again, and it quickly became clear I needed more cash to pay bills and fund our share of Jerry Benezra. I told myself I was really investing this money in the Labonte Case, our best hope for a substantial return. On September 12th, David and Dick Renehan went to court to argue the security issue over revealing or attaching individual lawyers' assets. Judge White would only compel H & W to provide us with copies of their insurance policies and documentation of any transfers of assets by individual partners since the date of my termination. David took this as a big defeat. "Nobody, let alone any law firm, has insurance covering damages for discrimination against persons with disabilities," he complained, and Judge White's order didn't really allow him to get at the partners' assets. Lora sent him a note to salve his bruised ego. "Judge White has every confidence in H & W's ability to pay. Alan and I are hoping she is right on!"

Soon after, David reported, to his chagrin, "Renehan told me that he would be seeking direct appellate review." He wanted to take the case right to the Massachusetts Supreme Judicial Court, bypassing the lower Appeals Court. Could they do that? "The SJC can hear a case directly, without appeal court review, if they are convinced a special point of law is at issue."

And we both knew that this special point of law might be centered on the doctrine of judicial estoppel if a handicap discrimination suit were brought against an employer by an employee who has obtained disability benefits. Like me. "Estoppel" means basically that a legal action can be stopped in its tracks and shunted off to an abandoned siding, even *after* a jury has reached its verdict.

Hill & Barlow submitted their petition for direct review to the SJC in late September. Sure enough, the essence of their argument was, first, whether my right to sue was estopped by my prior disability claim, and second, whether the trial court had ruled properly on other post-trial motions on damages, particularly those concerning punitive damages awarded by a presumptively over-generous jury.

Next, after negotiating a confidentiality agreement, H & W turned over copies of their insurance policies and some personal financial statements on each partner's asset transfers since my firing. It would soon be clear that they had no insurance to protect against our claim. I gave the financial statements to a close friend of mine in Cohasset, Bill Haynes, whom I first met at Glastonbury Abbey. He was a CPA with the respected Boston firm of Livingstone & Haynes. Bill had always struck me as a guy who had everything totally together, serene in his retirement. But I discovered he had been diagnosed with prostate cancer, which was why he was no longer actively practicing.

We sat out on his deck near the sea, while he talked turkey to me. "I can't tell from these statements if these people have enough money to cover your claim. Your best chance is to attach the assets of the law firm itself. They undoubtedly have millions of dollars in accounts receivable."

Undoubtedly, as I knew only too well. Almost eight million, last time I tried to help them.

Bill said very seriously, "Have you considered a settlement?"

I had to smile. "They just don't seem to be interested."

"I've discussed your case in confidence with contacts I have in the city. The word on the street is the jury gave you too much in punitive damages. Two and a half million, and people say it should have been around a million. My advice is to negotiate for around two million."

I thought that over, in the peace of Bill's deck. "Maybe you're right." I could feel a deep calm coming from the salt marshes and ponds that stretched away toward the ocean horizon. "I'll speak with David again about it." It was so peaceful that I got to thinking, reciprocally, about Bill and his cancer. And the mutual dread of the diseases we both shared. "Bill, I've been invited back to Bosnia and Medjugorje to visit with their health minister, Spomenka's father, Dr. Bozo Ljubic." And on the spur of the moment, I asked, "Would you like to come along?"

Bill looked at me, and in a trice said, "Sure." Maybe he might want to think about it, get back to me? No, he insisted, "Just let me know when you're going, and I'll be ready."

That October, Bill and I flew over to Bosnia—two pilgrims, neither of us in too great shape—and on this trip, we ended up staying together in Medjugorje at the home of one of the visionaries, Vicka Ivankovic. It was now fourteen years since the original apparitions, and Vicka was a young woman in her early thirties. After I introduced Bill to her and the village, I stepped aside, left him to fend for himself and his faith, and Vicka took him under her visionary's wing.

I had my own appointment with Minister Ljubic. He turned out to be a tall, soft-spoken man, an orthopedic surgeon, who had good English. I'd been hoping we could find ways to work together to improve the broken health care delivery system in his war-torn land. But nothing developed out of our conversation, until he said his daughter Spomenka was coming to the United States to complete her high school education in Bethlehem, Pennsylvania. He planned on coming to visit her in Pennsylvania after going to a medical meeting in Canada. I offered to do whatever I could to help him with that visit, perhaps invite him to speak at BU. When his driver dropped me back at Vicka's house, I had to ask myself, "You had me travel all this way for a one-hour meeting? That could have waited until he arrived in the United States?" Surely, something more had to come out of this latest trip of mine.

I hadn't yet understood the compassionate point of the trip was really Bill. I'd gradually come to hear more of his own story, which had its hidden tragedy. Several years back, one of his four daughters had been murdered by a jealous boyfriend. She'd been found in a car parked in Cohasset just before Christmas. Bill had never gotten over her brutal death, nor his sorrow at the senseless loss. He told me that every morning he drove into Boston, he broke down in tears, could hardly make it to his office.

But on this visit to Medjugorje, he was actually starting to enjoy himself, despite his intractable illness. Every evening at dinner he had fresh stories of his newly ventured faith. Before we left, he managed to hike to the top of Mount Krizevac with a party led by Vicka. At the summit, under the concrete cross, Bill reported Vicka had experienced another apparition. He arrived back to our room at around one in the morning, in high excitement. "I ran all the way down the mountain." Not that easy for a guy with a stent in his urinary tract, but he was that exhilarated. "Vicka said Our Lady appeared to her there and prayed over us for a long time." I quietly said my thanks to *Gospa* for bringing my friend this brief respite from his sorrows, even in the face of his harrowing malignancy.

* * *

I called David after Thanksgiving to tell him my guy saw no tax consequences from the proposed changes Renehan had sent us. "We've already determined the jury's award is taxable income except for the damages for emotional distress." We puzzled over this, since Renehan must have already understood these matters, especially about the $550,000 for pain and suffering.

"Maybe," David speculated, "it's his way of raising the issue of settlement."

Of course! Our annual ride on the accounting merry-go-round. H & W probably needed to calculate the potential liability from our suit on their books for 1995.

"Call Renehan back," I said, "tell him what my tax guy says, and see if the other shoe drops."

It dropped. Renehan admitted the tax ploy was just his way of inducing a conversation about settlement before year's end. He made us an offer of $500,000. "He said they just wanted to 'Get rid of it,'" David reported back.

"If that's true," I said, "they're not going about it in the right way."

David agreed entirely. "By my calculation, they now owe us about $4 million," he figured, counting in the accruing interest. "I don't believe this reflects any serious desire, on their part, to settle." Once more, we agreed to blow them away.

"Don't worry about it," I assured David. "Just remember, if they'd offered this during the trial, we would've been dancing in the streets."

What that turndown starkly meant for Lora and me was that, a week later, we had to accept a low offer for one of our building lots in Greenfield. Ultimately the net proceeds came to $28,000, far less than we thought the property was basically worth, but I handed the check over to Lora and said, "Merry Christmas, honey." To keep the lawsuit alive, as well as ourselves, we had to continue cashing out our holdings.

Then, right after Christmas, the SJC approved Renehan's request to hear our case on direct appeal, and that began the rolling thunder that carried us through 1996-97—the stormy, final phase of the Labonte Case. David immediately saw all sorts of advantages. "Our appeal will be heard sooner. We'll know which judges will be reviewing our case well in advance, and once they rule . . . " Anticipating a loud clap at the last stroke of lightning. " . . . there will be no further appeal."

"So you don't see this," I probed, "as a negative thing?"

"Not really. We know H & W will be relying on some recent federal case decisions that shouldn't apply here. The SJC will be less reluctant than the Appeals Court to say they don't apply. Remember that Rapaport is on the job, content to argue the case in whatever court wishes to hear it!"

I laughed. "Go get 'em, tiger."

David began researching and writing our brief in deadly earnest. Renehan had submitted H & W's principal brief to the Appeals Court, back in December. Now that our case was entered on the SJC docket as SJC-07111, the brief was simply transferred. "Nothing new here, no substantive change in the basic issues," David told me. It was still the estoppel, appropriateness of punitive damages, and size of verdict. He called on Jerry Benezra for further help with his answer, but he was off consulting in China. David really faced the crucial questions alone. At root, how to knock down any newly decided cases that favored estoppel.

Our brief was due by February 29th, to be followed by H & W's reply, then oral argument before the SJC. We might hear their decision before year's end. David said, "And Alan, you won't probably be hearing from me until this is completed, but don't feel slighted. I'll be thinking of you every morning when I get up at 5:30 A.M. to work on the brief."

While David was rising early, "determined to make this the best brief I have ever written," I was getting deeper into the affairs of state in Bosnia-Herzegovina. Minister Ljubic arrived as our houseguest overnight in February and spoke before a distinguished panel of the Dean and other faculty at BU's School of Theology, where his appearance at this open forum was a resounding success. He spoke movingly of the war and his people's suffering with an authority that only a medical doctor clinically on the scene can command. Lora then drove him to Logan Airport for his flight to Pennsylvania, to be with his daughter Spomenka. Later, I got a call from Spomenka. "My father says he was so honored by the reception he received from BU, and my family is so happy for what you did." She now spoke very good English and invited Lora and me to stay that summer with her family in Siroki Brijeg. Her family, I'd by now learned, included her uncle, the president of Bosnia-Herzegovia, Mariofil Ljubic. Apparently I was garnering some small role in international diplomacy.

My mother slipped away in late March, just a week before her 95th birthday. She had spent the last three years in a congregate living facility in Worcester. I talked with her doctor earlier that week. "You're going to leave me and go be with Daddy, aren't you?" I remember how broadly she'd smiled and then nodded.

Meanwhile, I had to face an ever-deepening financial hole. We had early in February accepted an offer on our last building lot in Greenfield for $35,000. A slightly better price than we'd gotten for our first lot, and the moneys due to us would come in about thirty days. But pressing obligations, especially our legal bills, had to be paid now.

I was also well into my doctoral studies at BU, already planning preparatory work over the summer break for autumn classroom duty as a teaching assistant. The research project was winding down, quite successfully, since we had forty-three Massachusetts hospitals participating. My many hospital contacts, long established through the old healthcare lobbying group we'd formed in the 80s, had proven to be extremely useful in the recruitment effort. I'd been able to talk with many of my former colleagues one-on-one.

Work as a TA meant making up exams, conducting office hours for students, running labs and helping with everything including grades. One afternoon, I was informed the director of research for the School of Management, Dr. Lee Sproule, wanted to see me. I'd taken one of her classes in research methods, but only managed a B for the course. So I was flabbergasted when she asked me to be her TA for that very same class. As another professor in my department said, when he heard of the offer, "High praise from Allah!"

Through early April, David wrote our brief. The SJC approved two time extensions, plus the brief's expansion to fifty-five pages. I knew David had to attend to his other clients, so I stayed well out of his way. He gleaned key quotes from the 1300 pages of our trial transcript, identified forty-eight cases that best supported our position, and wove together a concise, logical, and masterful argument for our just cause.

The day the brief was due he encountered a computer glitch that pushed his hard drive into producing a master list of 2000 footnoted cases, all supposedly part of our brief. He had no idea where they came from, nor how to get rid of them. Neither did the tech support people he frantically called. "Send us a disk," they said, "and we'll figure it out." David had to solve the problem himself by manually creating a table of cases, and he just barely made the court's deadline for filing the brief.

In late July David found out about a case recently decided by that same First Circuit Court of Appeals in Boston, the court that had caused us so much worry with its findings in the *August* Case. This new case was *D'Aprile v. Fleet Servs. Corp.* The facts were that Ms. Beverly

D'Aprile, a senior system support analyst for Fleet Services, contracted MS. She worked for two months on a flexible part-time schedule, using her vacation time as a *de facto* accommodation, performing the essential functions of her job proficiently. But she ran out of vacation time, and Fleet Services stopped her flexible schedule, then terminated her because her MS prevented her from working a full weekly schedule. She applied immediately for disability benefits, then later brought suit. Fleet Services argued, from *August,* that she was estopped from suing for handicap discrimination.

But the Circuit Court found for D'Aprile because she had never claimed she was totally disabled, in fact "demonstrated her ability to work with the accommodation she requested." Here was exactly the departure from the *August* Case we were seeking. But, to David's frustration, the decision was marked "Not for Publication." It couldn't be cited by attorneys in other cases.

David turned tiger again, and began lobbying any number of public interest groups, employment lawyers, and academics to write to the First Circuit Court justices, requesting that the *D'Aprile* decision be published forthwith.

A letter from David began, "I have great news!" As always, his broadcast salutation. "The First Circuit Court has agreed to publish the *D'Aprile* decision." He still had to win SJC approval to file a supplemental brief, but he and Jerry Benezra were already at work on a draft.

Oral argument was now set for October 7th. David waited until October 3rd to file his motion for approval of our supplemental brief, along with the brief itself for the SJC to consider. This brought a sharp, pained reply from Renehan, opposing David's unwelcome, last minute move as "a transparent attempt to have the last word."

But the SJC approved our filing since David had "new information pertinent to our case." That he managed to root that "new information" just in time, was among his major achievements as a trial advocate.

The Massachusetts Supreme Judicial Court convenes on the fourteenth floor of the New Courthouse, ten floors above Courtroom 314 where my trial had been held over two years ago. As we soared upward in the elevator—Lora, myself, and Bill Haynes, who had asked to come along—I had a sense of reaching ever higher for elusive vindication. We waited outside for our turn to be heard, late in the morning. There would be fifteen minutes for each side, at the single rostrum down in the well before the long justices' bench on a raised dais.

Our case was called: *Alan J. Labonte versus James G. Wheeler.* I was surprised at how crowded the large hall was around us.

You could tell that Dick Renehan was the crowd favorite, a remarkably small man, with a cocky, Back Bay air, and plenty of aplomb. He had the cool to nod to David and wink, "Well, this is for all the marbles."

Chief Justice Wilkins summoned Renehan to the rostrum and he began dourly, in a small voice that twanged of Boston. "September one, nineteen-ninety-four was an historic day. The largest verdict in our history under a discrimination case was awarded against Hutchins, Wheeler & Dittmar for having fired their executive director. Even worse, the verdict was 3.3 million, and 2.5 of it was punitive damages."

"Worse for who?" Justice Fried promptly interrupted.

And Renehan bobbled.

"Worse for *who?* " Fried repeated, with a sly smile.

More bobbling, until Renehan had to, *hated* to admit, "The defendant . . ." That sly uptick from Charles Fried gave the first hint—David said later, still chuckling—that we had an even hand at work on this panel of three justices.

"Let me play my lead card," Renehan offered. "It is a very simple legal principle that says, You, Mr. Plaintiff, may not say to an insurance carrier, 'I am totally disabled. I cannot carry out the functions of my job,' then collect disability benefits, and at the same time, sue for discrimination. Is this that kind of a case? Controlled, as we say, by *August*, or can the plaintiff ease out of it under the recently decided *D'Aprile* Case?" He made sure to remind the justices "of one fact. At no time prior to January 27, 1992, did Mr. Labonte ever make a request for a change in his employment that would have accommodated his illness."

Now he began his *"Reader's Digest* version" of my case, walking the justices through a half dozen familiar quotes out of only volume seven of eight volumes of trial testimony. They were all statements about my "total" disability, precisely cited and pruned down to neat legal abstractions, aimed at buttressing summary judgment against my ever pleading discrimination because of my MS. The justices followed him cursorily, until he argued, "And here's the reason for it. Courts all across the country have said you cannot speak out of both sides of your mouth. You cannot say—for the purpose of getting insurance benefits—I'm disabled, and then turn around and say to a judge and jury, I could have performed the job."

Chief Justice Wilkins jumped right on that. What if "he could not perform the job in its fullest form, but could have performed the job if accommodations were made? Is that a proper question for the jury?"

Yes, Renehan allowed, if Mr. Plaintiff has already affirmed as much to the insurance company. "There are cases in which an applicant has said, 'Look, I can't do the job as it is now. I would need to be accommodated, but since I'm not getting accommodated, I have taken disability benefits." He argued I never did "draw that distinction."

Justice Fried asked, "Isn't there some burden on the insurance company to say, 'Look, it's okay you can't do the full job, but you could do part of it, couldn't you?'"

Renehan clung to what he asserted was my "statement that says for several months prior to being discharged, 'I was unable to carry out the responsibilities of my job.' And it doesn't matter what the insurance company does, Your Honor," because the plaintiff is affirming a statement "which is inconsistent with what he states in court. And I suggest to you, as a matter of policy, that is simply wrong."

"You think," Wilkins asked, "it's absolutely the bar?"

"It's an absolute bar," replied Renehan, "even under the *D'Aprile* Case that gives my brother so much comfort." He nodded toward David. "And the reason again is the integrity of the system. Either you were or were not qualified to work. If you were qualified to work and they wouldn't let you, you have a lawsuit. If you were not qualified to work, you're entitled to benefits. But you can't have it both ways."

Then Fried raised another possibility. "Did the insurance company come back and seek to reopen the case, saying 'We've been cheated?' And can they get back whatever they had paid, money having been received?"

That shocked me, speculative as it had to be, and Renehan dealt with it very delicately. "Since July of 1992 this plaintiff has been receiving $72,000 a year for disability. There has been nothing to my knowledge, and certainly nothing in this record, suggesting that anybody is trying to undo that." But the idea of my cheating had been planted, and subtly cultivated by Renehan, and I might yet have to confront that lingering implication. "And the reason, I'll put to you, is very simple," Renehan went on. "This gentleman has multiple sclerosis. His job was a highly stressful, very frantic kind of job. What he said to the insurance company was the truth."

He tied the bow. "And you know something? When you look, as I know Your Honor will, at the response brief just filed by my brother, he says, 'Why are we penalizing Mr. Labonte for having been truthful?' The fact is, I want to penalize him because he can't speak out of both sides of his mouth."

Having rounded off that sharp corner, Renehan made a feeble try to distinguish the *D'Aprile* Case. "In *D'Aprile* the plaintiff was literally working with accommodations part-time, and they suddenly pulled the rug out from under her. Mr. Labonte was never working with any accommodations." Then, to gainsay the ways in which we argued I *could* have been accommodated: "You can't redefine the job and come under this act. You can talk about *how* you're going to do the job, but not the *what*, the substance of the job."

And he ended abruptly, having devoted his entire oral argument to estoppel, never once raising the moot question of excessive punitive damages. Maybe that was the right, bold strategy—an all-out attack at the one crux that could cost us the entire verdict—but Renehan seemed aloof from the facts of the case, arguing from on high for an all-or-nothing legalistic damnation of my supposedly reprehensible double-talk.

But not David. David stepped to the rostrum without a note, determined to speak candidly and al fresco to the justices. He said later he never felt more strongly the advantage of having been the trial lawyer, able to muster all the factual minutia and legal nuances for appellate argument. He knew our case inside out, carried everything in his head, spoke from immediate memory. So he could address the bench directly, always looking straight at the justices, never bowing his head, even briefly, to catch sight of some helpful note, out of perplexity.

He went straight to refuting Renehan's argument from the *August* Case. "Chief Justice Wilkins put his finger on it a few moments ago. There is no inconsistency whatsoever because there is nothing inconsistent if the employee, when he's asked, 'Can you do the job?' answers, 'No, I can't because no one's offering me accommodation.' As Justice Fried pointed out, the insurance company does not ask that question about accommodations. Now maybe they should, but they don't ask that question. So when Mr. Labonte said to the insurance company, 'I am totally disabled, I can't be the executive director of Hutchins & Wheeler,' he meant 'without reasonable accommodation.'

"And that's what his doctors meant."

"The defendants spent the whole trial showing the jury—and waving around all these forms they were waving around this morning—that he said this to UNUM, and his doctors said that. Both of his doctors—Dr. Wolpow and Dr. Gross—testified before the jury that when they were filling out these forms to UNUM, *they weren't considering any accommodation.*

"They were saying Mr. Labonte couldn't do the job as it was. And we agree. There is no dispute. The whole point here, and the whole point of Chapter 151b, is that you've got to give the employee reasonable accommodation. Now if they had given him reasonable accommodation, and he still couldn't do the job, then there could be a problem. But they never, ever gave him reasonable accommodation."

Justice Ruth Abrams leaned forward with a succinct question.

"When did he ask for it?"

And I felt as if I had slipped back a few years into David's conference room, on the night of that mock trial. It was the same question Joe Limone had sprung on me and had thrown me back then: "Did you ever *ask* them to do anything for you?" Only we'd since been through two weeks of actual trial, and months of reflection, to finally frame the right answer.

David gave it for me. "He asked them to see his doctors, Justice Abrams. He didn't know what accommodations he needed, Justice Abrams, because he is a lay person, who only knew he had MS. He knew he was in trouble, and he said, 'Please see my doctor, Edward Wolpow at Mount Auburn Hospital. He's the expert. He treats fifty people.' But they wouldn't go near Dr. Wolpow. They never picked up the phone to call him. They never wrote him. They never met with him. They didn't care.

"They saw one doctor, their own client, Dr. Wepsic, who is a good fellow, gave them some good advice—all of which they ignored. He said, 'You've got to accommodate Mr. Labonte by changing his location, so he doesn't have to walk as much. You need to make sure he gets rest during the day.' And above all—this is so important and it came from a stipulation—he said, 'Don't discriminate against him.' He didn't use those words, but if you read the stipulation, he said, 'Judge him by his performance on the job, not because he has multiple sclerosis.'

"But that's exactly what they *did* do, and exactly what the jury found. The jury found they engaged in plain old blind discrimination—racial, sexual, or whatever—in this case, it was handicap. Almost as soon as he told them he had MS, they started to move away from him. They told him, 'Oh, we've got a long-term disability insurance policy.' They started having meetings about firing him. Now bear in mind he had just been given a raise and a good performance review, so he was a good performer. And the jury had plenty of evidence, members of the court, to show not only was he a good performer *before* he had MS. He was good *afterwards*.

"He fought like wild during those last six months. Maybe he wasn't doing a fabulous job, but he certainly was trying hard, and that was without any accommodation. It's very significant that he's working fifty-five hours a week now at Boston University, because BU has a very different attitude towards accommodating the handicapped than Hutchins & Wheeler. They've allowed him to work flexible hours Monday through Thursday, etcetera, etcetera.

"So you see, Your Honor, you ask whether or not he requested accommodation, he did the only thing he could do, which was to say, 'Please see my doctor.' Moreover, the judge charged the jury that if the employer knows the employee has a disability—and there's no dispute that was the case here—they have a legal duty under Chapter 151b to provide accommodation. That was the charge to the jury, and there was no objection. And the jury took that as the law of the land."

What struck me, profoundly, was that David's long declamation was really the same short answer I'd given Joe Limone at the mock trial. But it had been so thoroughly fleshed out, with the details of H & W reprehensible conduct, that the justices were absorbed as surrogates into the process of how to achieve reasonable accommodation.

"So you're saying," Justice Fried inquired, "that it's not the employee's obligation to present a plan of accommodation, which the employer must then implement. The ball is in the employer's court."

"Yes, Your Honor," David said, letting that ball land just where Fried had lobbed it. "The idea is, the statute envisions a dialogue that had the employer sit down with Dr. Wolpow and Alan Labonte and say, 'Well, you've got MS. Here are the essential functions of the job. Can you do them? Let's see if we can work something out.' The judge charged the jury that the law requires that these parties—I think the word used was *may*—may initiate a dialogue. But clearly once the employer knows there is a disability, they have a duty to accommodate. And I would think, as Justice Fried suggested, the ball is in their court."

And David never let that ball leave their court.

"There were so many simple things they could have done that would have worked. At trial our doctors said, they could have moved his office to lessen the amount of walking he had to do. Now this didn't take a genius. He was limping around the firm. They saw him limping, and they just let him limp. They didn't move his office. They didn't direct some of the billing partners to come to his office. They didn't direct other people like a new managing partner to help him. They didn't modify his hours at all. They didn't make sure he got rest. They didn't do anything because they didn't care.

"You know verdicts like this don't just drop out of the sky. This jury was very upset with what this law firm did to this man. They decided there should be punitive damages—and significant ones."

He adroitly broke new ground with the *D'Aprile* Case, showing how the First Circuit Court of Appeals had shifted away from *August*. "The First Circuit saw what was going on around the country. Handicap plaintiffs would be automatically thrown out because they had the temerity to apply for some long-term disability insurance and check a box, an ambiguous box that said 'Check here if you're disabled' on a form where they're not asked the right question." Which is, 'Could you work with accommodation?' "And the First Circuit said, 'Wait a minute, we didn't mean that in *August*.'"

All these cases, the First Circuit now says, are "very facts specific." "We have facts in dispute here," David pled. "To tell the handicapped plaintiffs they can't even get to trial because they filled out a long-term disability insurance application would be very harsh indeed. Seems to me that we ought to let the jury decide here because Mr. Labonte's case is a perfect example of somebody who, as the defendants would have it, should just be dismissed on summary judgment, but whom fourteen jurors unanimously decided deserved to recover.

"So it would be a terrible injustice to adopt some kind of *per se* rule, which my brother argued for, as I understood him, that all these people just get thrown out. Let's put the facts before the jury, let them wave all the UNUM forms around and focus on Mr. Labonte and make their argument. And in some cases the jury is going to decide that the person can't bring the case, and in others, that they can.

"But let's not take away the role of the jury. This court just decided two years ago in the *Dalis* Case that handicap discrimination cases and others get decided by juries. The decision says the jury is the sacred vehicle for deciding these cases and represents the conscience of the community. The only means by which a lay person can participate."

That went right straight to my heart again, how the jurors were "shocked and outraged by what had been done to Mr. Labonte.

"It is now clear from the court that started it all, the First Circuit that the doctrine of judicial estoppel doesn't apply to people like Beverly D'Aprile and Alan Labonte."

Then David made a staunch defense of our award of punitive damages, arguing the defendants have not raised the only salient legal point. Was there any "abuse of discretion by the trial judge" because "they know how tough it is to prove the standard" for such abuse? They would have to show that "no judge acting intelligently and conscientiously could have honestly reached the conclusion" that this verdict of $2.5 million is appropriate, and need not be scaled back.

As for what they did to deserve such punishment, "When you look at the facts, it's apparent why they also shy away from the facts."

David put their manifest offenses "in a nutshell." "They shunned him like a leper. They worked him very hard those last several months, even though they knew he needed a slightly less onerous schedule. And by the way, it's very significant for the year before Mr. Labonte's tenure as executive director—and for the two and a half years after—they let a man named Gaziano, the head of the trust department, and a non-lawyer—they let him be the executive director, spending only thirty-five to forty hours a week. So they had no problem accommodating Mr. Gaziano, but somehow or other, they couldn't do the same for Mr. Labonte."

At the last, "They fired him. They told him he was no good. These were people he said he respected, and so when he went to UNUM, he was truthful, as my brother admits. He said, 'They tell me I can't do the job, so I guess I'm not fit for this.' He thought he was losing his mind because people he respected told him he was doing a terrible job. They did a terrible thing to him. And this is one of the reasons the jury was very, very upset."

And he closed up both halves of his nutshell by saying, "When you're looking at the amount of the verdict, members of the court, keep in mind that these are not people ignorant of the law. They knew exactly what the law required. It's not a complicated law. They say, 'Oh, the law is hard to understand, and we didn't do anything wrong to Mr. Labonte.' Well, I just cannot accept that." Then he pressed down tight on the same point he'd sounded from the day we first met. "It's basically the rule of decency. It says, treat handicapped people decently. Treat them the way you would want to be treated if you had a disability.

We were all very *up*, buoyed by an optimism raised by the clear impact David's words had on the four justices. I was astonished at the amount of detail he'd packed into his presentation, and though you can never know for sure, I felt certain the sitting bench had been equally impressed. I took it as significant that Justice O'Connor, whom David counted our most likely disbeliever, hadn't opened her mouth once.

But it didn't follow that the SJC was in any rush to judgment. As autumn advanced, almost every afternoon, I logged onto the Internet, opened Netscape, and clicked the bookmark for *Lawyers Weekly*, a web page for attorneys and students of the law in Massachusetts. Then I selected among the options "Massachusetts Courts/Supreme Judicial Court (SJC)/Recent Opinions." SJC-07111, *Alan J. Labonte vs. Hutchins & Wheeler* always came up blank.

On November 11th, I gave a sigh as I finished scanning the latest cases, around two P.M., all decided the previous Friday. Nothing again. I sat there for another hour, gazing at the screen saver after the Internet timed out, brooding over the law's endemic delay since I had stumbled up Beacon Hill to file my claim with the MCAD. "For God's sake," I muttered irrationally, "we even lost our dog Strider." He was too old to make the move, not strong enough to survive the rigors of so big a change. Was the same now true of me? I had to wonder. Was I getting to be another old dog, lamer than ever in my right leg, going stiff in the left as well?

The phone rang, and it was David, crisp and clear, broadcasting again. "I have some exciting but sobering news. I just got off the phone with Dick Renehan. Now that we're on the brink of getting a final judgment from the SJC, they want to talk about settling. Dick offered $1,750,000. This is what I meant when I told you if these guys ever got serious, they could give us some sleepless nights."

I wasn't moved. "I can still sleep soundly on this one, David."

Because I was slowly beginning to have a change of heart. David and I agreed there were several issues to consider. Monetarily, if the damages awarded by the jury were adjusted for accrued interest at 12%, H & W had an exposure of $4.4 million. So they were taking the same miserly approach to settlement they always had. Their offer was only slightly more than one third of the total now due.

But non-monetarily, we were also deeply disturbed by H & W's determined fight to frustrate the legal right of persons with disabilities to sue for handicap discrimination. Increasingly, if for different reasons, we both saw a vital principle at stake here. Misapplication of judicial estoppel in a long line of cases, was causing widespread injustice. And H & W had fought hard both at trial and on appeal to deny handicapped people just this right to sue, so long as they were receiving any disability income.

David decided to keep his reply limited to their shortfall in offering $1,750,000 as a settlement. In a response he drafted that Thursday, he wrote, "This signals to us that H & W's evaluation of the case is so vastly different from ours that further negotiations would likely be unproductive."

I assumed that would be that, and took heart instead from a letter of commendation I had just received from Dr. Sproule for my services as her TA. More high praise from Allah for her former B-student.

Then, early the next week, but late in the day, I heard back from David. No broadcasting the latest news this time. He sounded very grave.

"Renehan called again today before I had a chance to send him my letter by messenger." They had gotten into a colloquy. "I told him what our reasoning was. How strongly we felt about the case, and the importance we placed on the SJC's ruling on judicial estoppel. And I thanked him for his efforts to bring about a resolution of our dispute, and the courteous manner in which he and his assistant Josh Davis had handled the appeal."

Typical, formal David, full of decorum.

"But before I could say goodbye, he gave me their final offer. Alan, it's $3 million."

Chapter Ten

O kay, over an offer of $3 million, anybody might lose a little sleep. But remarkably, we didn't.

After I gulped once, hard, I heard David say he had his own thoughts on the immediate prospect of three million assured bucks, but first he wanted to hear what I thought.

Then he quietly laid out three possible outcomes, if those four SJC justices were still left free to rule on our case. "They could rule against us—in favor of judicial estoppel—and you lose it all. They could rule for us—against estoppel—and stay with Judge White on her approval of the jury verdict for all damages, and you collect every penny. Four-point-four million right now, plus a few more dollars in added interest.

"That's your ideal either/or, but realistically, even if the SJC denies estoppel, they could still order that something in-between be done about the damages. They won't touch back pay or front pay, and nobody raised much question on appeal about the award for emotional suffering. So the way I see it likely happening, they could remand the case to Judge White for remititur on the punitive damages.

"Then you might well end up with something less than the three million that Renehan is offering." And three million did happen to be "a goes-into number," a sum easily divisible by three. That is, two million for the plaintiff, one million for the lawyer on contingency.

He was pretty much telling me what I already knew. We'd done calculations on the possible reductions in the award before this. And often enough, Lora and I, made guesstimates "just for fun," with Lora always coming in with the most conservative estimate.

What I was thinking about that $3 million was pretty straightforward. *If I take their money, I'm going to be just like them.*

David wasn't thinking exactly that way. He was thinking instead, as always, about the law. But he was coming out at the same place.

He explained that if I took the three million, that would be the end of it. There would be no further deliberation by the SJC on a mooted issue in a case that would be by contractual agreement dropped. All those depositions, the trial record, the jury verdict would cease to have any official existence, and the question of judicial estoppel would remain in legal limbo, unresolved. Everything about the *Labonte* Case would disappear down a black hole.

David had long admitted he wanted to see judicial estoppel invalidated as a matter of handicap law. The jury should decide the facts of each case on handicap discrimination, if not necessarily *August*, then surely *D'Aprile* and *Labonte*. He wanted to put better law on the books. Better for whom? As Justice Fried might have asked, in his continuing sly vein. For the plaintiff obviously, and for whomever plaintiff's future lawyer might be. Though he sincerely believed a change in the law was correct jurisprudence, David did have an interest.

But he was not going to advise his client—Alan J. Labonte—against any worries I might have about my own security and enrichment.

I made that quixotic decision all on my own.

What got to me, finally, was the caveat that I would have to sign away my right to say anything ever again about the *Labonte* Case. For $3 million, they wanted to buy my silence. They were trying to estop *me*. And I wasn't going to let them do that.

"You will be required to sign a legal contract to hold them harmless from any wrong doing," he explained the terms, yet again, "and agree to maintain complete confidentiality."

"In other words, I'm going to be paid to keep my mouth shut," I reacted, "while they go ahead and whitewash the whole nasty business." This reminded me of the original agreement that Charlie asked me to sign after I was fired. The big difference was that this was for $3,000,000, not $60,000.

"So to speak," David allowed.

"It's always been about money with these guys," I poured it on. "That's all that ever counted with them. And I'm not going to let myself be like them. I want to do whatever we can for the rights of the handicapped."

That was how I made my choice, and David went right along with me. I wanted to keep the same feeling that had welled up in my heart as I walked out of the New Courthouse after that jury verdict. I'd come there for justice, and by God, at this late date, I wasn't going to accept anything less than justice. Nor commit myself to some skulking vow of silence about justice that had not been done.

In the end, it didn't take but five minutes for both of us to agree.

And Lora was shocked.

When I got off the phone and went to tell her, she gave me one of her very long looks. "And you're telling me you're not a gambler?"

All four of us had a conference call that evening, and Lora gave free rein to her worries over parting with a "Sure Thing." Ultimately, our reasons to turn down the settlement prevailed.

David called Dick Renehan, early the next morning.

"Dick, if you'd been in on the case from the start," David told me he'd explained, "maybe it could have been different. But things have gone too far. We'll just have to let them take their course."

Renehan was really surprised.

Then, on a chilly morning in January, Bill Haynes had his wife call me. He was at home, under hospice care, in the last stages of his cancer. Once his wife reached me, he took the phone. "Been thinking about that offer that Hutchins & Wheeler made. It's probably still on the table. You should take it."

I knew how hard it must be for Bill, weakened by a lot of pain, to make any call, but this early in the morning, he was all business. Somehow I wasn't. "Let's talk about it this weekend," I put him off, "when I come by to see you."

That Saturday, I found Bill propped up in an easy chair, gazing out his picture window at the beautiful inlet of Little Harbor. His eyes were too large—childlike and deepened from his pain medication, yet still clear and focused. I bent down, kneeled down actually, so he wouldn't try to get up. After we embraced, and I sat down next to him, he was all business again. "Thought about what I said to you on the phone?"

"I have, Bill," I sighed, "but this case has taken on a life of its own. I feel like I'm only an observer now. In a way, that helps because I can react to my observations instead of my feelings. So let me tell you what my observations are.

"If I take that money, I'm sending a message to the community that H & W didn't do anything wrong. I just always had my price. And they got so tired of the whole damn thing that finally they just up and paid it. I'll never be able to tell my story, and we'll lose this opportunity to set an important legal precedent for handicapped people."

"You've already helped the handicapped by winning the trial."

I knew he was calculating how I should, by rights, now be helping myself. Three million in hand was far better than nothing out there in the judicial bushes. It was already one million better than the two million he'd advised me to negotiate for. But he knew better than to press that arithmetic on me. And maybe I had some different arithmetic that I was doing for myself. If I was deliberately passing on that third million, didn't that give me a million reasons, all my own, for doing what I believed was right?

"I know you're giving me sound financial advice, Bill," I admitted, "but I can't accept it. I feel I have to let things take their own course. In my heart, I've felt that way all along. I only want what the process is willing to give me, not what I can squeeze out of it."

He smiled sadly. Having done everything he could for me, his conscience was clear, and he could now face his Maker. Along with Our Blessed Mother, in whom I hoped I had helped him to find some comfort in Medjugorje.

"Like I said," I had to shrug, "it's out of my hands."

I did still play one game with myself. Late on a cold January night, I sat at my desk and worked out how a settlement of $3 million might be apportioned among the H & W partners. The same way, I assumed, they shared their sometime profits. At the top of my list, I put Charles Robins down for $300,000, Tony Medaglia for $240,000, and on through the roster. I knew what an enormous effect such hits would have on each partner. I hardly felt much sympathy for the guilty parties at the top of the list. They'd perpetrated this injustice, and had plenty of assets to draw on, come payback time. But others like Jack Clymer had gotten caught up in the internal political shenanigans, and other partners like John Thomson were swept along, with little knowledge of the intrigue or skullduggery. In sum, everybody had been put at short or long risk, and now that we'd refused to settle, that meant the law firm itself, even under the new leadership of Jim Dittmar, could take a hit from which it might have real trouble recovering. Well, so be it. I still had a million reasons, all my own.

By the end of January, Bill was gone, but I thought of our colloquy often as pressure built to accept H & W's offer. Now there was time pressure. By early February, the SJC had been deliberating for almost four months. David told me it was common knowledge within the legal community that the SJC had a self-imposed limit of 130 days in which to decide a case. What on earth, the Boston Bar kept asking, was taking them so long? Clearly disagreement, ominous enough among a quartet of justices, so likely to be divided. The possible splits and permutations on any opinion even among so few on this reduced panel were mind-boggling. Indicating the depth of the problem, the court issued a notice on February 5th, actually waiving the 130-day limit on reaching a decision in our case.

The delay added to our financial woes. By March, we were in pretty desperate straits, since I had run up our home equity loan to the maximum and drawn down all our tax sheltered savings. There was $800 left of our supposed retirement.

Next thing I knew, I got a call from a benefits examiner at UNUM. He sounded friendly enough, said that the company would like me to meet with one of their field staff. I said okay, but after I hung up, wondered, "Why would they want to talk with me at this time?"

On April 18th, an UNUM representative showed up on our doorstep in Cohasset. He asked me a series of questions about my disability, my health status, and my work schedule at BU. Then he showed me a report that UNUM had secured from a personnel agency. He informed me that the data contained in the report had been obtained from a geographic area outside Greater Boston, to ensure confidentiality. In content, the document stated that I was employable as a vice president within a healthcare organization, assuming an accommodation for my MS handicap. The agency further stated that they could place me in such an executive position within six months, provided that I was willing to relocate.

Was this just aggressive company policy? UNUM had embarked on a nationwide canvass of their beneficiaries to reduce disability payments, sometimes buying out the company's long-term obligations to disabled insurees, until the courts finally halted their harassing practices. Or was I hearing from UNUM via some whispered charge after oral argument before the SJC? Justice Fried had asked Dick Rehehan whether the insurance company could recover if it found it had been cheated of funds by a less than disabled beneficiary. Had H & W let UNUM know that Renehan had left this stain upon my integrity stand without unambiguous denial?

Either way, I couldn't believe it was happening. I squinted at this flimflam man, and said, "I don't think my doctors would agree with you."

He glared back at me. "Do you see any contradiction in the fact that you made a disability claim with UNUM and then filed a lawsuit against your former employer for handicap discrimination?"

"No," I replied. That was the burden of our legal case. "These things are mutually exclusive. UNUM insured me in my former position as a law firm administrator, as the job was constituted at that time. My lawsuit related to my employer's unwillingness to make any accommodation for my disability, which they are required to do by law."

Who's been feeding information to this guy? I began speculating.

"You will soon be contacted by another UNUM representative who will discuss the matter with you in greater detail," he spieled away. "In the meantime, you should consider your options."

I felt my blood rising. "Maybe you could explain them to me."

"Well," he pursed his lips, "you can't expect UNUM to just keep sending you checks. You need to decide whether you want to continue your education at Boston University or seek an executive position in a healthcare setting." Then, leaning forward in his chair, "And further, whether you want to negotiate a settlement of your claim with UNUM."

"Look," I said, thoroughly exasperated, "I have to tell you that my income from UNUM is very important to me. This financial support has made it possible for my wife and me to keep heart and soul together over these past few difficult years." I was struggling to keep myself from slipping into an abject plea or giving way to an angry outburst. "As grateful as I am to UNUM, I'm putting off further discussion of settlement, pending the final disposition of my lawsuit." Which was taking more time, not just months but *years*, than anybody could believe. "You can understand that, can't you?"

He looked at me for a silent moment more, and his eyes were cold. Then he rose to his feet, extended his hand, and politely issued a last threat. "Thank you for your time, Mr. Labonte. As I mentioned before, another person from UNUM will be contacting you in the future."

How does this guy sleep at night? I asked myself, after he left.

I called David the next morning and told him how creepy the encounter made me feel.

"What is it about you, Alan?" David tried to lighten my mood. "People just seem to think they've got a right to kick you around."

"Don't I know it."

"Listen, my friend, everything's going to be okay."

"I know these people can't make me do anything my doctors say I can't do." In brutal truth, my MS was "progressing"—that awful diagnostic term. I was limping badly, unable to walk beyond short distances. "It's maddening. Why am I presumed to be malingering, told I should be mitigating everybody else's losses? The thought of jumping into another dispute at this point in my life is absolutely abhorrent to me."

"Let me look into it, and I'll get back to you."

"While you're at it, how about giving the SJC a kick in the butt?"

"It's tough on me as well, Alan. You know I'm not very good when it comes to waiting for a court decision."

We'd been waiting now six months, and had to wait through one more month after another extension by the SJC of their own deadline. I drew a blank everyday on the *Lawyers Weekly* web page, while David worked on other cases to keep the wolf from his own door. Lora worked to sign up more real estate listings.

Until late Monday morning, May 5th, when David got a call from the SJC clerk that an opinion had just come down. There is never any oral presentation. David had to rush over to the New Courthouse from his One Boston Place office, to pick up the opinion in a brown manila envelope.

"When I got to the thirteenth floor, I didn't want to grab and open it right there, in front of the clerk," David told me later. "However, I did let myself ask him one question. 'Who wrote it?' He said Ruth Abrams. And I knew I could relax, at least long enough to get outside the courthouse, find somewhere I could sit quietly and read enough to learn our fate."

He found a chair, out in the chilly plaza, sat down and tore open the envelope. The first page a lawyer always turns to is the last, to find out whether the court has ordered action to kill, save, or further his cause. *The case is remanded to the Superior Court for further proceedings on the issue of remittitur or a new trial on damages.* So he knew our cause was still alive.

Then he flipped back to the first page, in a rush through fluttering paper—twenty-two pages altogether—skimming them in a controlled panic to discover how we had fared on the issues. Almost immediately, he understood we had prevailed on judicial estoppel. I had never said anything to indicate I was "totally disabled." On that question, Justice Abrams used judicious but strong language, which I read myself that afternoon when I got David's fax.

The law firm asserts that "neither [the plaintiff] nor his doctors ever qualified their numerous statements to [the insured]." This assertion is incorrect. On the form on which the plaintiff filed his claim for benefits, he stated that he was in need of a flexible work schedule. This request for accommodation, never considered by the law firm, was evidence that the plaintiff was not claiming to be totally disabled.

Justice Abrams went on to say I had shown that I "was capable of working a fifty-five hour week when allowed to utilize a flexible schedule and when his expected amount of walking was limited. He did so at Boston University after being terminated by the law firm." She picked up on David's point regarding the accommodation H & W had allowed Charlie Gaziano. "The person who filled his job at the law firm before and after the plaintiff devoted less time to the functions of executive director than the plaintiff devotes to his current position." All this, and other instances quoted in her opinion, provided evidence that I "could have handled the time requirements necessary to perform the essential functions" of my job.

> *The plaintiff's evidence was that he was disabled to perform the job without reasonable accommodation, but quite able to perform the job given some reasonable accommodation. . . . In these circumstances, estoppel is inappropriate.*

Together, David and I had made new law. "We conclude that the judge did not err in denying the law firm's claim that the plaintiff was estopped from pursuing a claim under 151b, by filing for disability benefits." So much for H & Ws attempts to silence me.

From the tenor of her remarks on estoppel, David felt a rising confidence in what he would find in the section on "Damages." But he was rudely surprised. He called as soon as he got back to his office. "Alan, the SJC issued their opinion today, and I've got good news and bad news."

"Go ahead and tell me the good news first, please."

He summed up everything, in his scrupulously succinct fashion. "On the issue of liability, the court has upheld the lower court's decision and the jury's verdict in so far as there was handicap discrimination. They have also held that judicial estoppel was in error, and did not prohibit you from pursuing a discrimination suit, and that there was emotional distress, and that punitive damages were justifiable."

I jumped out of my seat, despite my MS. "Wow, that sounds terrific! What's the bad news?"

"They have agreed that the damages for emotional distress are too high and should be reduced by the lower court. In addition, they have concluded the amount of the punitive damages should be reviewed by the lower court, using the standard that was established in the *BMW* Case."

Suddenly, astonishingly, we were back in the nasty midst of yet another dispute. Would this go on forever?

"Tell me again about the *BMW* Case," I blurted out.

"A doctor in Atlanta bought a brand new BMW with a few scratches in its finish that turned out to be caused by a failure to paint an undercoat. The seller, BMW of North America, tried to fudge its negligence and got caught. The doctor sued, and the jury awarded $4,000 in compensatory damages, but $4 million in punitive damages. Justice Sandra Day O'Connor has been laying for excessive punitive damage awards for years, and the Supreme Court overturned. It just recently got decided, right in the middle of our own adjudication."

"But I'm not missing an undercoat," I protested. "Hutchins & Wheeler didn't cheat me on a paint job. They nearly ruined my life."

"I know, Alan. But it's this new standard on punitive damages they want Judge White to apply."

I got a look at this new standard when David's fax arrived that afternoon. Because the *BMW* Case "was decided after the trial and after hearing on the motion for a new trial in this case," Justice Abrams wrote, "we conclude that there should be a rehearing on the defendant's motion for remittitur in light of the factors set forth in BMW of North America."

David suspected he saw the deft hand of Justice Fried, former Solicitor General, in this demand for a recount on punitive damages. The majority opinion in the *BMW* Case held that "three main factors should be considered in determining if a punitive damage award is excessive." They are "the degree of reprehensibility of the defendant's conduct," the ratio of the punitive damage award to the "actual harm inflicted on the plaintiff," with a comparison of "the punitive damages award and the civil or criminal penalties that could be imposed for comparable misconduct." In a nutshell, the Supreme Court, following language from the late Justice William Brennan, would not permit "a punitive sanction that is tantamount to a severe criminal penalty."

David thought we could live with those imposed restrictions on our punitive damages. After all, we had been assured of back and front pay—$235,000 altogether—and even if damages for emotional distress were sharply cut, say by half—that still came to a total of $500,000. Our award for punitive damages was five times that amount for "actual harm inflicted on the plaintiff." Who could object to that reasonable of a ratio, even in the parsimonious Massachusetts courts?

What bothered David far more was the SJC's conclusion that there was "insufficient evidence to sustain the jury verdict for emotional stress." The justices said that I "did suffer from depression," and required "counseling for that depression from a therapist," but noted that "his depression abated as he found a new job and began taking classes at Boston University."

> He was not hospitalized and never took medication to combat his depression. After being terminated, the plaintiff told his internist that he was "very motivated" to move on to new projects. He also expressed to another of his doctors that he was relieved to be free of the emotional stress of his position. Stripped of punitive aspects, this award does not relate reasonably to the emotional distress suffered by the plaintiff. His depression, while real and significant, did not rise to the level awarded by the jury.

So I was the victim of my own fraught struggle to overcome my inner demons. My successful return to mental health—after I'd once thought I was going insane, that MS was eating away at my brain cells—was to be held against me. This infuriated David. "In Massachusetts, the appeals court never interferes with what a jury finds on emotional suffering," he stubbornly argued. "They weren't at the trial. They didn't hear you testify about your own fears and confusion. They didn't see Lora, hear what she had to say, watch her break down and have to leave the witness stand." And so on. I might well agree, but I have to say, at that moment on a cold May afternoon, I felt a surge of relief at all David was telling me about the outcome. I set aside any feelings of disappointment or aggravated insult. It was really all good news, and I outright congratulated him.

"So, counselor, how do *you* feel about all this?"

"I feel great," he admitted, sheepishly. "I believe we've won a tremendous victory for handicapped employees. This decision clears up one of the hottest debates in handicap-discrimination law. From now on, we can count on being able to pursue a claim of handicapped discrimination even if a person has applied for disability benefits. We should be proud of ourselves." Then he paused. "I couldn't have done it without you, my friend."

Afterwards, I rang up Lora at work to give her the good news.

"Honey, I'm very proud of the way you guys persevered under so much pressure," she said. "What happens now?"

"The case goes back to Judge White, but we don't want a new trial. David says nobody would make all those mistakes, all over again, at a second trial. It's up to Judge White to decide, in light of the SJC opinion, what the appropriate amount should be for emotional distress and punitive damages."

After the opinion came in on the fax, a big jumble of flimsy pages, I took the pile into the bedroom, and plunked down in my favorite chair. I had to smile at David's handwritten note on the cover sheet. It said, "To Alan ('Deep Pockets') Labonte."

Reading through the faxed pages, I realized how forthrightly the opinion argued my willingness and capacity to do my job with accommodations. Justice Abrams attacked H & W's claim that "whether a certain function is an 'essential function' is solely the employer's judgment." Not so, since that judgment could be tested against "the work experience of previous incumbents and current work experience of incumbents in the same or similar jobs." And here was the glaring record on both prior and subsequent work experience from Charlie Gaziano, who was "able to complete the essential functions of the job in thirty-five to forty hours a week." She called them on other blatant misrepresentations.

According to the law firm, the plaintiff was told that he was terminated because his thinking was not as "crisp" as it needed to be. That evidence was contradicted by evidence presented by the plaintiff. The partner who worked closely with the plaintiff was unaware of any dissatisfaction with the work the plaintiff was doing.

That had to be John Thomson, bless him. Thomson had snuck in this good word on my behalf, even while testifying against me. That kind of thing is what defeated their manipulation of the facts, and shifted the focus to the larger issue: how my standing up for myself—refusing to accept H & W's shabby treatment—spoke for the rights of all handicapped employees, not just myself. Among the million reasons I had the right to feel proud of the course we'd chosen.

What's more, I realized, after a few quick calculations, I was covered, no matter what happened next. "Forget any emotional distress," I told myself. "Forget any punitive damages. The undisputed damages alone— for back pay, front pay, along with the legal costs, plus interest—must amount to about $750,000. Another goes-into. Easily one quarter of a million dollars for Rapaport and Rapaport, a half million for Lora and me. Not bad when you consider we started out asking for only $200,000 altogether." I leaned back in my chair. "So, whatever Judge White does, we're already golden!"

Then I fell asleep, right in the middle of saying a prayer of thanks that my burdens had at last been lifted. Some say if you don't finish a prayer, the angels will finish it for you. They must have said my remaining thanks that afternoon. I was tucked up in that big bedroom chair, with my tired feet raised. That always takes away the encroaching tension from MS that can run up my legs like a ground chill chasing after hot flashes. My brace and shoes were cast aside, along with any further care or worry I could possibly imagine. My brain just wasn't up to it. I slept away the rest of the afternoon in my stocking feet, and counted on those angels to provide me some peace, maybe even pick up after me.

Three weeks later, both parties were back in the New Courthouse before Judge White. At three in the afternoon, on May 28th, in Court Two, on the 12th floor, to argue remittitur. H & W had no more appetite for retrying the case than we did, and Dick Renehan had become downright friendly. He walked over to meet me personally. A bit to David's discomfort, but I could tell from Renehan's demeanor and handshake that he truly meant to pay his respects. He was the first to publicly recognize we had shown both character and courage in refusing their $3 million offer to settle.

"Your Honor," he opened his pleading, "my client admits they made a mistake."

It was a noble gesture, as close to an apology as I was ever likely to receive, but it didn't prevent Renehan from taking a hard line on what was due me for emotional distress. He instanced my full recovery from depression to pursue a new career path, the far more meager awards for emotional distress cited as precedents by the SJC, and proposed that the $550,000 be reduced to $15,000. On punitive damages, Renehan argued that his client had learned a valuable lesson but still had not done deliberate harm to me—nor ever any harm to anyone else—so gross as to evidence the reprehensible conduct the jury unreasonably sought to punish. He also argued front pay damages should be excluded from the formula of "actual harm inflicted" in calculating the award. He asked that those millions in punitive damages be lowered to $50,000.

David was still upset over the SJC's intrusion upon the award for emotional distress, believing the justices had neither cause nor sufficient knowledge of the facts to second-guess the jury. But he leaned toward caution and asked the sum be reduced to no less than $350,000, trusting the award would end up around $250,000 at worst.

On punitive damages, he stuck to his guns. He justified $2.5 million as fitting well within the parameters set by the Supreme Court in the *BMW* Case. Two-point-five million was three-to-five times the possible damages for "actual harm inflicted," a sound ratio in the case of such reprehensible conduct by the defendant. A *law* firm, after all, as we had long been saying. Lawyers who should have known better than to flaunt employer-discrimination laws and who clearly could afford to pay such punitive damages.

On June 19th, H & W issued me their first check for $619,048.86 toward payment of back pay, front pay, and legal costs, plus interest to date, to avoid paying any further interest on these assured judgments. I said to David, "This is the first sound business decision that these guys have made in the last five years." That money saved the bacon of both the Labonte and Rapaport households, as I had paid about one-third of the $619,048.86 to Rapaport & Rapaport. Later in the summer, we would hear Justice White's rulings on the larger damage awards.

Finally, in August, we heard how the real money would finally be handed around. But so much of our blood, sweat, and tears—from Lora and myself, and David and Diane—had gone into these last five years of struggle, that it was like a late accounting rendered for our shared lives. These would not be our winnings, our ship come in, any sort of bonanza. The real El Dorado, as always, lies further on. What this last installment would really cover were the costs of our mutual survival.

Judge White had reduced the award for emotional distress to $100,000. She did so, on the basis that I had "suffered through eight months of being shunned by his co-workers and supervisors, and eight months of physical pain and suffering with repeated limping around the office with no accommodation or support from the law firm until he was summarily terminated by his employer." David still smarts at her concluding I recovered fully from my depression, convinced that she should never have cut emotional distress below $250,000. But she did ignore the SJC's citing of "two not very recent cases where the awards were significantly less than $100,000," insisting that $100,000 was "fair and reasonable in this case and at this time."

On punitive damages, she rejected Renehan's argument that front pay should not be included in "the concept of actual damages." That might be the limited case under the federal Age Discrimination and Employment Act, cited by the defendant, but had nothing to do with Massachusetts law. She then reduced the $2.5 million award to $900,000. That amount, she wrote, conformed to "the three *BMW* factors."

On H & W's reprehensibility, she did allow there was no evidence that "any other handicapped worker had suffered at the firm's hand." She also recognized that the sheer adverse publicity would have a deterrent effect, "especially in this case since no law firm enjoys having its actions deemed discriminatory by a jury and so described and preserved in a reported decision of the state's highest court."

But beyond that, she was scathingly critical of their "callous disregard for Mr. Labonte's failing health."

She noted again how Tony and Charles Robins "did nothing more to learn about multiple sclerosis than to have a brief in-office lunch with a client who happened to be a physician who knew something about MS." She denounced their corporate behavior. "His employer ignored him and his obvious physical difficulties, continued to maintain his heavy workload, and, as the Supreme Judicial Court found, 'shunned' him and his problems." She then nailed them as deleterious lawyers, and read from the Supreme Judicial Court's document:

In this court's view, a law firm charged with upholding the law serves as an example to others. Here the defendant in its actions and failure to act did not comport with the highest standards required and expected of the legal profession. While there may not have been malice or ill will, there was certainly inhumane and callous treat-

ment of him, amounting to active indifference. That is the major factor, which the court considered in applying the reprehensibility factor and determining the $900,000 in punitive damages is not excessive.

That said it all, a shot fired straight across the Boston Bar.

On the second *BMW* factor, she set a close ratio of punitive damages to actual damages. Nine hundred thousand dollars "is more than two times but less than three times the actual damages which, after remission, stand at $335,000." That was "well within acceptable limits for punitive damages as reflected in the cases cited by both plaintiff and defendant." It also satisfied the third *BMW* factor, keeping within sanctions for comparable misconduct, either civil or criminal. Multiple damages for age discrimination are civilly awarded "up to three, but not less than two" times actual damages in Massachusetts, which sets no cap on punitive damages, leaving it to the court "to review the amount awarded to ensure that it is reasonable and 'not tantamount to a severe criminal penalty.'"

Some might argue, as David still does, that she had pared away too near the core of proven (at least to the jury) damages for emotional distress, but by keying the remitted awards to each other, she had arrived at a significant bottom line.

Together, they came to $1 million.

Exactly.

That million along with the other awards against H & W—back pay ($125,000), front pay ($110,000), legal fees ($233,039.50), and other disbursements ($6,710.73)—plus total interest of $491,751.58 brought the judgment to $1,996,501.81.

Almost $2 million. Just what Bill Haynes—God rest his soul and Lora—always the cautious bidder—predicted would be the final outcome.

No, I didn't get the original jury award, over $4 million, and I missed out on that extra million I could have had by simply taking H & W's out-of-court settlement of $3 million. But all along that extra million was a bribe to buy my silence, and help them hide their ignoble actions. What I have kept is my freedom to speak out, and what I gained was even more precious. I've now got a million reasons to tell it like it really is, and join in the continuing fight across this country for the rights of Americans with disabilities.

Since I'd already received $619,048.66 in July, the remaining amount due me was $1,347,452.95. On September 3rd, Hutchins, Wheeler & Dittmar, P.C. cut me a check in that amount.

Neither David nor I had ever seen such a large check, made out to someone we actually knew. To me. Up close and personal. We picked it up from the 101 Federal offices, and right there in hand, it made us distinctly nervous. This thin folio of green paper, serrated down the middle between the stub and the actual, negotiable instrument, a signed—two signatures—certified check for $1,347,452.95.

David drove us straight over to his branch of my Fleet Bank. I tore the folio in two, turned over the oblong, and wrote "For deposit only" on the back, then signed my name, and handed it, fully endorsed, over to David. I stayed in the car—weak from this giddy burst of stress on my MS—while David rushed into the bank to deposit our mil-point-three-four-seven, and change.

Then I drove back to Cohasset, in a benign state of near euphoria. When I arrived home, I looked again at the deposit slip receipt and the check stub, all set to show them to Lora, and my heart skipped a beat.

There was my signature.

I'd endorsed the stub instead of the check.

And David had deposited it.

We spent the rest of the day frantically calling various officers at several branches of the Fleet Bank to trace this wayward, unendorsed check. By then, missing in the system. We were reassured. Not to worry, even though the teller had initially failed to catch our mistake, there was no conceivable way in which an unendorsed check for over a million dollars would ever be cleared through the after-hours grid by the receiving bank.

The next morning I had well over a million dollars in my account.

We did manage ultimately to straighten out this whole delirious situation, so I could sit down and write David a check of my own. A more complicated goes-into. One third of the gross judgment was $446,944.25. But I had previously paid him fees of $11,443.50, to be deducted. But then again, I wanted to reimburse him for the other half of Jerry Benezra's fee, so that added $13,915.00. After all, as I well knew, disbursements should be paid by the client.

That meant I wrote a check to David Rapaport, Esq. for $449,415.75.

A few days later, I was rounding up all these papers to file away in my office, and happened to pull out a copy of our contingency fee agreement. Leafing through, I suddenly balked, and immediately called David.

"You may be a great lawyer, but you're a lousy business man!" I chortled.

"What's wrong now?"

"You never had me sign our contingency agreement!"

It says a lot about how much we trusted one another, after five years of working together, what a big laugh we both got out of that. I signed the agreement and sent it along in the mail.

Epilogue

It wasn't some formal contract that obliged David and me to keep faith and bear it out, even to the edge of likely legal doom. And certainly the four of us—the Labontes and the Rapaports together—formed an alliance that never got around to agreeing upon terms. There was no formal agreement. We just all knew what had to be done—for ourselves, yes, but also for all those with disabilities in America—and set out, in understood unison, to do it.

I've since said to David that it was a good thing he never told me the very long odds against our succeeding with our suit. Barely five percent of handicapped plaintiffs prevail in the federal courts these days, but I'm not sure even that would have discouraged me. Mainly because I came to this cause after painfully discovering, much against my own will, that I absolutely *had* to step forward and be counted among those people, *my* people with disabilities. And in the end, when the H & W lawyers tried to get me to settle the case, and we turned down their third million, that gave me a surprise bonus: a cool million reasons why—I knew, from then on—I had to tell my story.

David and I still get together to reminisce about the *Labonte* Case. There hasn't really been another such action since mine, David observes, once our $2 million judgment made it plain across the Commonwealth of Massachusetts how failure to reasonably accommodate employees with disabilities would be handled by the courts. David has become one of the leading legal lights on handicap discrimination, as well as other matters of labor law. He notes how much more ready and willing employers are to settle disputes out of court these days. Which is as it should be.

But he is not optimistic about future cases across the land. He is saying how the trend lately in the federal courts is turning away from vigilant enforcement of the Americans with Disabilities Act (ADA). The Supreme Court is steadily tightening the strictures on plaintiffs seeking to recover damages for discrimination under the ADA. Congress must amend the ADA, so that the right to trial by jury in handicap discrimination cases is federally preserved.

And I know David is right because I know how people react when they first learn they have MS. Exactly the same uncertain way I once reacted. They are suddenly and desperately afraid of losing their jobs. As the saying goes, "Diagnose and Adios." Nothing else but their fears for their immediate livelihood matters. They even try to hide their disability. They will do anything possible to show they are still up to par. They are ready to work hard and get the job done, even if they have to stay longer hours, make more demands upon themselves, turn workaholic in order to save themselves and their loved ones from the bitter fate that is already written in their blood, bone and brain. Hopefully, my experience will inspire and encourage others to disclose their illness to their employer and to seek a reasonable accommodation to it.

* * *

I am now a D.B.A. "Doctor of Business Administration" and a member of the faculty at Boston University's School of Management. Although I must avoid the rigors of classroom teaching, I greatly enjoy working one-on-one with graduate students and participating in research projects, particularly those aimed at improving health care delivery processes.

Through her real estate ties, Lora did find us a smaller house in neighboring Scituate, so we've moved out of Cohasset and consolidated our finances. That two million may have looked like a "deep pocket," but once we began dipping into it—to recompense David, pay off our debts, equip the new house, buy a new car to deal with my disability, and pay taxes—there wasn't a lot left. Our biggest hit came from the remitted damages for emotional distress, the only nontaxable moneys from the jury verdict. That $100,000—formerly $550,000—made it safely to our newly opened mutual fund account.

If Mary Marshall was surprised to discover the true size of our family during the trial, she'd probably be even more exasperated now. While Sloan has moved to Oklahoma, Lora's mother, Madelene, and sister, Gail, have moved in, so we presently have five sitting at the table every evening. And that's just great as far as I'm concerned. I love the closeness of our extended family and all the joy and warmth that they bring into our home. The added benefit for me is that there are even more hands (and legs) to assist me with my daily chores and also, but most importantly, there's the comfort of knowing that there are always people, close at hand, who care about me—to care for me.

Even UNUM finally decided they had better back off, after we confronted them with the certainty of a lawsuit if they chose to stop sending my monthly disability checks. And I always found it curious that during their most egregious efforts to force me into a settlement, some of their correspondence was copied to Charlie Gaziano.

My monthly checks were for *partial* disability, I should emphasize, since that is what my trial and the ruling decision from the SJC irrefutably established. I'm sensitive and proud, even a little prickly, when it comes to speaking out on that score, especially since my disability, while somewhat worsening, has gradually stabilized. I've had the benefit of excellent medical care, on a continuing basis from both Drs. Peter Gross and Ed Wolpow who have become two of my most trusted and cherished friends.

But I could never have done any of this, taken on even the least of my problems, even experienced the rebirth of my long-dormant faith without the love and support and companionship of my devoted Lora.

Today, I have braces on both legs, and am dependent on two forearm crutches, or a walker or my electric wheelchair for much of my daily mobility. I long for *Gospa* to call me back to worship among her visionaries in St. James Church and remain hopeful that, in spite of my physical limitations, I may someday move again in the rugged mountains and verdant valleys of Bosnia-Herzegovina and experience the embrace of our godchild, Vedran.

Not that my range, locally—or my maneuvering around on my own house—is that much restricted. I have an elevator chair that takes me up and down the stairs, and there are hand railings along all the upstairs corridors.

Outside the house, I get around on a large, red, four-wheeled, electric scooter. We recently bought a compact SUV and equipped it with an electric hoist that easily lifts my scooter in and out of the storage bay, so that I can readily cargo the thing into the BU parking garage or anywhere else that I need to go.

So I do get around. Here and there, and everywhere. I keep contact with those involved in the *Labonte* Case, even with Brock Brower, my collaborator on this book. A while ago, Brock called to say I just *had* to come into Boston and see what had finally happened to Hutchins & Wheeler.

When I entered 101 Federal Street, nobody recognized me in the hustle of the lofty, hushed lobby, though some did glance at me with that vague curiosity touched by a semblance of sympathy, as they always do at anybody in a wheelchair-scooter.

I rolled up to the alphabetical rosters, set like temple tablets in the marble wall's display.

At first I kept looking for Hutchins, Wheeler & Dittmar, reminding myself to stay up to date, but drew a complete blank. Meanwhile, my collaborator was frowning and pointing at another felt-ridged spot, way down on the sixth floor.

"They're gone," he marveled. "Charles Robins and Jim Westra. They were right there, just the other day."

"On six?" I puzzled.

"Set themselves up as a boutique, doing international law."

I turned back, scanning wildly, but still couldn't locate any of the big names. I kept on scanning, and began to catch a few, individual, familiar names scattered throughout the long rosters. Some of them—Mary Ellen O'Mara, Jack Clymer, John Thomson— were still up on the 28th, 29th, and 30th floors, but others—Fred Grein and David Rosenthal— were down on the 16th and 17th floors. I couldn't puzzle out how some had become so dislocated, or under what single rubric they might all now be identified.

Until I made out the partnered names listed prominently far enough to the left to be their capstone logo: Nixon Peabody.

Of course, it dawned on me that this was another merger along the constantly shoaling Boston Bar.

"Tony. Where's Tony?" I asked.

"Long gone." Brock replied.

"Where?"

"Goodwin Procter, became a partner in their corporate department. He went there with Jim Dittmar."

No more *Dittmar?*

The more I scanned up and down those pyramids of names, the stranger their fates became. I did spot a Robins, but it was *Mark* Robins, possibly the Robins' son? Most everybody else left among the H & W partners and associates were the stalwarts of trusts and estates, other slighter eminences. Still in the building, but they'd been redistributed, helter-skelter, scattered like the diaspora of Hutchins & Wheeler.

That wouldn't make me any more welcome around the old neighborhood, I sensed, but I rolled resolutely up to the lobby desk, just to ask a few questions. Nobody seemed to recognize me, and I surely didn't know any of these faces.

"Yeah, Mr. Charles Robins on the sixth floor, but they moved out last week," we were told. "Across the street." More expensive offices. "Weil, Gotshal & Manges, LLP," we were told. So was Robins moving up once more in the world of Downtown Boston, feeding on further mergers and acquisitions, and would he still be taking Eleanor along to do his checkbook?

Then I took a large chance. We turned toward the elevator, waited for UP, and rolled brazenly through the squeezing doors. We rode all the way to the thirty-first floor.

I powered my scooter out into the long hallway, thinking this is all they ever really had to do, locate me near enough to this bank of elevators. It would have been such a simple thing to do, yet it stood for so much else that H & W had never been willing to do. I looked around, a little warily, at my same old familiar floor, wondering whom I might chance but didn't want to run into, though I didn't need to worry.

The glass doors beyond the elevators were tightly shut. Locked, we found on reaching them, and there was no young woman sitting demurely at the reception desk. In fact, there was nobody anywhere.

Through the unshining glass, I could see the private stairway leading up to the once-gourmet 101 Federal Grille, dusty and destitute as a front stoop. And back there, out of sight, had to be my old office, with its sliver of a harbor view. Was my door still ajar for anybody to stop by and peak in, or locked to secure those supposedly confidential files, in the eerie, utter emptiness?

Here was just another floor for rent, I sensed, in yet another abandoned office complex.

I half pondered, "Did I cause all this? Had the Labonte Case brought down the entire law firm?" I knew the shoals of the Boston Bar always shifted with the huge pull of New England's economic tides—surely setting up a far greater current than any lone swirl a complainant like myself could start running. But did a law firm have any real future if those at the helm pitted themselves against a handicapped employee, then did all in their collective power deliberately to disobey the law?

Returning to the lobby, I rolled over to the marble desk to ask one more question.

"Yeah, Nixon Peabody moving out too," we were told. "In February. Going over to 100 Summer Street. Already closed that top floor."

I turned my scooter around from that desk, and headed toward the accessible doors, out onto Devonshire Street.

I reached the doors, and somebody, after the usual appraising smile, pushed them open for me.

I rolled away from there for the last time, glad to be—once more—the first out, ahead of them all.

And so it was over: the exciting new job, discovery that I had MS, being fired for cause, and sinking to total despair and depression. With medical and psychiatric help, striving to start a new life, rediscovery of God and the church in Medjugorje, and seeking a settlement from H & W. Then the trial, the victory, the appeal, and refusing a $3 million settlement in hope that our case would set a precedent aiding those with disabilities. In the end, a very satisfying result.

In reflecting back on what happened during the period that's recounted in this book, I can now see what a marvelous blessing the onset of MS really was and what a marked difference it has made in my life. And, I can certainly testify that given the opportunity, God can take the very worst of circumstances and bring about something wonderful. But I've learned that in order for Him to bring about His wondrous works, I had to affirm His plan and cooperate with Him. In this context, living with MS has become for me, like living with a friend.